MW00807622

The Essential
Tin Whistle Toolbox
by Grey Larsen

2 3 4 5 6 7 8 9 0

Visit us on the Web at www.melbay.com — E-mail us at email@melbay.com

table of contents

This book is lovingly dedicated to my mother, Beatrice V. Larsen.

acknowledgments and credits

I consulted with many people while working on this book. Some read and commented on my work in progress, others helped me find information, recordings, and photographs. Their help was of great value, and our conversations sparked many fruitful ideas. In particular, I wish to thank Steve Cox for his unflagging support, enthusiasm, and indispensable assistance. I also gratefully acknowledge the contributions of the following people:

Tim Britton, Mike Casey, Kathrina Cox, Jo Cresswell, Autumn Hills, Eleanor Hitchings, Linda Hitchings, Brad Hurley, Sharon Kahan, Cindy Kallet, Robin Larsen, Siri Larsen, Teal Larsen, Kathy Lynn, Michael Lynn, Caoimhin Mac Aoidh, L. E. McCullough, Bill Ochs, Jeff Sherman, Chris Smith, Elizabeth Sweeney of the Irish Music Center at Boston College, Sura Gail Tala, Philippe Varlet, and Lawrence Washington.

Scores of musicians have inspired me on my path. Chief among them are the elders and masters I have known well or even met briefly, for there is nothing as enlightening as sharing music, person to person, with one who has lived and breathed it for most of their life. These include Tom Byrne, Tom McCaffrey, Michael J. Kennedy, Phil McGing, Josie McDermott, Matt Molloy, Seamus Tansey, Cathal McConnell, Mary Bergin, Kevin Burke, Martin Hayes, Frankie Gavin, James Kelly, Liz Carroll, Seamus Connolly, Tommy Peoples, Paddy Keenan, Micheál Ó Domhnaill, Tríona Ni Dhomnaill, Paddy O'Brien, Noel Hill…the list could go on and on.

A special thank you to all of my students, who continually prompt me to think more deeply, examine more closely and stretch my understanding further.

Finally and foremost, my heartfelt thanks to my parents, my family, and my friends for seeing me through.

Photo Credits
Front cover photo by Rich Remsberg.

Figures:
Figure 1-8, photo © Peter Laban, Milltown Malbay, Co. Clare.
Brad Jacobs: Figures 2-1, 3-1 through 3-8, 8-9 through 8-11, and 9-2.
Figure 2-2 courtesy of the Dayton C. Miller Flute Collection, Library of Congress, Washington DC.
Rich Remsberg: Figures 2-3 through 2-5.

Other:
Irene Young: photo of Grey Larsen in *About the Author.*

Illustration Credits
Lisa Nilsson: Whistle drawing for the fingering chart and various diagrams in Chapters 7, 8, and 10.
Meghan Merker: Figure 3-9.
Fingering chart conceived and designed by Grey Larsen, executed by Rich Remsberg and Lisa Nilsson.

Other Credits
Design consultation: Meghan Merker, Gambler Graphics.
CD recorded by Grey Larsen at Sleepy Creek Recording, Bloomington, Indiana.
Indexing by Nancy Ball.

Introduction

WHAT IS THIS BOOK?

This is a book about learning to play traditional Irish music on the tin whistle. It is a book for the beginner and novice, but also for the intermediate player who may have already been playing for some years. The book starts with the beginner's first approach to the instrument and proceeds, step by step, to provide a wealth of information and guidance, examples and exercises, mapping out a route to genuine competence as a player of traditional Irish music. The journey includes very thorough instruction in the Irish ornamentation techniques known as cuts, strikes, slides, long rolls, and short rolls.

The book also offers a brief look into the history and development of the tin whistle in Ireland and a thorough orientation to traditional Irish music for tin whistle players. It does not cover the rudiments of music notation or ear training.

Section 1 features an orientation to traditional Irish music, briefly visits the history and development of the tin whistle in Ireland, explores everything having to do with holding, fingering, and sounding the instrument, supplies guidance and encouragement in practicing, and takes the first of two looks at the parallels between music and spoken language.

In Section 2 I share my insights into ornamentation. These ideas have led me to invent new ways to explain and notate ornamentation that are far more simple and clear than other approaches in use at the time of this writing.

Section 3 addresses tonguing, phrasing, and breathing.

In Section 4 I look into "muscle memory," revisit the subject of practice, and look again at the analogy between music and spoken language.

The book contains numerous musical examples and exercises. Many of them are excerpts from traditional Irish tunes. Transcriptions and recordings of these tunes, in their full form, are available online at <www.greylarsen.com/extras/toolbox>.

This book draws upon another of my books, *The Essential Guide to Irish Flute and Tin Whistle*. The scope of that book is far broader. Once you have worked your way through this book you may well want to move on to that one, for several reasons. You may be ready to delve into more advanced techniques of ornamentation (condensed long rolls, condensed short rolls, double-cut rolls, cranns, and others). You may be interested in playing Irish music on the flute – the Irish flute, or the modern, Boehm-system flute. You may want to study the playing of great whistle and flute players of the past and present. *The Essential Guide to Irish Flute and Tin Whistle,* along with its two companion CDs, explores all of this in great depth, and includes meticulous transcriptions of the playing of John McKenna, Tom Morrison, William Cummins, Séamus Ennis, Willie Clancy, Paddy Taylor, Paddy Carty, Josie McDermott, Matt Molloy, Cathal McConnell, Mary Bergin, Donncha Ó Briain, Desi Wilkinson, Breda Smyth, Seán Ryan, Conal Ó Gráda, Micho Russell, Joanie Madden, Kevin Crawford, Catherine McEvoy, Seamus Egan, and myself.

THE COMPANION CD

The companion CD contains most of the figures and exercises that appear throughout the book. A CD symbol paired with a track number shows where to find the recording.

Some CD tracks contain more than one musical example. In such cases, I give an index number for each example contained in that track, as shown here:

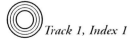
Track 1, Index 1

These recordings are provided for the benefit of every reader, not just those who do not read music. Even though the figures and exercises are notated in a detailed fashion, there are many elements of traditional Irish music that cannot be written down. Using both notated representations and recordings will help all readers to better understand the music.

COMPLEMENTARY TUNE COLLECTIONS

This book is complemented by my two tunebook and CD packages. These works, which present traditional Irish tunes that are particularly well-suited to the whistle and flute, respectively, contain the first large collections of transcriptions that make use of my notation techniques. (By the way, tunes that are well-suited to the flute are usually well-suited to the whistle, and vice versa.) For more information on these works, see <www.greylarsen.com> or Mel Bay Publications.

MORE TUNES AT <www.greylarsen.com>

There are additional tunes, in both audio and transcription form, at <www.greylarsen.com>. Please visit the site for more information on this and other items related to my Mel Bay books, and for information about recordings, workshops, and performances.

WHY IS THIS BOOK NEEDED?

There are numerous other books about Irish tin whistle playing. Unfortunately, many of them are at times superficial, confusing, or lacking in clear and complete explanation.

It is impossible to be good at playing tin whistle without basing one's learning on a foundation of extensive and continual listening. This book is intended to encourage and be a companion to such listening. But it also provides a wealth of information that for many is very difficult to obtain through listening alone, without regular, personal contact with experienced players.

This book also provides teachers of Irish tin whistle a solid pedagogical basis for their work.

READING MUSIC

There is a great deal of music notation in this book. As mentioned above, if you do not read music you can still use the book quite well because I play most of the notated exercises and figures on the companion CD.

I encourage everyone to learn to read music. It is an extremely useful skill, even for the traditional musician. However, it is very important to avoid becoming dependent upon written music. If you already are, then you need to begin to wean yourself. As you learn tunes, you should immediately start to internalize them. For much more on this subject, see Chapter 1.

The companion CD can be very useful in that regard. You can learn to play a musical example solely by listening to it over and over on the CD. Once you have learned it, you may check yourself with the music notation in the book.

ANALYTICAL LEARNING AND IMMERSION LEARNING

You certainly do not need to use this or any book in order to learn to play Irish tin whistle. This tradition has thrived and evolved for centuries with very little help from books. In Ireland, and in Irish communities outside Ireland, many musicians learn their music largely through immersion, the way that we all master our native languages. Most musicians who learn this way are not very self-examining about how they do what they do.

Analytical resources like this book should never supplant aural learning, but they can supplement it in important ways. This book supplies much-needed information for people who live far away from a thriving Irish music community. Even those who live in such communities will find plenty of new ideas, insights, and opinions here. I believe it is a very good thing for musicians to become aware of aspects of their playing that they may have been unconscious of for years. So, I hope this will be a valuable book for all players, regardless of their background and learning experiences.

Although traditional musicians, on the whole, tend to learn intuitively, it is interesting to note that music reading is more prevalent in the Irish music tradition than it is in many others. Instruction books and tune collections have played a part in the propagation of traditional Irish music since the 18th century. In our time, the tune collections of Captain Francis O'Neill[i], Breandán Breathnach[ii], and others can be found on the bookshelves of many traditional Irish musicians.

MANY WAYS TO REGARD A TREASURE

This book represents my own perceptions, opinions, and experience regarding traditional Irish music. As with any art form, there is room for a wide variety of viewpoints. Each one provides yet another way to illuminate a shared treasure, which, though deeply rooted in many generations of Irish culture, is alive and constantly evolving.

GENDER CONVENTION

In this book I have decided to avoid the cumbersome use of both genders for the personal pronoun. Instead of writing *he or she, his or her,* etc., I use the feminine gender. This way I can do my small part in helping to correct the imbalance caused by centuries of books that have used only masculine forms.

---

[i] Two of the tune collections of Capt. Francis O'Neill are particularly widespread. *O'Neill's Music of Ireland* was originally published in 1903 and contains 1850 tunes. *1001 Gems, The Dance Music of Ireland* followed in 1907. Both were published in Chicago where O'Neill served as Chief of Police. Both books have gone through several editions and are at the time of this writing published by Mel Bay Publications.

[ii] Breandán Breathnach, *Ceol Rince na hÉireann,* 5 vols. (Dublin: An Gúm). Years of first publication: vol. 1: 1963, vol. 2: 1976, vol. 3: 1985, vol. 4: 1996, vol. 5: 1999.

❖ section 1 ❖

---

first matters

chapter 1: orientation to traditional irish music for tin whistle players

As you embark upon the path of learning to play Irish music, you should realize that you are preparing to become a participant in a story that has been unfolding for centuries. In order to intelligently take part, you need to start developing a view of the big picture.

Seek Out the Older Players

In this pursuit, the key to all insight is listening. As you are learning your craft, it is inspiring to listen to the latest performers and their recordings. But it is even more important to seek out the older players (and not just whistle players) who may not come into your view so readily. The soul of the tradition rests in them, the ones who have lived the music for 50, 60, 70 or more years. They may be highly accomplished or they may play roughly and slow, but they are the keepers of the deepest wisdom and eloquence that you can experience through the music.

In an interview in *Fiddler Magazine,*[i] the great fiddler Martin Hayes tells about such a musician:

> One of my own favorites is a whistle player called Joe Bane. I have a tune on the album called "The Britches" [This refers to Martin Hayes' first album on Green Linnet Records, *Martin Hayes.*] It's very simple. Anybody could play it. Any beginner could play every note I play. It's not technically difficult. And it wasn't technically difficult the way he played it. But when he played it, it would bring a tear to my eye. He'd look forward to playing the tune all night at a session, and when the opportunity would arise, he'd go, "Ah, sure, we'll play 'The Britches.'" He'd be waiting to do this. He loved it. It was like a lullaby—there was sweetness in it, there was humility in it, there was joy and love, everything in it, and it was the climax of his day, of his week, to do this tune. He had no chops, he had no knowledge, no theoretical anything, but his space was magic. He didn't need to know any more technical anything. The only thing that was amiss around him was a world that didn't understand what was going on.

If you do not live in Ireland, you may be able to seek out Irish communities or Irish people nearby, attend concerts, festivals, music camps, summer schools, take part in dances, workshops, sessions. Hopefully, you will be able to travel to Ireland. There are a great many resources for broadening your knowledge.

Reading Music, and "What is a Tune?"

If you do not read music, you are in good company. Many traditional Irish musicians don't. But a surprisingly large number do, to some extent. I encourage everyone to learn this skill.

When we use music notation with Irish music, it should be only a supplement and convenience, a shorthand guide or reminder to memory. When used in these ways, it is very useful indeed. However, the most deeply vital aspects of this music cannot be written down and can only be learned through extensive listening.

If you are dependent upon written music, the time has come to begin to wean yourself from it. Below I offer some insights that I hope will help you do this.

The full embodiment of a traditional Irish tune cannot be written down. One of the reasons for this is that improvisation and variation are intrinsic elements of Irish music. There is no such thing as the definitive version of a traditional Irish tune. Often a particular setting will become established among certain comrade players, among players of a certain instrument or in a certain region, but even that setting is a vehicle for personal interpretation. In truth, a transcription of an Irish tune is no more than a frozen skeleton of a snapshot of a setting of the tune.

A tune is something very expansive and alive. Infusing each tune is an essence that makes it immediately recognizable, beautiful, and whole. Each tune also carries rich personal associations for the player. With musical maturity and experience, one comes to intuitively grasp the spirit of a tune and shape it in one's own way.

THE HABIT OF INTERNALIZATION

When you begin learning a tune, with or without the aid of music notation, you should immediately begin to commit it to memory, to internalize it, as a part of the act of learning itself. If you are using music notation, immediately start to let go of it. This may not be so easy at first if you are used to hanging your musical awareness on a visual representation and storing it there.

A natural way to learn a tune is to simply hear it many times, over a long period of time. Without making a conscious effort to learn it, the tune seeps into you. One day you may find yourself lilting or humming it. By then, you actually know it quite well. Next it is a matter of transferring it onto the whistle. Attending a regular session is a great way to give yourself the opportunity to learn this way.

For those times when you are actively learning a tune in a conscious, intentional way, here are some ideas that I hope will help you.

FIND THE TONAL CENTER

A good first step to reclaiming, internalizing, and developing your musical awareness is to find and hold onto the *tonal center* of a tune. The tonal center is the "home pitch," what some people call the *key* of the tune. (Below I'll explain why *mode* is a more appropriate term than *key* in Irish music.) If you were going to add a drone to a tune, the pitch of the tonal center would be the most natural choice for the drone's pitch. Many tunes end on the pitch of the tonal center, or at least come to rest upon it at the ends of some important phrases. When you land on the pitch of the tonal center you feel more resolved, at rest, at home, than with any other pitch. If you have trouble recognizing this feeling, then you need to tune in more to how the different pitches of a tune can make you feel inside your body.

Occasionally, you will run across a tune for which a tonal center is not obvious, or seems to shift. In other tunes the tonal center is clear, but changes with different parts of the tune.

For the vast majority of tunes, the tonal center is clear and unchanging. After learning about modes later in this chapter you will have more information about finding the tonal center.

THE DIMENSIONS OF MELODY

Here is a powerful and helpful insight from Robert Jourdain:

> …a melody's notes are largely perceived as offsets not from each other, but from an underlying tonal center. Melody is a harmonic phenomenon.[ii]

I would amend Jourdain's statement by substituting the word "pitches" for "notes." A note has pitch and duration. For the moment let's look at the pitch aspect alone.

The apparent contradiction of Jourdain's statement, that melody is a *harmonic* phenomenon, holds true because as we *retain* the pitch of the tonal center, we compare the pitch of the present melody note to it, and "hear" or sense the resulting harmony, or "vertical" interval, created by these two pitches. (An *interval* is simply the distance in pitch between two notes.) At the same time, we track the "horizontal" intervals that occur sequentially in time, i.e. the distance in pitch between one melody note and the one that precedes or follows it.

So, the process of memorizing melodies, which seems daunting to so many, begins with the task of internalizing and retaining only *one* pitch, that of the tonal center. From there, it becomes a two-dimensional process of hearing or sensing vertical (simultaneous) and horizontal (sequential) intervals, instead of a one-dimensional procedure of memorizing a long sequence of discrete, unrelated single pitches. The two-dimensional picture reveals the connections and relationships between the melody's pitches and allows musical meaning to emerge.

Your ability to internalize melodies will improve even more as you learn to recognize the sound and "flavor" of each of the twelve musical intervals. I recommend that you also learn their names. The smallest interval is known by three names: a semitone, a half-step, or a minor second. Each of the larger intervals can be measured by how many semitones it contains.

- The minor second (also known as the half-step or semitone) contains only 1 semitone.
- The major second (also known as the whole-step) contains 2 semitones.
- The minor third contains 3.
- The major third contains 4.
- The perfect fourth contains 5.
- The tritone (also known as the augmented fourth or the diminished fifth) contains 6.
- The perfect fifth contains 7.
- The minor sixth contains 8.
- The major sixth contains 9.
- The minor seventh contains 10.
- The major seventh contains 11.
- The octave contains 12.

You can see and hear these intervals and their constituent semitones clearly by studying and experimenting with the fretboards of guitars or other fretted instruments of western Europe, almost all of which have twelve frets to the octave.

It's not necessary that you mentally count or memorize the number of semitones in each interval you hear. But just as it is a carpenter's business to be able to look at a board and know whether it is two inches wide, or four, or eight, it is your business as a musician to gradually gain the ability to hear an interval and know whether it is a minor second, a major third, or a perfect fifth, etc., in other words, to mentally "size it up," to know or feel what the distance is between the two pitches. Knowing what intervals are, knowing their sizes and names, developing your sense of their "flavors" or "colors," and knowing that there is a sensible and proportional system to the relationships between them will enhance your ability to learn by ear, an ability that everyone has.

Enter now another dimension: pulse and rhythm.

Aside from some slow airs, all Irish tunes have a *pulse,* a steady recurrent beat. When we tap our foot we tap out the pulse. The pulse is subdivided into either two, three, or four units of duration which most transcribers of Irish music represent as eighth-notes, or sometimes as sixteenth-notes.

As stated above, a note has both pitch and duration. A melody then, or a tune, is formed by a succession of notes (pitches and durations).

Rhythm is difficult to define succinctly. In *The Harvard Dictionary of Music,* Willi Apel attempts this by stating that "rhythm is everything pertaining to the temporal quality (duration) of the musical sound."[iii]

This broad definition will work for our present purpose, which is to integrate the *rhythms* of the notes with the two-dimensional "interval map" of the melody. This sounds complex, but it needn't be experienced that way. What we are doing is stretching our powers of attention so that as we learn a tune, we create an on-going, three-dimensional melody in our mind's ear.

GETTING MORE PHYSICAL

Music is a profoundly physical experience. It is made up of air compression waves that affect our bodies and make them vibrate. Over-dependence upon music notation dulls our perceptions of the physical sensations of music and causes us to externalize and conceptualize it, to remove ourselves from it in a very real sense. Learning music by ear again, for we all did so as children, brings us back into full, physical contact with music.

So, as you are learning a tune, immediately bring your focus to the physical nature of the sound:

- The relationship of each note to the tonal center (higher than, lower than, the same as)
- The feelings and sizes of the vertical intervals between each melody note and the tonal center
- The feelings and sizes of the horizontal intervals that join the successive notes of the tune

- The shapes and phrases in the melody
- The pulse of the tune
- The subdivision of that pulse (into two, three, or four smaller units of time; described more later in this chapter)
- The rhythms formed by the melody notes as they overlay the pulse
- The patterns of your finger movements as you play the melody
- Your overall physical experience of the music

Store this awareness inside of yourself instead of externalizing it, relegating it to written music. If you enjoy computer metaphors, store the tune on your huge internal hard drive, not on a removable disk that you put away in some desk drawer. The more you cultivate this internalizing mode of learning, the more natural and sophisticated it will become. It's amazing just how vast our internal memory banks are. There is room for many hundreds of tunes.

OTHER AIDS TO MEMORY

Each tune has one or more names which belong with the tune for specific reasons. Often those reasons are unknown or obscure to us, and many people seem to have trouble maintaining the connections between tunes and their names. Make an effort to establish this connection early on, even if a name's meaning is mysterious to you. You may remember the tune better by connecting it to an image, a person, even to an uncertainty or a curiosity, to a special meaning the name may have for you, and to the larger world of the tradition. Connect the tune also to the time, place, people, and circumstances that surrounded you as you first heard it or began to learn it.

Notice these things about the tune: its tonal center, its mode, its first few notes, its meter, and dance tune type. Link all of these things to the name of the tune. Later, remembering or hearing the first few notes of a tune will bring it all back to you in a flash.

Luckily, the structural aspects of Irish tunes, compared with the structures of classical music, are quite simple and even formulaic in some respects, and therefore easy to remember. Understanding these structures will aid your learning a great deal. It's what happens within and through these simple structures that is so endlessly various and beautiful.

Despite my caveats about music notation, I make extensive use of it in this book. The combination of music notation, the audio CD, and these words on paper are the next best thing to personal contact. Thankfully, these three modes of demonstration, when used together, actually can convey a great deal of useful information.

SOME NOTATION CONVENTIONS

There are many good books that teach the rudiments of reading music. I am not going to duplicate their content here. However, I would like to explore a few aspects of music notation that are particularly relevant to this book.

THE MODAL NATURE OF IRISH MUSIC

In today's common practice of classical and popular music, almost all tonal music is considered to be in either a major or minor *key*, that is, based upon the central use of certain major or minor scales. The major and natural minor scales, the two predominant scales used in popular western music today, have early historical roots and are only two of seven *modes* that came to form the tonal basis for Gregorian chant and the rest of western medieval and renaissance music. These modes are also found in many of the world's ethnic musical traditions.

The word *mode* has a number of meanings, but in this case we'll use it to refer to "the selection of tones, arranged in a scale, which forms the basic tonal substance of a composition."[iv] There are many more than seven modes in world musical traditions, but for the moment we need only be concerned with the seven so-called *church modes* of western European music.

The vast majority of traditional Irish music makes use of only four of these seven modes: the Ionian (which we commonly call the *major* scale), the Dorian, the Mixolydian, and the Aeolian (which we commonly call the *natural minor* scale). In fact, the first three of these account for most of traditional Irish melody. Ocassionally you will encounter tunes in the Lydian mode.

Each of the seven modes, shown below, contains a unique sequence that includes five major seconds (or whole-steps) and two minor seconds (or half-steps, semitones) that occur as you ascend through its scale. The minor seconds in the following three figures are indicated by slurs.

One of the simplest ways to listen to and get to know these modes is to play ascending scales on only the white keys of a piano. Starting on C and playing in this manner, you hear the notes of the C Ionian mode. Starting on D, you hear the D Dorian mode, and so on. Note well the locations of the half steps in each mode.

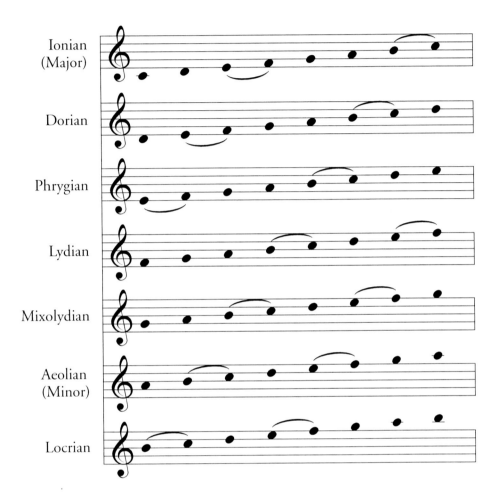

Figure 1-1: The seven so-called church modes, as played on the white keys of the piano.

 Track 1

THE TONAL CENTER OF THE MODE

Each mode has a tonal center, which is the first, lowest note of its scale. In Irish music this tonal center can reside on any one of various pitches, most commonly D, E, G, A, or B. We often say that a tune in the Mixolydian mode with a tonal center of D is "in D Mixolydian." Similarly, a tune in the Dorian mode that has a tonal center of E is "in E Dorian." The tune will usually come to rest on the pitch of the tonal center at various points, especially at the ends of some of its important phrases.

As mentioned earlier, it is very important to sense, identify, and retain this tonal center. The notes of the tune gain "meaning" in their relation to it. Keeping track of the tonal center and each note's intervallic relationship to it (the vertical intervals) will greatly enhance your ability to learn, internalize, and remember tunes.

Those who are familiar with the major and minor keys (i.e. the Ionian and Aeolian modes) may find it helpful to understand the Dorian and Mixolydian modes in terms of how they differ from the Ionian and Aeolian. The Mixolydian mode is like the Ionian (major) with a flatted or lowered seventh note (lowered by one semitone). The Dorian mode is like the Aeolian (natural minor) with a raised sixth note (raised by one semitone).

17

These comparisons are shown below. Play through them on an instrument or sing them. Note how only the position of the second half-step differs in each comparison while the position of the first half-step remains the same.

Figure 1-2: Comparisons between the Ionian and Mixolydian modes, and the Aeolian and Dorian modes.

 Track 2

The combinations of mode and tonal center most commonly encountered in Irish flute, tin whistle, and uilleann pipe music are shown in Figure 1-3. Those containing G-sharps (i.e. A Ionian and B Dorian) are encountered less often than the others.

Figure 1-3: The modes most commonly encountered in Irish flute, tin whistle, and uilleann pipe music. Note well the mode signatures.

"MODE SIGNATURES" INSTEAD OF KEY SIGNATURES

Note that in Figure 1-3 I have used the appropriate "mode signatures" for each mode instead of using accidentals. The term "signature" refers to the sharps or flats placed at the beginning of a piece of music that determine the normal state of that piece's pitches. "Accidentals" are sharp or flat signs that indicate a temporary (within one measure) semitone raising or lowering of a pitch from its usual state (i.e. natural, sharp, or flat) as shown in the mode signature.

Take special note of these mode signatures. Musicians who are used to operating on the assumption that every signature indicates a major key or its relative minor key will have to expand their thinking somewhat.

You may have noticed that there are no flats in these mode signatures. Modal scales that include flats, such as G Dorian, D Dorian, and F Ionian, are encountered in the special repertoires of the fiddle, banjo, and accordion and are not often played on the whistle.

Throughout this book I will be using mode signatures. Therefore, when you see a signature of two sharps, for example, don't assume that the tune is in D major (Ionian) or B minor (Aeolian). It could just as easily be in E Dorian or A Mixolydian. There is a growing trend toward using mode signatures, as they result in fewer accidentals and they reflect the true modal nature of Irish music.

PENTATONIC MODES

Some tunes use fewer than seven notes, such as tunes that are in a five-note, or *pentatonic mode.* There are two such pentatonic modes common in Irish music.

The first is formed by omitting the fourth and seventh notes of the Ionian mode. In the tonality of D this yields a scale of D, E, F-sharp, A, and B. I call this the "Ionian Pentatonic" mode. The second is formed by omitting the third and sixth notes of the Dorian mode. In the tonality of E this yields a scale of E, F-sharp, A, B, and D. I call this the "Dorian Pentatonic" mode. Note that these two examples, which are shown below, contain the same pitches and therefore share the same mode signature, though they have different tonal centers.

Even though neither of these pentatonic modes contains a C-sharp, C-sharp is indicated in their mode signatures. If a player were to use a C as either a passing tone or as a variation of a tune in one of these modes, it would properly be a C-sharp, not a C-natural.

In practice, I find that there are not so many Irish tunes that adhere strictly and totally to either of these pentatonic modes. Most of them include at least one instance of one or both of the missing notes. Many tunes have one part that is in a pentatonic mode while its other parts are not.

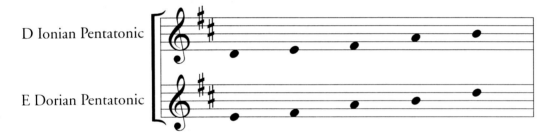

Figure 1-4: Examples of the two pentatonic modes found in Irish music,
the Ionian Pentatonic and the Dorian Pentatonic.

The Ionian Pentatonic mode is commonly encountered with a tonal center of either D or G. The first part of the reel *The Banshee* is in this mode.

The Dorian Pentatonic mode can be found with a tonal center of D, E, G, A, or B. An example of a tune in this mode is *Tom Billy's Jig.* Transcriptions and recordings of these two tunes are available online at <www.greylarsen.com/extras/toolbox>.

OUTSIDE THE MODAL BOUNDARIES

There are many Irish tunes that don't fit neatly into the profile of any of these modes. Some use *both* major and minor thirds and/or sixths. Some employ notes that fall in between the half steps. This happens in particular in the area of C-natural to C-sharp and F-natural to F-sharp on the whistle, flute, and uilleann pipes.

C-natural is an especially variable note on the uilleann pipes that, according to Breandán Breathnach, possesses "...several colors... which are exploited to the full by the skillful performer. It lies approximately halfway between B and D…"[v], in other words, approximately halfway between the equal-tempered C-natural and C-sharp. In fact, at least half the time, C-natural is played according to our modern intonation expectations, but often, especially in tunes with a tonal center of G, A or D, the sharper "piping C" is used by traditional whistle and flute players. The pitch of C-natural can change even during the course of a single note.

On the whistle, you can finger C-natural by using a *cross-fingering* or by *half-holing*. A "cross-fingering" is a fingering in which there is an open hole above one or more closed holes ("above" meaning closer to the mouthpiece).[vi] "Half-holing" refers to the practice of only partially covering a tone hole in order to play a pitch that is in between the pitches produced by fully covering the tone hole in question and fully uncovering that same tone hole.

You can play this "piping C" by using special cross-fingerings that we will explore later. All of these fingering options produce Cs with differing tone and pitch colors, and these relate quite directly to the tradition of uilleann piping. All of this will become more clear as you work your way through the book.

One more observation about C-natural and C-sharp: When playing C as a quick passing note between B and D, Irish whistle and flute players will usually play the note as a C-sharp, even if C-sharp is not in the mode of the tune. This may be in large part because playing B—C-sharp—D makes for an easier fingering sequence. The C-sharp goes by quickly enough that its altered pitch does not seem all that apparent. But, this use of C-sharp is actually an important element of style, not just a fingering convenience. If you play such notes as C-naturals, they often just sound "wrong" to someone with an ear that is finely tuned to traditional Irish music. Examples of this use of C-sharp occur in the jig *The Cliffs of Moher* and the slip jig *Hardiman the Fiddler*. Excerpts from these tunes appear in this book. Transcriptions and recordings of the complete tunes are available online at <www.greylarsen.com/extras/toolbox>.

MOST WHISTLES SOUND ONE OCTAVE HIGHER THAN WRITTEN

The most common and useful tin whistle is the small one in D. This instrument plays one octave higher than the flute, fiddle, pipes, etc. When reading tune transcriptions, this whistle sounds one octave higher than the notated music.

The much larger low D whistle, which plays one octave lower than the small D whistle (i.e. at the same pitch as the flute, fiddle, pipes, etc.) has become increasingly popular at the time of this writing.

Whistles come in a variety of keys other than D. For the purpose of music notation, these "non-D" whistles are considered to be *transposing* instruments, that is, "instruments for which the music is written in another key or octave than that of their actual sound."[vii] (By this definition, the small D whistle is also technically a transposing instrument.) All the whistles are treated as if they were D whistles even if they produce music that is either higher or lower in pitch level than that of the small D whistle.

For example, the C whistle is one whole step lower in pitch than the small D whistle. The lowest note of a C whistle is, naturally, a C, and is played with all six tone holes covered, the fingering that produces D on a D whistle. For the purpose of music notation, this lowest note of *any* whistle is considered to be a D. Therefore, when reading a tune you would use the exact same fingerings, no matter what key of whistle you choose to play it on. Let's say you are playing a tune that is in D Ionian. If you play it on a C whistle, you use the same fingerings that you would use to play it on a D whistle, but the music comes out in C Ionian.

USING NON-D WHISTLES TO PLAY TUNES THAT ARE IN "DIFFICULT" MODES

Now, here's a different situation. Let's say there is a great tune in D Dorian that you want to play on the whistle, along with other musicians. Playing in D Dorian is usually impractical on the D whistle because in this mode you often encounter F-naturals, which are relatively difficult to finger.

To solve this problem, you can play the tune on a C whistle, playing it as if it were in E Dorian (which necessitates using different fingerings), a mode that is very well suited to the whistle. Since the C whistle is a whole-step lower than the D whistle, and since you are now fingering the tune in a mode that is a whole-step *higher* than where it is notated, these two factors cancel each other out and the tune "comes out" sounding in D Dorian, right where you want it to be.

In case you are having trouble following this, let's use music notation to illustrate. Below is the first part of *Tuttle's Reel,* in D Dorian. Note the mode signature for D Dorian: no flats. (The key signature for D minor, i.e. D Aeolian, has one flat.)

*Figure 1-5: The first part of **Tuttle's Reel,** which is in D Dorian.*

Track 4

Note that there are a number of F-naturals in this tune. Though it is possible to play them on a D whistle, using half-hole fingerings, it is rather difficult. It is much easier to play the tune on a C whistle by fingering the tune as if you were playing a D whistle in E Dorian, as notated below. Note the mode signature.

*Figure 1-6: The first part of **Tuttle's Reel,** transposed up to E Dorian.*

Track 5

Played this way on a C whistle, the tune will sound in D Dorian, as shown in Figure 1-5. This strategy also solves the problem of the low C in bar 4 of Figure 1-5, which is too low for the D whistle.

Tonguing and Slurring

To **tongue,** in the musical terminology of wind instruments, means to use an action of the tongue to articulate or separate notes. You can use the tongue to stop and to start the flow of air.

To **slur** means to connect two or more notes such that only the first note of the group is articulated. A slurred group of notes is played using an uninterrupted, continuous stream of air. Only the first note of a slurred group is tongued.

Note: some people use the word *slur* (or *smear*) to mean a gradual, continuous pitch change. I call such pitch changes **slides.** Chapter 9 is devoted to an exploration of slides.

I follow common practice for notating slurs: an arched line above or below the noteheads of the slurred group. The arched line itself is called a slur. The first, and *only* the first, note within the slur is articulated. The rest are smoothly connected to this first, articulated note.

All notes that are not within a slur are articulated with tonguing.

A typical example of slur notation is shown below.

Figure 1-7: An example of the use of slur notation.

 Track 6

In this example, the letter "t" (for *tongue*) appears below each note that is articulated. Notice that only the first note of each slurred group is articulated. (These "t"s do not normally appear in written music. They are placed in this example only to help clarify the meaning of slur notation.)

The Classification of Instrumental Irish Music

Broadly speaking, instrumental Irish music can be divided into two categories: *dance music* and *non-dance music.*

Non-dance music includes slow airs, marches, planxties (tribute pieces), and most of the other compositions of O'Carolan, and other harpers, which have found a home in the repertoires of traditional musicians. In this book, we will work with dance music only.

In fact, the bulk of instrumental Irish music played in Ireland today is dance music. A large portion of this body of music is made up of the three most common dance tune types: *reels, double jigs,* and *hornpipes.* Other tune types which may be common, depending on the locale, are *slip jigs, single jigs, slides,* and *polkas,* as well as *set dances, flings, highlands, schottisches, germans, barn dances, mazurkas, varsoviennes, strathspeys,* and *waltzes.* For information on these tune types, see my book *The Essential Guide to Irish Flute and Tin Whistle.*

Pulse

All Irish tunes, except for most slow airs, have a steady recurring beat where we are inclined to tap our foot. This is the *pulse,* the heartbeat of the music. Most of this music is dance music.

Meter: Duple or Triple

As you listen to a wide variety of Irish music you will find that the pulses in most tunes are grouped in pairs. You would count them, "**one,** two; **one,** two." The first pulse in each pair is stronger. It carries more stress or weight than the second pulse.

In some other tunes the pulses come in groups of three. You would count them "**one**, two, three; **one**, two, three." Again the first pulse of these groups of three carries the most weight.

This regular, consistent grouping or patterning of the pulse is called **meter**. If the pulses of the tune are grouped in pairs, we say the tune is in *duple meter*. If the pulses of the tune are grouped in threes, we say the tune is in *triple meter*. *Quadruple meter* can be said to occur in Irish music, in tunes such as slides and some marches, but these tunes can also be felt to be in duple meter. The question of quadruple meter vs. duple meter is mostly one of how one chooses to notate a tune, not of how one hears or feels it.

Many other kinds of meter exist, but they are not found in Irish music.

Don't Confuse Meter and Tempo

Some people confuse the words *meter* and *tempo*. **Tempo** simply means the speed at which a piece of music is played. This can be described subjectively, with phrases such as "moderately fast," "very slow," etc., or can be quantified as a number of beats per minute (bpm). Bpm numbers are shown on metronomes.

Subdivision of the Pulse: Simple or Compound

In all Irish tunes which have a pulse, that pulse is subdivided into either two, three, or four shorter notes of equal duration. When the pulse is subdivided into two or four notes, this is called *simple* subdivision. When the pulse is subdivided into three notes, this is called *compound* subdivision.

Summary of Meters

The following table summarizes the dance tune types, their meters, and the subdivision of their pulse.

Meter	Tune Types	Time Signatures
Simple Duple Meter	Reel	2/2
	Polka	2/4
	Hornpipe	2/2 or 4/4
	March	2/2 or 4/4
	Schottische, Highland, Fling, Highland Fling	4/4
	German, Barn Dance	4/4
	Strathspey	4/4
Compound Duple Meter	Double Jig	6/8
	Single Jig	6/8
	Slide	12/8 or 6/8
	March	6/8 or 12/8
Simple Triple Meter	Waltz	3/4
	Mazurka, Varsovienne	3/4
Compound Triple Meter	Slip Jig, Hop Jig	9/8

Table 1-1: Summary of meters, tune types, and time signatures.

The Essentially Melodic Nature of Irish Music

In traditional Irish music, melody is king. A solo rendition of a tune is complete in and of itself, and functions perfectly well without accompaniment.

The great flute player Matt Molloy was quoted as follows in a 1979 interview:[viii]

The real art form, as far as traditional music is concerned, is actually playing solo, that's what it's about. It's the interpretation that you can give a melodic line, the basic line there of a tune. You stand or fall on your interpretation of that particular piece. It's no use playing it the same way I play it. Or me taking something and playing it similar to someone else. You have to put your own particular stamp on it. And be that good, bad, or indifferent, at least it's you. It's your personality. Ultimately that's what you stand or fall on.

Harmonic accompaniment, other than the drone of the pipes, may have begun in America "where Irish musicians were a staple element of minstrelsy, musical theater, and vaudeville during the 19th century."[ix] Percussive and harmonic accompanists must be very careful to support and not to overpower or restrict the melody.

THE LEGACY OF IRISH BAGPIPING

The Irish bagpiping tradition has played a seminal role in the development of the playing styles of all other melodic instruments used in traditional Irish music today, especially in the areas of articulation and ornamentation. As a wind instrument, the tin whistle bears a more direct relationship to the pipes than do the string or free reed instruments.

The modern Irish pipes are referred to as the *uilleann pipes,* the *union pipes,* or simply the *Irish pipes. Uilleann,* apparently a form of an old Irish word for "elbow," makes reference to the right arm's pumping of a bellows which fills a bag, held under the left arm, which in turn provides a continuous supply of air to the instrument. The melody pipe is called the *chanter.* Three *drone* pipes supply a constant accompaniment by sounding a note that is in unison with the low note of the chanter, usually D, as well as notes one octave and two octaves below this pitch. The *regulators* are specialized, keyed chanters that make possible the occasional additions of one, two, or three harmony notes to the melody and drones. The keys of the regulators are usually played with the heel or wrist of the lower hand. All of this can be seen in Figure 1-8.

The history of the uilleann pipes is a developing field of study. Current research indicates that the uilleann pipes' closest ancestor was probably the pastoral bagpipe. For much more on this, see my book *The Essential Guide to Irish Flute and Tin Whistle.*

The melody of the pastoral pipes was a constant, unbroken stream of sound. All articulation, by necessity, was created *solely* by movements of the fingers. The same was true of the *píob mór,* another Irish bagpipe that preceded the uilleann pipes historically, and which may have played a role in the development of the uilleann pipes.

In contrast to the pastoral pipes and the *píob mór,* the uilleann pipes evolved the capacity to play separated notes as well as connected notes: *staccato* as well as *legato.* (For definitions of these terms, see Chapter 12, p. 164.) This gave the instrument expressive possibilities that many believe make its music the most highly developed form of piping in the world.

Figure 1-8. Declan Masterson playing the uilleann pipes at the 1991 Willie Clancy Summer School, Milltown Malbay, Co. Clare. The seated listener is Drew Hillman.

An Inherited Legato Aesthetic

Still, uilleann piping was deeply affected by the pastoral bagpipe and *píob mór* traditions. It inherited a fundamental and deeply held aesthetic from these ancestral bagpipe traditions, and combined it with its staccato capability to create a new synthesis, one that is also shared by Irish tin whistle players: **The music, in all its variety, springs forth from an underlying foundation of legato playing. The appropriate use of staccato playing exists in relation to that foundation, and takes on its meaning in contrast to it.**

This legato aesthetic is essentially different from that of modern classical music. The classical wind player is taught that all notes are to be tongued unless there is an indication in the notated music, such as a slur, to do otherwise. Most Irish players use tonguing intuitively as an expressive device *against a general backdrop of slurring*. Classically-trained musicians who wish to learn to play traditional Irish music must come to understand this critical distinction.

Tonguing, in fact, is used extensively in both classical and Irish traditions, but in each it is thought of in a very different way. Much of the tonguing used in Irish tin whistle playing goes unnoticed, because on the whole traditional players use a very connected kind of tonguing that does not take the music away from its fundamentally legato nature.

It seems to me that the traditional Irish musician has much more variety of articulation available to her than does the classical wind player. In classical wind instrument playing, notes are *either* articulated *or* slurred. In Irish traditional music notes can be both articulated *and* slurred, because of its fingered articulations: the cut and the strike (see Chapters 7 and 8). Classical wind players do not have a common practice of fingered articulations.

Where Do You Breathe?

The flute and whistle are the only instruments of traditional Irish music that are not suited to non-stop playing. They share a vast repertoire of tunes with the fiddle, pipes, accordion, banjo, concertina, etc., and the tunes have no built-in breathing places. We must create our own by leaving out notes or shortening longer notes. I address this subject in depth in Chapter 13, *Musical Breathing*.

Lilt, or Swing

Irish dance music is rarely, if ever, played in an absolutely even rhythmic fashion, i.e. with all eighth-notes being exactly identical in duration. The same is true of many varieties of folk, ethnic, and popular music. Classical players, who are generally used to playing evenly, tend to notice this uneven quality right away. Musicians who are used to playing unevenly sometimes are not aware that they are not playing evenly.

This pattern of variance is often referred to as the *lilt* or *swing* (or sometimes *sway*) in a player's style. Each player has her own quality and degree of lilt and it varies with the speed of playing, mood, whom she is playing with, whether or not she is playing for dancers, and other factors.

Classically-trained musicians who are new to traditional Irish music often find the lilt of Irish music to be very elusive. Lilt is an aspect of the music that cannot be learned in an analytical, self-conscious fashion. It cannot be written down. It can only be internalized by immersion, by ear, just as an accent in speech is picked up unconsciously. It helps to feel these rhythms in your body, so if you have an opportunity to learn to dance to Irish music it will no doubt be very helpful.

Lilt is an element of musical personality and it naturally differs from player to player. If you do a lot of listening it will emerge in your playing over time.

Variance of Stress or Weight

Lilt involves not only the variance of duration, but also the variance of the stress or weight that is given to notes. The notes that are given more stress and longer duration are the notes that fall on more important subdivisions of the beat. To make this more clear, let's look at reels and jigs.

Reels are usually notated in 2/2 time, with each half-note pulse subdivided into four eighth-notes. If you are an English speaker and you say the word *generator* over and over, you will notice that you do not give each syllable absolutely the same weight and duration. There is a lilt inherent in the delivery of the word. The first syllable gets the most weight and duration. The third gets a bit less, but still more than the second and fourth which are roughly equal to each other. This pattern of varying duration and stress could be represented thus: **GEN**-er-a-tor, **GEN**-er-a-tor, **GEN**-er-a-tor. The use of boldface and capitalization indicates added stress and duration. This resembles the lilt of reels.

Jigs are notated in 6/8 time. The measure contains two dotted-quarter-note pulses which are each subdivided into three eighth notes. Again, if you are an English speaker, say the word *energy* over and over and notice the lilt inherent in that word: **EN**-er-gy, **EN**-er-gy, **EN**-er-gy. The first syllable gets the most stress and duration. It borrows some time from the second, which gets the least amount of stress and duration (notice that syllable's smaller type size.) The third syllable is stronger and longer than the second, getting approximately one-third share of the available time. Musically, it functions as a *pick-up note* that leads you into the next pulse. This scheme resembles the lilt of jigs.

PLAYING "ON THE FRONT OF THE BEAT"

Lilt is heard in the uneven subdivision of the pulse and the variance of stress. It is also heard in another way. If you listen carefully, you will notice that traditional Irish musicians tend to play "on the front of the beat." That is, they tend to place on-pulse notes a very slight bit early. This lends the music a feeling of "leaning forward," of forward motion and momentum. Some Irish musicians speak of a feeling of "lift" on the downbeat.

By contrast, blues musicians, to give one example, often do the opposite. They tend to play on the back of the beat, placing on-pulse notes a very slight bit late. This creates a "laid-back" feeling.

Sometimes you may notice that an Irish player who is tapping her foot seems to be playing a little ahead of the beat that her foot is setting. This is probably not evidence of sloppy foot tapping, but instead shows how she is playing on the front of the beat.

In an ensemble setting, different players may not always swing to the same degree and in the same ways. If they are very experienced playing together, they will intuitively find a way to fit their "swings" together to create a group lilt that gives great cohesion and energy to their sound.

"EVEN" PLAYING IS RARELY REALLY EVEN

Throughout this book I notate jigs, slip jigs and reels in even eighth notes and I often recommend playing the notes in an "even" fashion when you are learning the basic physical motions and coordination of a new technique. In these situations I believe it is best to practice slowly in a truly even rhythm, along with a metronome. Once you are comfortable with a technique, it is fine to use it in accordance with whatever lilt you may normally employ.

The faster an Irish musician plays, the more even her playing tends to become. If this didn't happen, then fast playing would sound too stilted.

TUNES WITH AN OVERTLY UNEVEN SUBDIVISION OF THE BEAT

There are tunes that are played in an overtly uneven fashion, such as hornpipes, mazurkas, schottisches, flings, barn dances, and germans. These tunes are normally played much more unevenly than reels, jigs, etc. There is no consensus on how to notate them. I prefer to notate them with even eighth notes and occasional triplets, a notational style which does not reflect the reality of their sound, but which I believe is the best compromise. I elaborate upon this subject in my book *The Essential Guide to Irish Flute and Tin Whistle*.

NATURE AND MUSIC SEEK A BALANCE

As you begin to pay attention to the lilt of good players, you will notice that it is changeable and flexible. There are some times when a heavier swing is called for and others when a more even delivery is appropriate. Even within a single tune there is such variance. If you adopt a "signature lilt" and adhere to it at all times, your playing will seem rigid and contracted, instead of flexible and expansive. Aim to be supple and let your lilt adjust itself to the nature of the moment. Let the music breathe.

As you can see, lilt is a complex and elusive thing, comprised of several interactive and changeable elements. It is not hard to hear it, but it is difficult to describe it in words.

AN IMPORTANT ELEMENT OF PERSONAL AND REGIONAL STYLES

Lilt is clearly an important element of personal style. It is sometimes an identifiable element of regional style as well. For example, Galway players, such as the late flute player Paddy Carty, tend to play more evenly than Sligo players, such as flute player Seamus Tansey. However, such generalizations are of limited use because they tend to break apart as you listen closely to individual players, especially in modern times as the definitions of regional styles are blurring due to decreasing isolation.

---

[i] Mary Larsen, "Martin Hayes, A Lilt All His Own", *Fiddler Magazine*, Spring 1994: p. 9.

[ii] Robert Jourdain, *Music, the Brain, and Ecstasy* (New York: Avon Books, 1997), pp. 281-282.

[iii] Willi Apel, *Harvard Dictionary of Music*, (1944; 20th printing, Cambridge, MA: Harvard Univ. Press, 1968), p. 640.

[iv] Willi Apel, p. 452.

[v] Breandán Breathnach, *Folk Music & Dances of Ireland*, (Dublin: The Talbot Press, 1971), p. 14.

[vi] John Smith and Joe Wolfe, in the International Congress on Acoustics, Rome, Session 8.09, pp. 14-15, describe cross fingering in this way: "Opening successive tone holes in woodwind instruments shortens the standing wave in the bore. However, the standing wave propagates past the first open hole, so its frequency can be affected by closing other tone holes further downstream. This is called cross fingering, and in some instruments is used to produce the 'sharps and flats' missing from their natural scales." In the case of C-natural, the most commonly used cross-fingering on tin whistle has T2 and T3 covering their holes with all other holes open.

[vii] Willi Apel, p. 756.

[viii] This is from an interview with Matt Molloy by Sean McCutcheon, a flute player from Montréal, that took place on September 26, 1997. I found it on Brad Hurley's website, "A Guide to the Irish Flute", <http://www.firescribble.net/flute/molloy.html>.

[ix] L. E. McCullough, *The Complete Tin Whistle Tutor* (New York: Oak Publications, 1976), p. 4.

chapter 2: a brief look into the history and development of the tin whistle

The tin whistle also goes by the names *pennywhistle, whistle,* and sometimes *tin flute*. In Irish it is known as the *feadóg* or *feadán*. It is undoubtedly the most affordable of the traditional melody instruments of Irish music, and for that

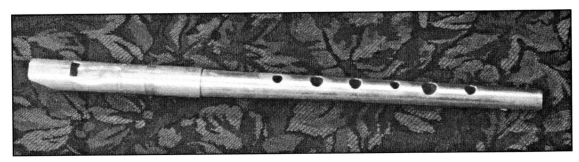

Figure 2-1. A small D tin whistle made by Michael Copeland, c. 1995, Conshohocken, Pennsylvania.

A FIPPLE FLUTE

The tin whistle is an end-blown, vertically-held, six-hole *fipple flute,* in the same family as the recorder and numerous other fipple flutes found throughout world musical traditions.

In fipple flutes, tone is produced by blowing air through a special mouthpiece that makes use of a small plug or block (the fipple) that is made of wood or other material. Sometimes the fipple is instead built into the shape of the mouthpiece itself, as is the case with the one-piece plastic mouthpieces of Generation and similar brands of factory-made whistles. A small air channel is created between the fipple and the inside wall of the instrument. The air stream is shaped by and directed through this channel to a sharp edge or blade that splits the airstream, causing the air column to vibrate and produce sound.

A VERY LONG HISTORY

L. E. McCullough, in his book *The Complete Tin Whistle Tutor,*[i] gives a fascinating summary of the history of the tin whistle, tracing its origins back to whistle-like instruments that are described in written records in Ireland dating as far back as the third century A.D. The *feadán* is mentioned by name in the 11th-century Irish poem "Aonach Carman," contained in the *Book of Leinster,*[ii] as is the *cuiseach,* an instrument made of reeds or corn stalks from which the pith had been removed.[iii]

There is no doubt that this simple type of fipple flute has been hand-crafted by ancient peoples around the globe for many centuries. Much attention has come in recent years to the 12th-century bone whistles unearthed in the old Norman quarter of Dublin. Certainly, Irish people made their own whistles out of bone, wood, or reeds before factory-made tin whistles came on to the scene.

The manufactured tin whistle seems to have had its origins, at least in part, in the *flageolet,* a wooden fipple flute that reached its peak of popularity in Europe during the Renaissance and Baroque periods and which underwent a revival in the late 1700s and early 1800s. Flageolet maker Andrew Ellard was active in Dublin from 1819 to 1838 and Joseph and James Corbett made flageolets in Limerick between 1801 and 1814.[iv]

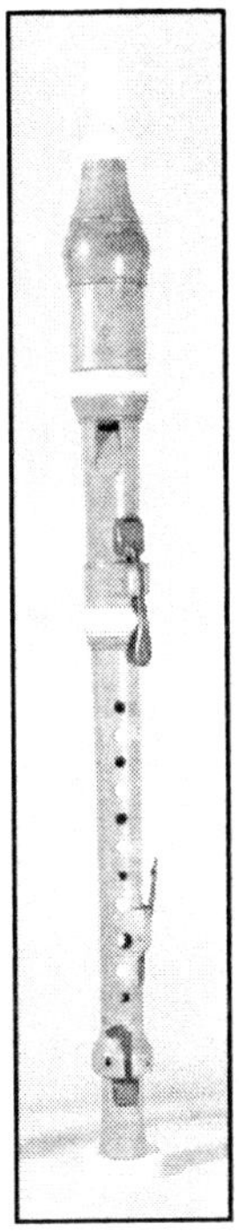

Figure 2-2. Anonymous 19th-century flageolet, from the Dayton C. Miller flute collection, Library of Congress, Washington, DC. The instrument was made in two sections. The upper section has the mouthpiece and fipple, a C-natural key, and a two-part sponge chamber (for absorbing breath condensation). The lower section has E-flat and F-natural keys and ivory finger studs. Made of boxwood with silver keys and ivory ferrules, finger studs, and mouthpiece.

At present, the earliest known evidence of the flageolet's use in traditional Irish music seems to be the reference to the "flagelet" in the subtitle of the 1804 uilleann pipe tutor and tunebook *O'Farrell's Collection of National Irish Music for the Union Pipes*.[v] The subtitle reads:

> Comprising a Variety of the Most Favorite Slow & Sprightly Tunes, set in proper Stile & Taste, with Variations and Adapted Likewise for the German Flute, Violin, Flagelet, Piano & Harp, with a Selection of Favorite Scotch Tunes, Also a Treatise with the most Perfect Instructions ever yet Published for the Pipes.

MANUFACTURED TIN WHISTLES

Inexpensive manufactured tin whistles became available in Ireland certainly no later than the mid-1840s with the introduction of instruments such as the English-made Clarke tin whistle. Unlike the flageolet, which was made of wood turned on a lathe, these whistles were made out of sheet tin rolled around a mandrel and could be produced, and purchased, at very small expense, hence the name pennywhistle. This name may also have come from street musicians who would play tunes on the whistle in exchange for the pennies of passersby.

The tradition of Irish people making their own whistles has persisted even into our time. L. E. McCullough writes that

> …uilleann pipemaker Patrick Hennelly of Chicago recalled that as a young lad in Mayo, he often made musical instruments from ripe oat straws simply by pushing out the pith and then fashioning the lip and fingerholes with a penknife, and, indeed, the basic structural principles of such instruments must have been discovered fairly early and by many people.[vi]

HIGHER REGARD FOR THE TIN WHISTLE

It appears that, until the 1960s, the tin whistle was not taken very seriously by most people in Ireland, being seen more as an introductory instrument for aspiring pipers and flute players as well as a good starting instrument for children. The Irish music revival of the 1960s and 70s, however, brought to light such masterful whistle players as Seán Potts, Mary Bergin, Paddy Maloney, Micho Russell, and Donncha Ó Bríain, who showed the world how highly developed and expressive tin whistle playing could be.

In response, there has been a tremendous flowering of innovation in tin whistle making, especially since the 1980s, resulting in a standard of quality never seen before. Now it is possible to buy fine hand-crafted whistles made of metal, wood, or plastic that are capable of responding to the finest nuances of a masterful player. Inexpensive whistles also abound in a wider variety than ever before.

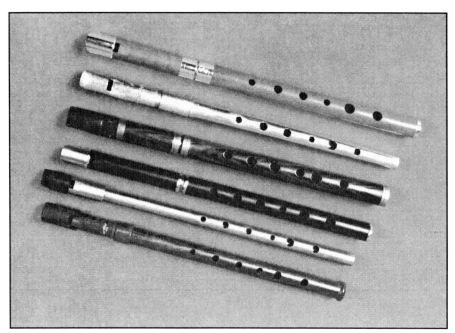

Figure 2-3. Six tin whistles in D. From top to bottom: Abell, Copeland, O'Riordan, Schultz, Sindt, and Susato. All of these have tuning slides and all have cylindrical bores except the Copeland and Susato, which have conical bores.

A VARIETY OF SHAPES, SIZES, KEYS, AND PRICES

The small whistle in the key of D, which plays an octave higher than the flute, fiddle, pipes, etc., is by far the most popular and useful. No whistler should be without a good small D whistle. Whistles are made in a wide variety of keys, including low-D whistles that can play in unison with the other standard melody instruments of Irish music.

There is a very broad array of whistles available today. Some have cylindrical bores and others conical. There are many inexpensive mass-produced whistles and an ever-growing selection of fine, more expensive, hand-made instruments. Improved mouthpieces for inexpensive whistles are being made, and whistles often come with several differently pitched bodies that can each be used with a single headjoint.

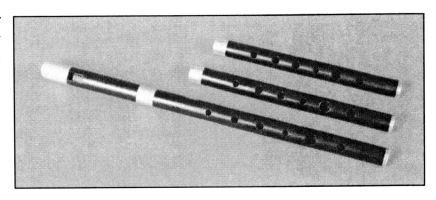

Figure 2-4. A set of three whistles bodies, in the keys of E-flat, D, and C (top to bottom), that share a single headjoint. Made by Chris Abell in grenadilla and silver.

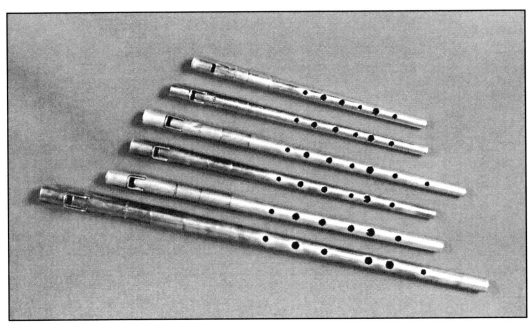

Figure 2-5. Not quite a complete set of whistles by Michael Copeland. From top to bottom: Small D, C, B-flat, A, G, and Low D. Note that this particular B-flat whistle has a seventh hole which gives it a low note of A-flat.

It may be prudent for many to start off with an inexpensive instrument. But if you decide to pursue more serious playing, you owe it to yourself to get a good hand-made instrument, one that plays well in tune, has a tuning slide, and will respond well and quickly to the subtleties of your playing. While these instruments cost quite a bit more than the mass-produced ones, they are still a bargain compared to other high-quality musical instruments.

THE ACCESSIBLE MODES

The tin whistle is somewhat limited outside of its natural scale and several closely related modes. (For information on modes, see Chapter 1.) One can obtain chromatic notes by the half-covering of tone holes and by using cross-fingerings, but these techniques are impractical for some musical situations. This is one reason why whistles in keys other than D can come in very handy. For instance, one can play D Dorian tunes by playing them as if they were in E Dorian on a tin whistle in the key of C. (For more on this subject, see Chapter 1.)

On a D whistle, one can easily play, without half-hole fingerings, in the following modes:

- D Ionian (major) and Mixolydian
- E Dorian and Aeolian (natural minor)
- G Ionian (major)
- A Mixolydian and Dorian
- B Aeolian (natural minor)

Tin Whistles are Simple-System Instruments

As stated elsewhere, the tin whistle and simple-system flute share the same fingering system, one which is almost the same as that of the uilleann pipes. As a result, fingering techniques on the whistle and Irish flute are nearly identical and both are very closely related to those of the uilleann pipes.

[i] L. E. McCullough, *The Complete Tin Whistle Tutor* (New York: Oak Publications, 1987), pp. 6–8.

[ii] Gearoíd Ó hAllmhuráin, *A Pocket History of Traditional Irish Music* (Dublin: O'Brien Press, 1998), p. 13.

[iii] Breandán Breathnach, *Folk Music & Dances of Ireland* (Dublin: The Talbot Press, 1971), p.5.

[iv] McCullough, p. 8.

[v] O'Farrell (first name unknown), *O'Farrell's Collection of National Irish Music for the Union Pipes* (London: John Gow, 1804). Compiled, edited and reconstructed by Patrick Sky (Chapel Hill, North Carolina: Grassblade Music, 1995).

[vi] McCullough, p. 6.

chapter 3: holding and blowing the tin whistle

A PHYSICAL RELATIONSHIP, AND MUCH MORE

The first time you pick up your tin whistle, or any musical instrument, and hold it in your hands you have begun a physical relationship with it that will hopefully last for years. If you are a beginner, you have the golden opportunity to form good habits and avoid bad ones. If you have already formed some unfortunate ones, now is the time to discover what they are and to begin your liberation.

Playing music is an athletic activity. As we learn to play, we train groups of muscles to work in exquisite coordination to perform the most subtle and complex maneuvers, sometimes in extremely brief moments of time. Playing the whistle is also an aerobic activity. In this chapter we will explore the particular nature of the sustained deep breathing that tin whistle playing requires. For now I will simply observe that keeping yourself in good shape with regular aerobic exercise will only enhance your playing.

Playing music is also a mental, emotional, and spiritual activity. We tend to talk about these as separate aspects and label them with separate words, but, in fact, playing music is a completely unified experience. At its center is a beautifully subtle interaction between one's self and one's instrument. As you mature as a musician, you become more and more skilled at sensitively expanding that interaction outward to include other musicians and listeners.

And finally, your sense of the core experience changes. You reach a point where you feel that you are not creating the music yourself, but that you have tuned yourself so well that you have *become* an instrument and music is simply flowing through you. All master musicians experience this.

But you must begin with the physical aspect of your relationship with the whistle, and mastering it will take time. You will need to adopt the attitude of *always* "tuning in": always noticing the nature of the sounds you are producing and what is happening in your body when you produce them, always noticing the connections between your sound and your body. It may seem obvious, but many people forget that *when you play you must always listen:* to your sound, which you hear through the air and through your bones, and to the sensations of your own body. Starting with this core of inner sensitivity, you learn to expand your listening attitude outward, and ultimately other people will find it a joy to play music with you, dance to your music, and listen to you.

This attitude of focusing on sound and the physical sensations within your body requires a quiet, undistracted mind. Most of us can achieve this inner quiet in moments here and there. As you bring your attention and intention to practicing this, you will find that you can sustain internal quietness for longer periods of time. For many, closing the eyes while playing helps considerably.

Both physical and mental relaxation are essential to this process and, of course, are woven into one another. When you begin by giving your attention to physical relaxation, mental relaxation tends to follow.

Of course, there is a difference between being physically relaxed and being limp. When you sit or stand in a relaxed manner, there are many muscles that are working to hold you up. But none of them are overly tense, and those that don't need to work are relaxed. This state of balance, with no distraction caused by unnecessary muscle tension, is what I mean by physical relaxation.

A BRIEF NOTE ON POSTURE

As a whistle player, your starting point for a relaxed body and the optimal use of your energy is an upright spine. This is central to allowing the free movement of your diaphragm and allowing the relaxation of your air passages, shoulders, arms, neck, and head. When you play, sitting or standing, make sure to keep both feet flat on the floor.

We'll talk a bit more about posture as it relates to breathing later in the chapter. Now let's look at how to hold the whistle in a relaxed and secure way.

THE FINGER HOLES, AND A CHOICE FOR LEFT-HANDED PEOPLE

The six finger holes of the tin whistle are covered and uncovered by the middle three fingers of your two hands. Most people find that it feels most natural to use their dominant hand for the three holes at the bottom of the instrument, i.e. the holes furthest from the mouthpiece. Since most of us are right-handed, that means using the right hand for these bottom three holes.

If you are left-handed you may feel it is more natural for you to use your left hand for these bottom holes. Many left-handed people do play this way, while some others use the right-handed hold.

However, I offer a word of caution here for left-handed people, especially those who think that they may one day play the flute or uilleann pipes (or another woodwind instrument). These other instruments are not as symmetrical as the tin whistle and are almost always designed to be played right-handed. Many flute embouchure holes are designed to be blown into from only one direction, and the keywork on multi-keyed flutes is built right-handed by default. You can go to the expense of having an instrument builder make you a left-handed instrument, but it may cost a pretty penny.

So, I advise you to give the right-handers' way a fair try and see how it feels. Switch back and forth and experiment a bit in this early stage if you wish. But don't delay very long in making a decision and sticking with it. We establish important neural pathways and connections from the earliest stages of learning and practicing a new instrument.

FINGERING NOTATION

In this book I will call the hand nearest the whistle mouthpiece the *top hand*. The hand nearest the other end, the foot of the whistle, I will call the *bottom hand*. Either of these can be the right or left hand, though, by far, most people play with the left hand as the top hand and the right hand as the bottom hand.

I call the top-hand index finger T1, the top-hand middle finger T2, and the top-hand ring finger T3. Similarly, I call the bottom-hand index finger B1, the bottom-hand middle finger B2, and the bottom-hand ring finger B3. See Figure 3-1.

COMFORT AND STABILITY: THE ATTRIBUTES OF A GOOD WHISTLE HOLD

When you hold your whistle you want to be comfortable, as relaxed as possible, and have no worries, conscious or subconscious, about dropping the instrument. You also want to keep the whistle still while your playing fingers do their jobs.

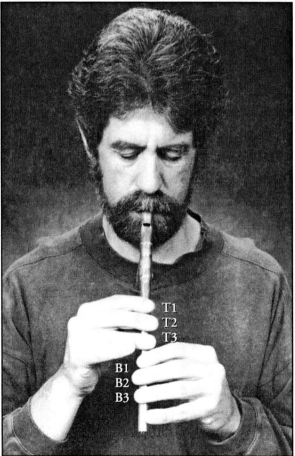

Figure 3-1. The right-handed hold (top) and the left-handed hold (bottom), with fingering indications.

What Parts of the Fingers Cover the Holes?

Generally speaking, cover the holes with the fleshy pads of the first joint of each finger, not with the fingertips. There should be a gentle arch to each finger, though the degree of that arch or curve will usually differ from finger to finger.

Hands and fingers come in many shapes and sizes of course. The arch of some fingers may be very slight. For most people, T2 and B2 are their longest fingers. Therefore, these fingers may naturally have a higher arch than the other fingers have.

Avoid "buckling" or "caving in" of any of the finger joints. This can be a sign of tension. In general, relaxed fingers don't want to buckle, they want to be curved.

To illustrate this, let your arms hang loose by your sides and imagine that your hands are apples hanging from their branches. Let gravity assist you in relaxing your hands. Notice the curvature of your relaxed fingers.

With larger, low pitched whistles you may have to change your hand position to be able to seal the holes reliably. Especially with low D whistles (one octave lower than and twice as long as the small D whistle), the holes of the bottom hand often require quite a stretch. In such cases, try extending your fingers out over the whistle further than usual and sealing the holes somewhere around the second joint of the finger.

Resting Position for the Playing Fingers

When any of the six playing fingers are not in motion or covering their holes they should be in *resting position,* gently curved and hovering, relaxed, very near their holes, about one-third to one-quarter inch above them. When you are relaxed, this is the position your fingers naturally want to assume. In resting position, your playing fingers are poised and ready for action.

The Four Anchor Points of the Tin Whistle

Now comes one of the most crucial elements of your physical relationship with the whistle. When you learn to hold the instrument so that you can be relaxed throughout your hands, wrists, arms, and upper body, and never be in fear of dropping it, you open the way for establishing the habit of physical and mental relaxation that is essential for being fully musical.

The six fingers we use to cover and uncover the finger holes should have *absolutely nothing* to do with holding or stabilizing the instrument. Their *only* job (and a very big job it is, as you will see as you work your way through this book) is to freely interact with the finger holes. Don't burden them with anything else!

When you use the four anchor points to hold, support, and stabilize the whistle, your playing fingers can be relaxed and free.

The four anchor points are:

1. Your lips
2. Your top-hand thumb
3. Your bottom-hand thumb
4. Your bottom-hand pinky

Figure 3-2. The proper way to hold the tin whistle. All fingers are relaxed, and in this case the playing fingers are in resting position above their finger holes. The whistle is held stable using the four anchor points and the whole body is relaxed.

We will examine these four anchor points in turn. But first, try this exercise to quickly establish the basic hold.

HAVE A SEAT: QUICKLY ESTABLISHING THE BASIC HOLD

1. Sit at a table and pull your chair right up close to the edge. Place this book before you on the table, an inch or two from the edge, and place the bottom of the whistle squarely on the table top right before you. Sit high enough that, leaning over the edge of the table, you can position your head so that just the tip of the mouthpiece is held gently, centered between your lips. Holding the whistle this way (no need to blow), remove your hands. The whistle is gently held upright.

2. Now, approach the whistle with your top hand and, *without* your thumb touching the whistle, gently lay T1, T2, and T3 on their respective finger holes. (See Figure 3-1 above if you need to be reminded of where they go.) Cover the holes not with your fingertips but with some part of the fleshy pad of the first joint of each finger. Your hand should remain very relaxed. Your fingers should be fairly flat but hopefully will have a gentle arch to them. Completely straight fingers are usually a sign of tensed muscles. Of course, the size and shape of hands and fingers vary considerably, as do the sizes of whistles in different keys, so you will have to work out your own way to comfortably cover the holes of the particular whistle you are playing. Your top hand pinky should just hang in the air, relaxing comfortably however it will, not touching the whistle at all. It is the only finger that gets to just come along for the ride and snooze.

3. Once your fingers are comfortable, make sure the thumb of your top hand is relaxed, and then allow it to touch the underside of the whistle wherever it will rest most naturally. That is its optimal spot.

4. Next, approach the whistle with your *bottom* hand and, without your bottom-hand thumb touching the whistle, gently lay B1, B2, and B3 on their respective finger holes. Once again, use the fleshy pads of your fingers to cover the holes as described above. As with the top hand, your bottom-hand fingers should be fairly flat but will have a gentle arch to them as well, especially B2.

5. Once those fingers are comfortable, make sure the thumb of your bottom hand is relaxed and allow it to touch the whistle wherever it will rest most naturally. That is *its* optimal spot.

6. Now, lay the relaxed pinky of your bottom hand on the body of the whistle, somewhere below the B3 hole, wherever it wants to lay. If your hands are small it may only touch the body of the whistle with its tip. That's all right. It is important, though, that it be squarely *on* the whistle, not slipping off. You will probably need to experiment some with the bottom hand position in order to find the most comfortable way to cover the finger holes and rest the pinky on the whistle body.

   If, with this relaxed hold, your bottom hand pinky simply will *not* reach the whistle, then you may want to explore anchoring with B3 instead, covering its hole, as an alternative to anchoring with the pinky, when you are playing notes higher than E. (When playing E, B3 must be off of its hole.)

7. Now, with all of your fingers in place and keeping them very relaxed, straighten out your poor aching back and simply lift the whistle with you. This is it: the basic hold.

   Now we'll examine the mechanics of this more closely.

THE FIRST ANCHOR POINT: THE LIPS

The whistle should never touch your teeth. Place the whistle in the center of your lips, not off to one side or the other. I will explain the reasons for this soon.

There is no need to squeeze *at all* with your lips. Doing so will create unnecessary and potentially harmful tension in your face, head, and neck. Simply place the tip of the mouthpiece between your lips. If you are relaxed you can feel the very slight weight of the mouthpiece resting on your lower lip.

Only the tip of the mouthpiece should be placed between the lips, just enough of it so that your lips can make an airtight seal around the windway (the opening in the tip of the mouthpiece that forms the beginning of the air channel). Most of the inexpensive whistles have a straight windway. Note that if you have a whistle with an arched or curved windway, you may have to place the mouthpiece a tiny bit further into your mouth in order to be sure you are completely sealing the entire perimeter of the windway with your lips.

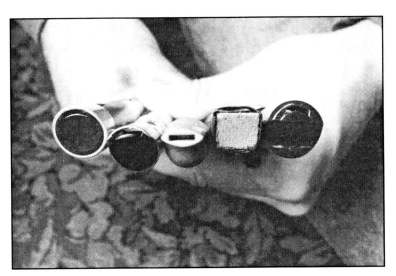

Figure 3-3. The straight and curved windway openings of several different models of whistles. Left to right: Abell, Copeland, Generation, Clarke, Susato.

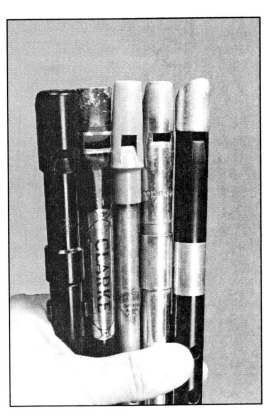

Figure 3-4. The mouthpieces of several different models of whistles. Left to right: Susato, Clarke, Generation, Copeland, Abell.

Regardless of the shape of the windway, make sure there is no air escaping from your lips that is not traveling through the whistle.

Everyone's lips are different, but for me I need only place about one-quarter inch of the mouthpiece between my lips to achieve this seal. Experiment and find out what works for you.

Now, remove the whistle but keep your lips as they were when sealing the windway. When you blow air through your lips you will see that this kind of blowing resembles the way you might cool down a spoonful of hot soup held a few inches away from your lips, or the way you might try to gently alter or blow out a candle flame a few inches away from your mouth, or the way you might spit out a watermelon seed. Feel the shape of the airstream by blowing this way against the palm of your hand.

As you get comfortable with the whistle you are going to learn to use the opening, or *aperture*, between your lips to help control and shape the flow of air. Now is the time to realize something important: **You will often want to blow a stream of air through the whistle that is *narrower* than the windway.** I'll explain the reasons for this later in the chapter.

You will control the size and shape of the airstream by changing the size and shape of the aperture between your lips. *If you place the whistle too far into your mouth, your lips will have no way to shape the airstream.* Try placing the whistle in too far, blow some air, and you will see what I mean. If you play this way, as many people unfortunately do, the shape of your airstream will be invariable, restricted by the size and shape of the windway itself. You will see soon that a more focused airstream can be very useful.

HOLDING ANGLES

Now try this. While holding the whistle as shown in Figure 3-2 (p. 36), blow air *straight* through the windway of the whistle. Sit or stand up straight, looking straight ahead, and keep your arms and upper body relaxed. If you do these things, you will find that you are holding the whistle at an angle approximately like that shown in Figure 3-5.

Still looking straight ahead, notice that if you now raise or lower your hands, and thereby change the angle of the whistle in relation to your torso, two things happen. First, the air stream now has a kink or bend in it. The air has to go around a bend as it escapes the aperture between your lips and enters the windway. Playing this way will reduce the responsiveness of your whistle and adversely affect its tone and volume. Second, if you hold the whistle at one of these incorrect angles for very long you may begin to feel tension and fatigue developing in your arms, shoulders, upper back, and perhaps elsewhere.

Figure 3-5. Holding the whistle at a proper angle so there is no kink or bend in the airstream.

38

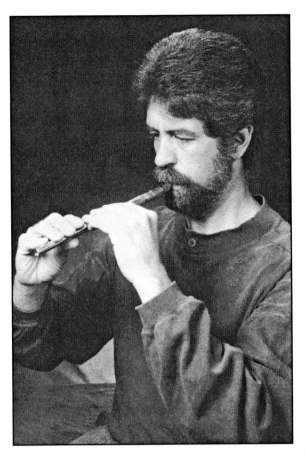

Figure 3-6. Two incorrect holding angles which cause a kink or bend in the airstream and, possibly, bodily discomfort.

Experiment with this angle, paying attention to preserving a straight airflow through the whistle and the relaxation of your body. As everyone's body is different, your correct holding angle may not be exactly the same as mine, but it should be close. As you find your correct position, close your eyes and *remember how it feels*. Take your time. You can also form a mental image of it by taking a look in a mirror. Do you see raised shoulders or other signs of tension?

You may not always play looking straight ahead. It is natural enough to find yourself looking a bit downward at times while you play. But notice that when you do so you need to adjust your upper body so that you are still blowing your air straight through the whistle. Notice also that this posture tends to close your throat a bit and restrict the capacity of your lungs. It is certainly better to play looking straight ahead and with an erect, upright posture. Similarly, twisting your body towards the right or left while playing restricts your lung capacity and puts stress on your spine.

Once you have fully explored this holding angle, let's take a look at a different one. See Figure 3-7.

Notice that the whistle is held straight up and down. The tip is not pointing to the left or right. The instrument is in line with the spine and the direction of airflow. This angle is also important in achieving the optimum responsiveness, tone, and volume of your instrument.

Figure 3-7. The whistle held in line with the spine and the direction of airflow.

THE SECOND ANCHOR POINT: THE TOP-HAND THUMB

If you need to, return now to our tabletop exercise to re-establish the basic hold (see pp. 36-37).

The job of your top-hand thumb is three-fold.

- First, it helps to support the weight of the whistle, along with your bottom-hand thumb and lower lip.
- Second, it serves to maintain the position of the top hand. When playing C-sharp, the thumb will be the only part of the top hand that is touching the instrument. If it were not touching, then after every C-sharp you would have to re-establish your top-hand position.
- Third, it supplies a tiny, but necessary, amount of opposing force to T1, T2, and T3, making it much easier for them to seal their holes securely.

The thumb's exact placement on the back of the whistle is unimportant. What is important is that it is as relaxed as possible and is not causing any strain to the rest of the hand. There is no reason to squeeze with your thumb. If you are squeezing with your thumb you are also squeezing with at least one of your other fingers. This means undue hand tension, which you must eliminate.

THE THIRD ANCHOR POINT: THE BOTTOM-HAND THUMB

The job of your bottom-hand thumb is also three-fold.

- First, it helps to support the weight of the whistle, along with your top-hand thumb and lower lip.
- Second, it serves to help maintain the position of the bottom hand, a job that is shared in this case by the bottom-hand pinky. When playing the notes from G up to C-sharp, inclusively, B1, B2, and B3 will be off the whistle and the bottom-hand thumb and pinky maintain the bottom hand's position.
- Third, it supplies a tiny but necessary amount of opposing force to B1, B2, and B3, making it much easier for them to seal their holes securely.

As with the top-hand thumb, the bottom-hand thumb's exact placement on the back of the whistle is unimportant. What is important is that it is as relaxed as possible and is not causing any strain to the rest of the hand.

THE FOURTH ANCHOR POINT: THE BOTTOM-HAND PINKY

This seems to be the most controversial anchor point, though all of the fine, experienced whistle players I have seen use it, or, in some cases, B3 as an alternative to the bottom-hand pinky. Whereas the thumbs and lips are obvious anchor points, most novices don't think of using the bottom-hand pinky. Not using it, or another approach that leads to the same result, gives rise to several kinds of problems and unconscious compensations.

The weight of the whistle is ably supported by the lower lip and the thumbs. The thumbs exert a small upward force on the whistle. A small downward force is needed to balance the hold and make the instrument secure. If you do not use the bottom-hand pinky to supply that downward force, it must be supplied by one or more of the playing fingers or by clamping down with the lips on the mouthpiece. The playing fingers need to be completely unencumbered to do their myriad of playing jobs. Trying to hold the whistle securely in place with the lips compromises the embouchure and causes facial tension, plus it just doesn't work very well. Remember that unnecessary tension inhibits musicality. (The term *embouchure,* used mainly in connection with the flute and brass instruments, refers to changes made in the disposition of the lips and mouth to affect the sound and response of the instrument.)

Players who don't anchor with the bottom-hand pinky unconsciously compensate for not doing so. The situation is not very problematic while playing D, E, or F-sharp, but once B1, B2, and B3 are off their holes, the whistle becomes more and more unstable as more of the top-hand playing fingers are lifted from their holes.

Some players have a bottom-hand pinky that is not quite long enough to comfortably reach the whistle without a shift of hand position that adversely affects the positioning of the B1, B2, and B3 fingers. If this is the case with you, you may wish to anchor with B3 instead. Or you may wish to anchor with B3 for F-sharp and anchor with your bottom hand pinky for G, A, B, C, and C-sharp, i.e. when B1, B2 and B3 are all off of their holes.

Without the bottom hand pinky (or B3) on the whistle, it becomes increasingly difficult to hold the whistle steady and secure as you move from G to A to B. When playing C-sharp, with all of the playing fingers off the whistle, you get into real trouble. In these situations many players unknowingly use the side of their B1 finger to exert some downward force, or squeeze the whistle between B1 and the bottom-hand thumb. Needless to say, this is an awkward and clumsy strategy. Using the bottom-hand pinky prevents these problems and insures that the whistle is always steady and secure.

The only time when the bottom-hand pinky should be lifted off the whistle is when performing something called a strike on the note E. This subject is covered in Chapter 8.

TAKE CARE OF YOUR BODY

Like any other athletic activity, playing the whistle, though it may seem quite harmless, subjects you to the stresses of very repetitive movements and postures and certain immobile body positions. Holding unnecessary muscle tension or assuming and holding uncomfortable positions can lead to physical pain and problems. *Always listen to your body*. It wants to relax.

POSTURE AND BREATHING

With any wind instrument it makes sense to have full and unimpeded use of your lung capacity. This is especially true considering the nonstop nature of most traditional Irish music. With the tin whistle you need to be able to inhale deeply and very quickly in order to not interrupt the flow of the music.

Having an upright spine enables you to use your diaphragm to breathe deeply and to relax your entire air passage. Don't stoop over when playing. If you are sitting, sit near the edge of your chair. Some people find that it helps their playing posture to imagine that they have a string pulling up from the top of their head toward the ceiling. Think of being as tall as possible.

GETTING COMFORTABLE WITH FINGERING AND PLAYING THE NOTES OF THE LOW REGISTER

Before you proceed further in this chapter it would be wise to make sure that you can comfortably and reliably finger and sound all the principal notes of the low register of the whistle. (You don't need to refer to a fingering chart just yet, but if you would like to, you will find one in Appendix A on pp. 180-181.)

Starting with C-sharp (all holes open), work your way down the D Ionian scale by covering one finger hole, then two, then three, etc., in the sequence given below. As you progressively add fingers, leave in place the fingers that are already covering their holes.

Make sure that each finger is sealing its hole completely before adding another finger. If you are getting a weak or squeaky tone, or one that is too high, it's very likely that one or more of your fingers is not completely sealing its hole. Don't worry – this is a very common occurrence among beginners. As you add fingers, one or more fingers that are already covering holes can shift a bit without you knowing it, especially if you are still getting accustomed to holding the whistle correctly. A tiny finger shift of this kind is enough to cause a hole to become partly uncovered. Complete sealing of the finger holes is essential for good tone.

1. All holes open (zero holes covered – the note C-sharp),
2. then, cover with T1 (one hole covered – the note B),
3. then cover with T1 and T2 (two holes covered – the note A),
4. then T1, T2 and T3 (three holes covered – the note G),
5. then T1, T2, T3, and B1 (four holes covered – the note F-sharp),
6. then T1, T2, T3, B1, and B2 (five holes covered – the note E),
7. then T1, T2, T3, B1, B2, and B3 (all six holes covered – the note D).

For most people, completely sealing the finger holes does not come naturally at first. It takes some time to develop the needed tactile sensitivity, control, and coordination, so go easy on yourself.

To sound the notes of the low register you need to blow with a moderate force, enough to fill the instrument and produce a solid, low tone but not so forcefully that you jump up into the high register. Some experimentation will reveal a way of blowing that is usable for now.

ADJUSTING THE OVERALL PITCH OF THE WHISTLE

Some whistles are made in two pieces to allow for easy adjustment of the overall length of the whistle for tuning purposes. You can adjust your overall pitch higher (by pushing in to shorten the whistle) or lower (by pulling out to lengthen the whistle) to match the pitch of other instruments. Experiment and find a position that works well most of the time. You can then fine-tune the instrument as required. Note that excessive lengthening of the whistle can adversely affect the *intonation* (or "in-tuneness") of the intervals of the whistle's own scale.

Clearly, when you shorten or lengthen the whistle you are raising or lowering the pitch of all its notes. However, it is not obvious, yet is important to know, that this pitch change is not uniform. The pitch of certain notes changes more than the pitch of others. For any given note, the closer the lowest uncovered tone hole is to the foot of the whistle, the smaller the change in pitch.

Here is an example. On my small D whistle, with the tuning slide closed (i.e. fully pushed in) the distance from the cutting edge of the blade to the center of the B3 hole is about 8.5 inches. This is the length of the vibrating air column that produces low E, B3 being the highest uncovered tone hole. The distance from the cutting edge of the blade to the center of the T1 hole is about 4.25 inches. This is the length of the vibrating air column that produces C-sharp in the low register, T1 being the highest uncovered tone hole.

If I pull out the tuning slide by one-quarter inch, I increase the lengths of these air columns to 8.75 inches and 4.5 inches respectively. In the case of the low E, this is a lengthening of about 2.9%, while for the higher C-sharp it is a lengthening of about 5.9%. It follows that lengthening the whistle by one-quarter inch will lower the pitch of the C-sharp quite a bit more than it will lower the pitch of the E. If you lengthen your whistle as far as it will safely go, you will experience this effect in the extreme.

If you have a one-piece whistle with a plastic mouthpiece that is glued onto a metal tube, you may be able to melt the glue so that the mouthpiece becomes movable. Try dipping the mouthpiece into very hot water to melt the glue, taking care not to melt the plastic. Then remove the mouthpiece and clean the molten glue out of it and off of the metal tube. When you put the mouthpiece back on you will hopefully be able to adjust its position in order to adjust the overall pitch of the whistle.

TAKING A BREATH WHILE PLAYING

You will take frequent and quick breaths while playing the whistle. When you take a breath, keep the whistle in place. Let the mouthpiece rest on your lower lip and open your mouth just a tiny bit so you can take air in quickly. Breathing in a musical manner is covered in Chapter 13, *Musical Breathing*.

CLEARING THE WINDWAY

If the tone sounds stuffy or you can't produce any sound, there is probably a build-up of saliva or condensation in the windway of the whistle. This happens quite routinely, especially when you are salivating more than usual, such as soon after eating. It also happens more when the whistle is cold. There are two good ways to clear the windway.

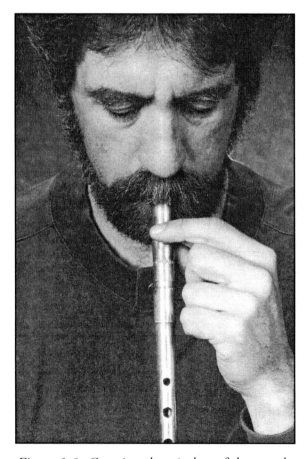

Figure 3-8. Covering the window of the mouthpiece while blowing to clear the windway.

42

One is to simply inhale *through* the whistle, keeping the whistle at your mouth as you do in normal playing. This way you will suck back in the moisture that is causing the problem. This is the method to use when you don't want to interrupt your playing. It is not a good way to get a fast, deep breath, however.

The other way to clear the windway is to stop playing, place a finger over the window of the mouthpiece, and blow forcefully enough through the whistle to force out the clogging moisture (see Figure 3-8). If you don't place your finger over the window you will produce quite a loud and shrill noise.

THE TWO REGISTERS, OR OCTAVES, OF THE TIN WHISTLE

In traditional Irish music we confine ourselves to playing in the lower two octaves of the instrument's range. It is possible to play into the third octave, but such notes, which are quite loud and shrill, are not called for in traditional Irish playing. If you wish to explore them, feel free, but warn the neighbors first. And you might want to have some earplugs close at hand for yourself.

A quick glance at the fingering chart shown in Appendix A (pp. 180-181) reveals that the fingerings for the two registers are basically the same. The ways that you alter and control the airstream determine the register and the intonation of any given note.

"KICKING UP" INTO THE SECOND OCTAVE

Whistle players commonly say that you just "blow harder" to move from the first to the second octave. What actually happens when one blows "harder" in this way is something quite subtle and complex, though it is something that most players learn to do unconsciously, as I did.

By the way, it's interesting to know that when you "kick up" into the second octave you are forcing the air column inside the whistle to vibrate at the first overtone of a fundamental note. When you play in the low octave you are playing fundamental notes. I won't get into the physics, acoustics, and music theory of these matters here. If you are curious, I recommend that you read one of the many good books that address those subjects.

When I examine how I move from the lower octave to the upper octave I find that there are three, or sometimes four subtle changes happening at the same time that combine to provide the necessary increase in air speed. By the way, it is an increase in air *speed,* and not air volume or pressure, that is required.

Let's look at the example of moving from low E to high E, blowing a continuous stream of air with no tongue or throat articulation on either note.

First, I notice that my abdominal muscles push out my air a very slight bit harder.

Second, I notice a change in my throat. Looking in the mirror, I see my Adam's apple rise and retreat a bit into my neck. This throat change is more dramatic than the abdominal one. I decrease the amount of space inside my throat, changing the shape of the back of my tongue, which in turn forces the air to travel faster through the throat. Reducing the diameter of this air passage by even a few millimeters has a large impact on the speed of the air traveling through it.

Third, I notice a very slight narrowing of the shape of the aperture between my lips, which forces the air to travel faster through it.

A fourth change that can be used, though it is not used in this example, is to give the higher note an attack with a quick puff of air from a tongue articulation.

The first two changes, in the abdomen and the throat, happen quite automatically. Even in beginning whistle classes I have found that absolute novices do these things naturally and without awareness when prompted to move a note from the low to high octave. (Actually, it was a student in one of these classes that noticed the throat change and pointed it out to me. I had been unaware of it for over twenty years.)

As you notice the changes that happen in your throat, take care to just observe them. Don't try to tighten your throat or you could inadvertently introduce undue muscle tension.

The third change, the aperture or embouchure change, doesn't come naturally to all players. First of all, many whistle players, as mentioned earlier, hold the mouthpiece too far inside their mouth to be able to affect the airstream in this way. Some others use aperture-changing techniques quite naturally and unconsciously. All players should become aware of these techniques because they are very useful, in more ways than just helping to produce the octave jump.

Tin Whistle Embouchure

These aperture-changing techniques can be properly called tin whistle embouchure.

A commonly held myth is that the tin whistle is just a "blow and go" instrument, one that can offer great sophistication in fingering and embellishment possibilities but is strictly primitive when it comes to blowing. When you take a closer look and do some experimentation you discover instead that there are unexpected possibilities in nuance and fine control in the blowing of the instrument, particularly with fine handmade whistles. Inexpensive, mass-produced whistles tend to be less responsive to embouchure changes.

The whistle's range of dynamics and tone colorations is smaller, to be sure, than that of many other instruments, but it is significant nonetheless. The use of these possibilities, whether conscious or not, is one of the things that distinguishes fine whistle players.

The abdominal breath support and throat narrowing combine to speed up the flow of air that arrives at the front of the mouth. Now, with embouchure changes, you can further speed up the air flow *without* having to blow more forcefully, thus using your air supply more efficiently. This means you won't run low on air as soon. Plus, you can focus the airstream.

Both the speeding up and the focusing of the air stream help correct for pitch. Try this. Blow a low E and then increase the air speed, *only* with the abdomen and throat, just by the *minimum* amount required to cause the jump into the second octave. You'll hear that the high note is very flat in pitch. More air speed is required to bring its pitch up to the correct level. This means, if you are *not* using embouchure, that you need to support the breath more with your abdominal muscles and/or narrow your throat more to create enough air speed to bring the note up to the correct pitch level. If you use embouchure to aid in the process, you don't have to expend as much energy with your abdomen or use up as much air to achieve the same result.

Narrowing the airstream with the lips also has the added benefit of giving the tone of the instrument more focus and clarity. This effect can be heard when playing notes in the low octave as well as the high. I also notice that, when blowing with a more focused airstream, a fine whistle will respond more quickly to finger movements.

Your lips can narrow the airstream in both the horizontal and vertical dimensions. I was recently surprised to find, upon checking in a mirror, that the narrowing I do occurs as much or more in the vertical axis as in the horizontal. The muscles used are much the same as the ones used in controlling flute embouchure, i.e. the muscles of the lips and the lower cheek areas. There is no need for tension in your upper cheeks.

Playing a Whistle in Tune

As you now see, after trying the pitch experiment described above, the tin whistle does not play in tune of its own accord. It is a variable-pitch instrument.

Electronic tuning machines attempt to measure the fundamental frequency of a note and compare it to the pitch standard that we call *equal temperament*. This provides us with a useful starting point, a good way to establish whether *overall* we are playing our whistle sharp or flat of the generally accepted pitch level of A440. Once we have warmed the whistle up to room temperature, and then to breath temperature, then adjusted our tuning slide or mouthpiece so it seems we are playing at the right overall pitch level, we then need to attend to the intonation of the individual notes that we play.

You may have noticed that when different players try out the same whistle, one may make it sound more in tune to your ear than the other players do. No whistle has inherently perfect intonation; perhaps it is more accurate to say the meaning of "in tune" is subjective. It necessarily changes from situation to situation and it often involves compromise when playing with other people. Experienced players do their best to play whatever sounds sweet to their ear in any given situation. That personal judgment of good intonation usually does not conform to equal temperament. Instead, we tend to prefer the sound of "pure intervals." **It may be more useful to think of playing in-tune intervals rather than in-tune notes, for it is the relationship between notes that we are really tuning.**

For instance, sometimes the third degree of the Ionian mode (or major scale)—let's consider F-sharp in the D-Ionian mode—sounds better to our ears, in relation to D (the tonic note), if it is played slightly flat of an equal tempered F-sharp. In another mode, such as E Dorian, a sweet or correct sounding F-sharp may be sharper that the sweet F-sharp of D Ionian. Why this is so is a long story, one written about much by others, having to do with pure intervals and the harmonic series. I won't delve far into this controversial area. Suffice it to say that equal temperament is a rather artificial, though very useful, system that is not based closely on the natural harmonic series. It was developed initially for keyboard instruments. When given a choice, our ears usually prefer the sweeter, pure intervals.

When we play unison melodies with fixed-intonation equal-tempered instruments such as accordions, concertinas, and keyboard instruments, we need to adjust to them, or at least compromise. When we are accompanied by instruments such as guitars and bouzoukis, we may also need to make some adjustments. The open strings of fretted string instruments are not always tuned to equal temperament, but their frets are placed in order to produce equal-tempered intervals. This is a tricky area. As always, let your ear lead the way.

Add to these considerations the fact that whistle makers have had their own differing opinions and aesthetics on how to adjust the inherent intonation of their instruments. (With inexpensive, mass-produced whistles, similar choices have been made, but there are also quality-control problems inherent in the manufacturing process that often result in poorly-tuned and inconsistent instruments.)

You may have noticed that with old simple-system flutes, F-sharp tends to be flat, A tends to be sharp, C-natural tends to be sharp, and C-sharp tends to be flat. At least that's how these notes sound compared to equal-tempered notes. Those same pitch "distortions" are typically found in tin whistles and the uilleann pipes as well. A very similar pattern is even observed in Irish fiddling. However, since fiddlers determine their intonation by finger placement and by comparison of fingered pitches to those of the open strings, these pitch "distortions" are clearly a matter of choice, though probably an unconscious or conditioned one. It seems that there is a kind of natural intonation "profile" or "dialect" that is inherent in the design of the simple-system instruments (whistle, flute, uilleann pipes) which is also inherent to some degree in the nature of traditional Irish music as a whole.

We can certainly say that tin whistles do not naturally play in an equal-tempered scale. It is tempting to surmise that at least some of the intonation oddities of tin whistles were, and are, in fact intentional. Most Irish musicians prefer the subtle intonation "personality" that the simple-system instruments share. It takes time and experience to learn how to play the tin whistle "in tune," but the kind of "in-tuneness" that most of us strive for, consciously or not, is not the same as the equal-tempered ideal that Boehm worked so hard to achieve in his new flute. Modern flute players who succeed in sounding traditional do so, I feel, in part by emulating the simple-system intonation profile.

If you are a beginner, it will be hard for you to judge the intonation of a whistle and hard to know how well it fits your own emerging aesthetic. For that reason, it may be wise to start out on an inexpensive whistle. But once you gain experience, and if you decide that whistle playing is important enough in your life, you would be well advised to invest in a good, handmade instrument. Try out different models and ask more experienced players to try whistles out for you and give you their feedback.

All of this boils down to the fact that you yourself must make a whistle play in tune, to your own standards, by controlling your embouchure. To make a note sharper you must increase the speed of the airstream, and to make a note flatter you must decrease that speed. These adjustments can be made by subtle and quick changes in your throat, mouth, and lips. If you are listening well and you care about intonation, you can probably learn to make these adjustments unconsciously, especially as you get to know your whistle and its intonation profile more intimately. As always, listening is the key to success.

Get to Know Your Whistle

Now that you are aware of a wide range of blowing and embouchure techniques, you can explore them on your whistle and discover how it responds. Try the following experiments, without tongue articulations. Introduce tonguing later, if you like, and see what effect it has.

- Find the *minimum* amount of air-speed change required to kick any given note up into the second octave.

- Listen to how flat the upper-register notes are when played with this minimal amount of air-speed change.

- Try this with different notes and notice how things change, especially in your throat, as you move up and down the scale.

- Find out how much more air speed is necessary to bring high register notes into good tune with the low register notes of the same pitch. Try blowing them *too* sharp and see how that feels. Explore the limits, and always listen.

- Try tuning the high register notes using embouchure, and without using embouchure. Notice the differences in tone quality when you do and don't use embouchure to tune the notes.

- Try playing some long notes while moving in and out of using embouchure to alter the tone quality. Try to do this while keeping the pitch stable and see how your air usage changes.

If you are new to the whistle these may be difficult experiments. But try them, and return to them as your experience deepens.

The use of these techniques will eventually become second nature to you. Irish music often requires us to change rapidly, and sometime repeatedly, between the two registers. You will discover ways to use these techniques that enhance your agility and fluidity as a player.

Normal Breathing: Shallow and Automatic

There is no more normal an activity than breathing. We are always breathing, but we rarely attend to it.

Normal breathing is fairly shallow. At rest, we inhale and exhale about a pint of air. In between the exhale and the next inhale we pause for a brief period of repose, roughly equal in length to the inhale and exhale phases. It's a regular cycle: inhale, exhale, rest; inhale, exhale, rest.

Whistle Breathing: Deep and Controlled

In whistle playing, an entirely different kind of breathing is required. We must learn to quickly take in a much greater quantity of air, sometimes as much as eight pints, in half a second or less. We must also learn to release the air in a very slow and controlled manner. The pace of whistle breathing is irregular, being determined by the phrasing and register of the music. And, *especially* in Irish music, there is no rest period between one exhalation and the next inhalation.

When playing the whistle, you should inhale through your mouth rather than your nose. You can take in air much more quickly this way. It is not necessary to open your mouth very far.

You can inhale through both your mouth and nose, but if you do you will have to then close off your nose on the exhale so that you don't waste valuable air that should be traveling only through the instrument.

Try this simple, powerful visualization technique to help your body learn how to take a very deep, quick breath. With your hand find the spot near the base of your throat where your collarbones come together and form a "V". Feel that soft, indented area of your throat with your fingers. Now, imagine that there is a hole there. Put your whistle to your lips and take a quick, deep breath, imagining that you are taking in all of your air directly through that hole, not through your mouth. Feel the breath hit the back of your lower throat as it rushes in. Something about this visualization cues the body to open the throat, which enables you to take in more air in the short amount of time that is available to you.

BREATHING, AND LEAVING OUT NOTES

As you have probably observed, there are almost no breathing places built into traditional Irish music. We have to create our own. With very few exceptions, such as some places in slow airs and other slow and moderate tunes, it does not work to sneak breaths between notes. Doing so almost always disrupts the flow and energy of the music, drawing attention to your breathing and away from the music. We whistle players must learn how to leave out notes, and shorten longer notes, in a musical and tasteful way. When this is done well, most listeners will not even notice that you are breathing.

This is a crucial subject. An in-depth discussion of it requires knowledge of ornamentation. Therefore, I have placed Chapter 13, *Musical Breathing,* after the chapters on ornamentation. If you wish, you may skip ahead and look at that material at any time. However, you will get more out of it once you have worked your way through the intervening parts of the book.

EXERCISE: GET ACQUAINTED WITH YOUR DIAPHRAGM

Breathing is activated by changes in air pressure within the lungs. Expanding the chest capacity causes the air pressure within the lungs to drop in relation to atmospheric pressure, and as a result air rushes in (inhalation). Reducing chest capacity causes the air pressure within the lungs to increase, and so air rushes out (exhalation). Two actions can increase chest capacity and thereby cause inhalation: raising the ribcage, and lowering the floor of the lungs by contracting, or lowering, the diaphragm. The diaphragmatic action is vastly more effective, though both come into play.

If you are unfamiliar with the action of your diaphragm, try this exercise. Lie on your back and breathe normally through your mouth, placing your hand on your abdomen. Feel your abdomen rise as you inhale and fall as you exhale. When you inhale, your diaphragm contracts and draws itself down (toward your feet), expanding your lungs and pushing against the abdominal organs, which in turn push against the abdominal wall, causing your hand to rise. When you exhale, the diaphragm relaxes and rises, allowing the lungs to contract, and your abdominal wall falls back.

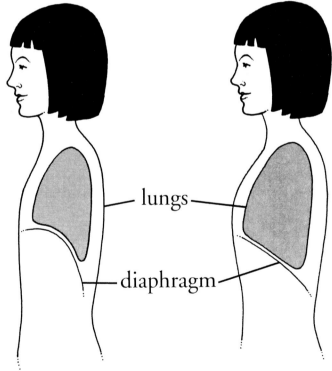

Figure 3-9. Left: During exhalation, the diaphragm relaxes and ascends, taking on a domed shape. The lungs deflate and the chest cavity contracts. Right: During inhalation the diaphragm contracts, flattens and descends. The lungs inflate as the chest cavity expands.

Try this again, this time taking deeper and slower breaths. Feel how your abdomen expands much further. Continue deep, slow breathing and restrict the movement of your ribcage by pressing down on it with your hands. There is not a major change. Now press your hands firmly against your abdomen and try to continue deep breathing by elevating your ribcage only. Your air capacity is greatly reduced this way.

To feel how your back also moves when you breathe, place your hands under your waist area and get a friend to place their hand on your abdomen just below your ribcage. Take a deep, slow breath and notice how you can feel the expansion in your back as well as your front.

Now roll over onto your stomach and place your hands by your sides. Have a friend place their hands on your shoulder blades and provide some moderate weight. Again take a slow, deep breath and feel the expansion in your back.

When you exhale, your diaphragm relaxes and rises. It does not "push" the air out of your lungs. The muscles of your abdominal wall and ribcage act in tension with the diaphragm to accomplish this and give support to the breath, helping to control the rate and pressure of exhalation.

RESISTANCE IS NEEDED FOR SLOW BREATH RELEASE

If we are to release our breath in a slow, controlled manner, something must resist its natural outrushing. In flute playing, this is almost entirely achieved through *embouchure,* the disposition and manipulation of the lips to control air flow. By creating a very small opening between the lips, the volume of air escaping can be reduced while its speed is increased. This makes for more efficient use of your limited reservoir of air. Such embouchure control is also possible and useful in tin whistle playing.

You can observe a similar phenomenon when using a garden hose. When you make the hose's opening smaller by covering part of the hole with your thumb, the water is focused into a narrower stream which is forced to shoot out of the hose faster. In the case of the garden hose, the volume of water passing through it remains constant. Playing the whistle is a more subtle pursuit than watering a garden: we can control both the speed of air flow *and* its volume.

Keep your chest expanded while your abdominal muscles are contracting during the exhale. If, after expending all the air you can with your diaphragm, you find that you still need more, you can exhale a little more by contracting your ribcage. Hopefully you will create breathing places frequently enough that you will not find yourself in such need.

The whistle itself provides very little air resistance. Many other wind instruments, such as oboe, clarinet, and other reed and brass instruments, provide much more.

WHY THE TIN WHISTLE IS LIMITED IN COMPARISON WITH THE FLUTE

The flute player has a much broader range of dynamic and tonal expression than a tin whistle player has. This is due to the flute player's ability for fine control of three variables: the shape and direction of the airstream and the distance of the airstream from the cutting edge of the embouchure hole. The tin whistle's windway, not the whistle player's lips, directs the air flow to the whistle's cutting edge. The direction and distance of the air flow in relation to this cutting edge are fixed by the physical dimensions of the whistle's windway and mouthpiece, though the shape of the airstream is somewhat controllable with embouchure.

On the bright side, these same limitations make the whistle much easier to play than the flute.

BREATHING EXERCISES

Good breath control is essential in tin whistle playing. Playing the larger whistles sometimes requires even more air than flute playing does.

In *The Flute Book,*[i] Nancy Toff gathers together eight breathing exercises from various modern flute teachers, all of which can be helpful for developing breath capacity and control for whistle players, too. I will paraphrase four of them here.

For the first exercise, stand erect with your feet slightly apart and inhale slowly and deeply through your mouth, expanding your abdomen. Slowly exhale. Repeat this, gradually increasing the frequency and reducing the duration of your breaths until you are panting. Place your hands on your hips so that you can feel expansion both in the front and back of your abdomen.

In this next exercise, which Nancy Toff calls "The Hiss," stand and place your hands on your hips, as above. Inhale, form your embouchure, and hiss like a snake as you exhale. This hiss, along with support from the abdominal muscles, restricts the airflow and helps you develop those muscles.

Noted flute teacher Sarah Baird Fouse has developed an exercise called "The Thinker." Sitting in an armless chair, place your elbows on your knees with your jaw resting gently in your cupped hands. This posture constricts your abdominal muscles, something you want to avoid when playing. But in this posture your abdomen can only expand at waist level. When you breathe deeply you cannot fail to feel these crucial muscles working.

Finally, with your whistle, play a low G (or another note of your choice) as long as you can and time yourself. An easy way to do this is to set a metronome at 60 beats per minute and count the clicks, which occur once each second. If you do this frequently and keep a written record of your time, you should see progress as your breathing muscles and your embouchure develop.

SUBTLE BREATH PULSE OR WEIGHT

The flow of air that you blow is much like the hair of the fiddler's bow as it travels across the string. Just as a fiddler can change the pressure and speed of her bowstrokes to emphasize certain notes and to impart rhythmic stress, weight, or impulse, you can give such life to your music with changes in the qualities of your breath. Just as a fiddler can "lean into" the bow, you can "lean into" the breath.

Flute players have much more capability in this regard than whistle players do, but even very subtle touches, as are possible on the whistle, can help bring your music to life beautifully. One way that good handmade whistles show their worth is that they offer you more capability to lean into the breath without adversely affecting pitch.

I elaborate upon the subject of subtle breath pulse in Chapter 10 in the sections *Rhythmic Emphasis Within the Long Roll* and *It's Alive—It Has a Pulse,* which appear on pp. 136-137. I suggest you work your way through the book to that point before delving into this aspect of breath and embouchure control.

---

[i] Nancy Toff, *The Flute Book* (Oxford: Oxford University Press, 1996), pp. 84–85.

chapter 4: on practice

PRACTICE STYLES

The word *practice* appears many times throughout this book. Clearly, practice is essential. What *you* mean by practice depends upon your reasons for playing this music and your goals. Some people enjoy a very relaxed approach and are content with slow or sporadic progress, while others are driven to learn voraciously and progress quickly. Most of us find ourselves somewhere in between.

Whatever your learning style and your drive, no doubt you hope to continually improve your skills and deepen your insights. That means "doing your homework," attentively listening to the older players as well as the new, and honing your own skills so you can play in a conscious and ever-improving way. It also means venturing out of your practice space to play with other people so that you can partake of the entire experience of community music making that is such an essential part of the "practice" of Irish music.

For now let's turn our thoughts to private, at-home practice.

ABOVE ALL, LISTEN

Though it may appear that practicing is a process of repeating the physical movements involved in playing, in fact effective practice is at least 90% attention, mental focus, and listening. It may sound obvious, but listening, *truly attentive, inquisitive listening,* is the cornerstone of effective practice. Physical repetition will not do you much good if you are not listening well and paying attention to yourself. In fact, it may serve to reinforce bad habits instead.

Throughout this book, I will be hammering away at how important it is to immerse yourself in listening to the fine players of the past and present. Being in their physical presence is the best of all and you should seek out such opportunities as you are able.

Even when your playing is rudimentary, you can be a virtuoso listener. Soak up the sounds of great whistle and flute players. With the help of this book you will be able to understand most of what they are doing.

PRACTICING SLOWLY BRINGS YOU FASTER RESULTS

This is a challenging and encouraging paradox. You will find its truth very liberating if you can muster the discipline to follow it. We all want to be able to play fast, but it is far more important to play well and beautifully. What is the point of playing poorly at a fast pace? Playing beautifully at a fast pace is magnificent, but slow practice is the thing that will get you there sooner.

W. A. Mathieu writes beautifully about this in *The Listening Book.*[i] He says,

> …you cannot achieve speed by speedy practice. The only way to get fast is to be deep, wide awake, and slow. When you habitually zip through your music, your ears are crystallizing in sloppiness. It is OK to check your progress with an occasional sprint. But it is better to let speed simply come on as a result of methodical nurturing, as with a lovingly built racing car.

> Yet almost everyone practices too fast …We want to be the person who is brilliant. This desire is compelling, and it can become what our music is about…

> Pray for the patience of a stonecutter. Pray to understand that speed is one of those things you have to give up - like love - before it comes flying to you through the back window.

When you play slowly you can much more easily notice and pay attention to the sounds you are making and the physical movements and positions that you are using to make them. How can you change and improve if you are not aware of these things?

To the extent that you can, you should practice playing well instead of playing poorly. This may sound ridiculously obvious. But the repetition of playing well is what builds the desired skills. Repetition of poor playing reinforces itself.

SOME WORDS OF WISDOM FROM MARTIN HAYES

Martin Hayes is one of the finest musicians, and he is deeply insightful and highly articulate about his art. In an interview in *Fiddler Magazine*[ii] he was asked how he chooses the pace for a particular tune. This was his response.

> …I tend to not start out at maximum speed and maximum volume, but somewhere at a medium to slow speed and volume. When I want to heighten the expression into excitement or vigor, I can do that. I can strive upwards and outwards…I think it's foolish to start out at full speed and at full volume. You're eliminating all sorts of possibilities…Playing a tune at full speed would be like driving through a country road at full speed. You may get the excitement of driving fast through a country road, but there's a lot of little gaps and avenues and trees and houses and such that you miss along the way. And it's like that with a tune. There's all these little dips and hollows in the tune that are self-explanatory, but time should be taken to go through them slowly. They explain themselves, they interpret themselves. They almost show what should be done.

THE METRONOME: A GREAT TOOL

A metronome can be a great aid to slow, conscious practice. By keeping a steady beat for you, it frees up part of your mind which you can then devote to deeper listening and observation.

Let's say you are sitting down to practice a phrase of a tune. Use the metronome to help you find a comfortable speed at which you can play your best. Stay and play at that tempo for a while, listening to and reinforcing your best playing. When you are ready, increase the speed just a notch or two and see how that feels. If the new tempo is too challenging, return to the slower tempo. If you can do fairly well at the new tempo, if it stretches you but doesn't break you, stick with it until it feels quite comfortable. Then stay there for a while before moving on to try a faster tempo. And so on.

When doing metronome practice and gradually increasing your speed, you may enjoy trying the following approach. Start with a *very* slow tempo. Then adjust the metronome faster by three notches and play there for a while if you comfortably can. Then adjust the metronome slower by two notches. Play there for a while and notice the differences in your playing and sound. Then increase by three notches, decrease by two, increase by three, decrease by two, and so on.

Don't be in a rush. Our muscles learn more slowly than our minds, but muscle memory is very long-lasting and dependable. There are intriguing physiological reasons for this, which will be discussed in Chapter 15, in the section *The Physiology of "Muscle Memory"* (see pp. 178-179).

A metronome provides a rigid time reference, and that can be extremely revealing. When you *externalize* the definition of the beat to a machine, you come to see how your internal sense of the beat can tend to speed up or fluctuate. It's hard for us to maintain a steady beat at an unusually slow speed. We want to speed up, even when we are not ready to. Of course we don't want to play like machines, but machines can help us gain insight into how to play better as humans.

PAY ATTENTION TO YOUR ENERGY

A short period of conscious practice is much more beneficial than a long period of practice when your attention is flagging. It does you little good to practice if you are not focusing well. If you find that your mind is spinning its wheels, take a break and come back later, refreshed.

It seems that some part of our mind keeps on practicing, even while we are away from our instruments. Many people have had the experience of working very hard on a particular challenge, not making much headway, and then have come back after hours, or even days, to find that in the meantime they have somehow progressed to a higher level.

FIND A PLEASANT PRACTICE SPACE

Since you want to make practicing an experience that you will look forward to, do what you can to find the best practice space. Ideally, you should find a room that is quiet and private, a place free of distractions and away from others if they make you feel self-conscious. It should be well-lit and ventilated and not too cramped. The acoustics are very important. If the room is too dead (too absorbent of sound) it may be unflattering and discouraging. If it is too reverberant it may hide your true sound from you, though reverberant stairwells and the like can be a lot of fun to play in now and then.

A MIRROR CAN HELP IN SEVERAL WAYS

One of the drawbacks of practicing whistle is that we tend to stare out into space while we play. Since we don't have our instrument in the center of our field of vision, as, for example, fiddlers do, it is easy for us to become distracted. Closing your eyes can help a great deal.

Or you might take the opposite approach and play in front of a mirror. Not only does the reflection engage you visually and help keep you focused on what you are doing, like the metronome it externalizes an aspect of the experience, allowing you to see what your body is *actually* doing, not just feel what you *think* it is doing. Comparing your body's sensation of itself with an objective visual reflection of it can be very enlightening.

The mirror not only reflects your image, it reflects your sound back to you, making it easier to hear the details of what you are doing. When a wind player plays while walking around in a room, you will often notice that she unconsciously gravitates towards a wall. The wall reflects her sound back and she can hear the details of her playing more clearly.

ISOLATE CHALLENGING AREAS

One sign of flagging attention is finding yourself playing through an exercise or a tune, repeatedly glossing over places that you don't really play very well. When you catch yourself doing this, stop. Take a break if you want to. When you resume, listen for a problem spot and stop when you come to it.

Take a close listen, examine the challenging area and try to isolate the note, notes, or technique that is catching you. Work on a very small group of notes, maybe just two or three, that contains the problem area. Use a metronome to stay at a slow enough tempo to do good work. Perhaps a mirror will help you see what is going on. When you have begun to make some good progress with the challenge, slightly expand the passage you are working on by adding a note or two before, then a note or two after. See how the problem manifests in this slightly larger context. When you are comfortable, expand the passage some more and see what that is like.

LISTEN TO YOUR BODY

Watch out for physical pain. This is a signal telling you to take a break, check for undue muscle tension, poor posture, etc. Get up and move around; shake out your arms, hands, legs. Stretch. Maybe it's time to stop practicing for the day. There are a lot of resources available that can help musicians prevent or deal with stress-related injuries and problems. Hopefully you can prevent such trouble from occurring.

ANOTHER USEFUL TOOL: AN AUDIO RECORDER

Most traditional musicians these days own and use some type of audio recorder. Such devices are certainly very handy for capturing music that you wish to learn later. Beware, however, of becoming over-dependent on them. It's all too easy to record someone playing a tune and then not really listen to it as it *happens,* since you know you can listen to your recording later. In your archiving zeal, don't forget to live in the moment.

If you have the opportunity to attend a regular session, try learning tunes gradually by simply soaking them in through repeated exposure. One day you will realize that you have already learned the tune in your head. You will realize that you can hum or lilt it. Then it is simply a matter of translating it onto your instrument. Even if you do not have contact with other Irish musicians, you can learn this way by listening repeatedly to favorite recordings, letting the music wash over and through you until you have absorbed it.

On a trip to Ireland in 1979, I left my cassette recorder home because I wanted to work on training myself to listen more deeply, as musicians must have done in older times, before the age of tape recorders. I did learn some tunes that way and learned them very well, but I'm afraid many escaped me entirely. My intentions were noble and it was great ear training, but it was also a rash decision, considering the fact that I was not able to visit musicians repeatedly during my fairly brief stay. Moderation in all things is a wise policy.

It can be very revealing to record yourself. As you listen back you will no doubt hear things that you didn't notice while you were actually playing.

Some recorders are equipped with a variable speed control. It can be very instructive to slow down the playback of a great player. For the computerized, there are also ways to capture music and manipulate it with software, some of which is free or very inexpensive.

GIVE YOURSELF POSITIVE MESSAGES

A musician always has more to learn, no matter how many years she has been practicing her art. Everyone is a beginner in some sense.

Even if your playing skills are rudimentary, your listening abilities are not. If you didn't have wide-open ears you wouldn't have been drawn to embark on the serious work of learning a new musical language and how to play a musical instrument.

Be encouraging to yourself. One can always find fault if one wants to, but one can also find progress, commitment, and devotion. Give yourself positive messages.

TAKE COMFORT IN "MUSCLE MEMORY"

Many people find it frustrating that it seems to take so long for them learn to perform unfamiliar physical actions, even though they can quickly understand them conceptually. There are important physiological reasons for this, which we will explore in Chapter 15.

For now, just know and take comfort in the fact that learning an unfamiliar physical skill actually requires you to build new neural pathways in your body. No one can quickly make such physical changes to their nervous system. The good news is that once these new pathways are established, they are extremely durable. Once you thoroughly learn a new physical skill, you will not forget how to perform it, even if you lose your clear grasp of the concept.

---

[i] W. A. Mathieu, *The Listening Book* (Boston: Shambhala Publications, 1991), p. 101.

[ii] Mary Larsen, "Martin Hayes, A Lilt All His Own," *Fiddler Magazine*, Spring 1994: p. 50.

chapter 5: getting comfortable with fingering

How Does the Whistle Produce Tone?

When a musical instrument produces a tone, it does so by setting the surrounding air into motion. Some part of the instrument system vibrates and transfers that vibration to the air. With a fiddle, the wooden soundboard vibrates to set the air into motion. With a bodhrán, the vibration of the goatskin drumhead excites the air. With an accordion, it's the metal reeds hidden inside the instrument.

With tin whistles, however, it is not a part of the instrument itself that causes the surrounding air to vibrate. When you play the whistle you set the *column of air* inside the instrument into vibration, which in turn sets the surrounding air into motion. Tin whistles are essentially containers for the vibrating body that produces tone: an air column.

So, you could say that when you play the whistle, you are playing a column of air. More accurately, your mouth and lungs and the blade are setting the air column into vibration, and your fingers are simply changing the length of that air column. The air column starts at the mouthpiece and extends down the whistle until it encounters an open finger hole. As far as the air column is concerned, the whistle ends at the first open finger hole.

The Finger Holes and the Whistle's Natural Scale

With all finger holes closed, the air column is as long as it can be, and it vibrates to produce the whistle's lowest note: D. As you uncover the holes one at a time, starting with B3 and progressing upward toward the mouthpiece, the vibrating air column becomes shorter and shorter and produces higher and higher pitches: E, F-sharp, G, A, B, and C-sharp. These ascending pitches, starting with low D, form the D major scale, or the D Ionian mode.

This is the *natural scale* of the tin whistle, the pitches produced beginning with the air column at maximum length (all holes sealed), and becoming shortened progressively, one increment, or finger hole, at a time. The Ionian mode is the whistle's natural scale only because of the particular positioning and sizing of the finger holes. Another arrangement of hole positions and/or sizes would yield a different scale.

The whistle's arrangement of finger holes corresponds roughly to the arrangement of the white keys of a piano, or the string scheme of an Irish harp, or closer yet, to the frets of an Appalachian dulcimer. These are all ingenious systems for producing a series of discrete, predetermined pitches. But the whistle's finger hole method seems to be the oldest, dating back at least to Neanderthal times.

I find it quite amazing how quickly the air column responds to the covering and uncovering of the finger holes. In effect, it responds instantaneously.

Completely Sealing the Holes

The success of tin whistle fingering depends upon the total, air-tight sealing of the holes by the fingers. When one of your fingers is not *completely* sealing its hole, you will get an unintended sound. The nature of that sound depends upon which hole or holes are not well sealed and which other holes are covered or uncovered at the moment. You may get an unstable, weak, unmusical sound, or perhaps a stable pitch of some description – but not the one you were intending to play.

With experience, your ability to completely seal the holes will become second nature, but nearly all beginners have some trouble with this. It takes time to develop the ability to move individual fingers without changing the positions of others. In the beginning, it is almost certain that placing a finger or group of fingers on their holes will at times cause another finger to inadvertently move slightly off its hole, resulting in an air leak. Even the tiniest of air leaks can cause a problem.

The challenge of moving only *one* finger at a time and reliably sealing its hole is not terribly daunting. However, moving a *group* of fingers in synchronized unison is a bit trickier. Making numerous such movements in sequence is trickier still, at least in the early stage of learning. In time, all of this becomes easy.

MOVING GROUPS OF FINGERS IN PRECISE COORDINATION AND SYNCHRONIZATION

We coordinate the movement of groups and combinations of fingers in many day-to-day tasks: making a fist, grasping a rope, picking up a cup, typing on a keyboard. But I can't think of any common day-to-day task that requires near-perfect synchronization of our finger movements. Since we don't normally need such skills, we tend to not develop them.

But playing well on the whistle (and most other musical instruments) does demand precise coordination and synchronization of finger movements.

In lifting or putting down a group of fingers, when one or more of the group moves out of synch with the others, you will produce one or more brief unwanted notes. If you are listening attentively, you will hear them. Pay attention to these stray notes – they will show you where you need to improve your fingering technique.

If you are an adult beginner, and especially if you have never played a musical instrument before, you may feel foolish or inept when you come up against such fingering challenges. After all, you may think, what could be simpler than moving a couple of fingers? But don't feel foolish or call yourself uncoordinated. This is simply a new situation that calls for new skills. The physical skills needed for handwriting are quite complex and sophisticated, and it took us all quite a while to learn them. Most of us were young children then, and we didn't expect ourselves to be competent in all things. Be easy on yourself.

To the uninitiated, playing the whistle looks easy. Many think, "It is such a simple instrument, almost a toy. And it's inexpensive, so it can't be *that* hard to play." Since some whistles do look like a child's toy, when we find that in fact it is actually not so easy to play, we may feel all the more foolish. One might wonder, "Is there something wrong with me?" But don't give in to such thinking. The tin whistle is a musical instrument, as valid as any other. Learning to play any instrument well is challenging, no matter what your age.

NAMING THE NOTES

Clearly, you don't need to be able to read music to be a fine tin whistle player. But even if you never intend to read music, it is very helpful, useful, and important to learn and memorize the commonly accepted names of the notes you play, and to learn to *automatically* link those names to the fingerings of the notes.

This is beneficial for two reasons. First, it will help you to "think music" more clearly and learn tunes more readily, and second, it will greatly enhance your communication with other musicians.

Let's consider the first of these reasons a bit further.

It is simpler and less cumbersome to think of a note as "G" rather than "that note I get when I cover only the top three holes of the whistle." In a similar way it helps to think of "the color of the sky when it is daylight and it is not overcast" as "sky blue." Simple names, standing for relatively involved ideas such as colors, numbers, musical pitches, or tin whistle fingerings, allow for a kind of mental shorthand. They allow us to think more efficiently.

In the western world, the commonly accepted system for naming consecutive ascending pitches uses the first seven letters of the alphabet – ABCDEFG. These are not just arbitrary names, but a pattern of names that we already know extremely well, having learned the alphabet as young children.

Using this convention, we can deduce certain things about sequences of ascending notes almost without thought. For example, we deduce that the note B is higher than the note A, since B comes later in the alphabet that A, and more specifically that B is higher than A by one step of the scale, since B follows *immediately* after A in the alphabet. Similarly we know that the pitch C is two steps higher in the scale than A, since the letter C comes two steps later in the alphabet than A. We deduce such things so automatically because we have already thoroughly memorized the names and sequence of the letters of the alphabet.

How would the absence of note names affect musical thinking? It's hard for me to know exactly, but I believe it would prevent the development of a certain clarity and rapidity of musical thought. It seems to me that once you simply and instantly know that F-sharp is the note produced by covering holes with T1, T2, T3, and B1, leaving the B2 and B3 holes open, your mental process is greatly simplified. Instead of thinking of, or visualizing, six objects (the finger holes) and two states (covered or uncovered), you just command yourself to "play F-sharp" and your fingers automatically go where they need to go. (The register of the F-sharp, whether high or low, is determined by air control, not by fingering.)

If tin whistles (of the same size and pitch) were the only instruments in existence, it would make sense to name the whistle's lowest note for the first letter of the alphabet. But since there are a wide variety of instruments in the world, and they are designed in so many different ways in relation to pitch, it makes sense to subscribe to the common naming standard that applies to all instruments and voices in the western world. It just so happens that the note western musicians have agreed to call "A" is not the lowest note of the D tin whistle. The lowest note of the D tin whistle is, of course, what we have agreed to call "D."

Some Good News

Using these letter names and the two words that modify them – "sharp" and "flat" – makes clear something else that might not otherwise be readily apparent: the tunes we play actually use only a small number of pitches, usually about seven. Sequences of these pitches combine in many wonderful and complex patterns, but the palette of pitch "ingredients" in the music is fairly small, and therefore quite manageable.

Each pitch can occur in both the low and high register of the whistle. These low and high instances of a pitch share the same name *and*, almost always, the same fingering. These things help reinforce the fact that "low G" and "high G" are simply different forms, or registers, of the pitch "G", one octave apart from each other.

Whistle players are very fortunate that the high and low register of each pitch share the same fingering. With many instruments such direct fingering correlations do not occur. For example, on the fiddle, low D is played on the open D string (i.e. with no fingers depressing the string), while the D one octave higher is played on the A string with three fingers depressing the string.

We are also lucky that there is only one fingering for almost every note. With many instruments, especially string instruments, there may be several alternate fingerings for any given note.

To Use This Book Well, You Will Need to Memorize the Names of the Notes

One of the most important reasons for memorizing the names of the notes is to facilitate communication among musicians. That goes for communication between you and me, too. You will have to memorize these names to make full use of this book, because I refer to notes by letter name, not with such phrases as "the note you get when only T1, T2, T3, and B1 cover their holes."

A Fingering Chart

Referring to a fingering chart can help you visualize and memorize the relationships between notes, their fingerings, and their names.

You will find a fingering chart for the tin whistle in D in Appendix A, pp. 180-181. The first page of the chart is for the low register of the whistle, the second page for the high register. You will find information about the chart and its symbols in the caption on the first page of the chart.

17 Finger Coordination Exercises

The ability to move various combinations of fingers in precise coordination and synchronization is essential for good whistle playing, and not just combinations of fingers of only one hand or the other, but often fingers of both hands. If you are a beginner, gaining these skills may seem daunting to you, but I assure you, in time and with practice such dexterity will become second nature.

I have devised 17 exercises for developing finger coordination, but due to space limitations, am not able to include them in this book. However, the music notation for these exercises is available online at <www.greylarsen.com/extras/toolbox>, along with thorough explanatory text and sound recordings of each exercise.

ECONOMY OF MOTION

When moving from one note to a different one that requires you to cover a larger number of holes, do *not* lift any fingers that you don't *have* to lift. For example, when moving from low G (T1, T2, and T3 covering their holes) to low E (T1, T2, T3, B1, and B2 covering their holes), do not lift and replace T1, T2, and T3. Those three holes need to be covered for both fingerings, so just leave them covered. Simply put down B1 and B2.

This is a perfect example of a vital principle that we should apply when playing any instrument: *economy of motion.* Playing is challenging enough. It makes no sense to create unnecessary work for ourselves.

When we are beginners, there are so many things to attend to that it may be hard to sense opportunities to apply this principle, or even the reasons for applying it. When you become a more advanced player and want to play with agility and speed, the reasons for practicing economy of motion will be eminently clear. If you attend to economy of motion now, as best you can and whenever you can, you will be very grateful later on. Undoing unwanted habits takes much more work than establishing good ones in the first place.

FINGERING LOW C-NATURAL

There are two approaches to fingering low C-natural: by using a *cross-fingering* and by *half-holing*. A "cross-fingering" is a fingering in which there is an open hole above one or more closed holes ("above" meaning closer to the mouthpiece). "Half-holing" refers to the practice of only partially covering a tone hole in order to play a pitch that is in between the pitches produced by fully covering the tone hole in question and fully uncovering that same hole.

For the easiest low C-natural cross-fingering, cover holes only with T2 and T3, leaving all other holes open. This fingering works well with well-made whistles, but with many inexpensive mass-produced whistles, it unfortunately yields a C-natural that is too sharp. In such a case, one or more fingers must be added to bring the pitch down. (See the alternate cross-fingerings for low C-natural shown in the fingering chart on p. 180.)

The cross-fingering for low C-natural is more versatile that the half-hole fingering, and it should be your default choice. However, the half-hole fingering (played by only partly covering T1, with all other holes open) can be quite wonderful and evocative in many situations. (High C-natural is generally played using the half-hole fingering just mentioned.) I'll address the use of the half-hole fingering for C-natural in Chapter 9.

FINGERING HIGH D

The lowest note of the high register is high D, one octave higher than the lowest note of the whistle, low D. There are two fingerings one can use for high D. One is the same as the fingering for low D. The other is also the same, except that you uncover, or "vent", the T1 hole (see the fingering chart). This, too, is a cross-fingering, since there is an open hole above the closed holes.

I generally prefer the latter, vented cross-fingering for high D. I find that it makes the note "pop out" more readily and sound more clear. But often it is more convenient to not vent the D. Sometimes, when high D is preceded or followed by a fingering in which T1 is closed, economy of motion suggests that you not vent the D (i.e. leave T1 down). However, if you favor the sound of the vented D, you may choose to disregard the more economical fingering and opt instead for the sound you prefer.

THE D MIXOLYDIAN MODE

If you change the C-sharp of the whistle's natural scale, the D Ionian mode, to a C-natural, the mode becomes the D Mixolydian mode. There are hundreds of wonderful tunes in this mode.

In the following figure I provide the name of each note, below the musical staff. Low register notes are labeled with capital letters (A, B, C, etc.), and upper register notes with small letters (a, b, c, etc.). This is consistent with the conventions of "abc notation," a music notation system in common use on the internet as of this writing.

Also, a number appears above each note. This number shows how many fingers must move in order to advance to that note from the preceding one.

Play the notes of this mode, as shown in Figure 5-1.

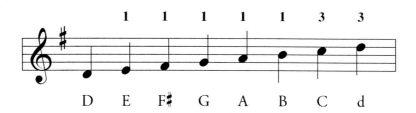

Figure 5-1: The D Mixolydian mode.

 Track 7

Note that the last note, high D, is represented by the small letter "d," since it is in the high register.

The finger movements indicated by the numbers above these notes assume two things (which may not be the case for you): that you are using the T2, T3 cross-fingering for C-natural, and that you are venting the high D. Here is a situation where it is easier to vent the D than not. If you did not vent the D, you would have to move four fingers to get to high D instead of three, since the note that precedes high D is a cross-fingered C (T1 open). Economy of motion suggests that you vent the D.

OPPOSING FINGER MOVEMENT

Very often you will need to move two or more fingers at the same time *but in opposite directions*. Changing from a "natural" fingering to a cross-fingering, and vice versa, sometimes creates this situation. Again, it is not common in everyday life that we need to move fingers in opposite directions with precise synchronization, so many people have not developed such skills. The 17 exercises available at <www.greylarsen.com/extras/toolbox> thoroughly address the practicing of opposing finger movement.

chapter 6: the language analogy

Many writers have explored the common ground between music and spoken language. Though they have a great deal in common, in important ways the two are fundamentally different. Words are symbols that represent objects, actions, and ideas. Musical sounds, when not coupled with lyrics, are not usually involved with the symbolic representation of anything.

Yet when musical sounds are put together they take on intricate and multidimensional relationships with each other that resemble the patterning of speech; and when we speak, we "perform" the sounds of language in real time. The similarities between music and spoken language are indeed many.

FOOD FOR THOUGHT

Since spoken language is such a rich and omnipresent aspect of our daily lives, examining its resemblance to music can yield potent insights. In this chapter, I will introduce some of these ideas as food for thought, notions to chew on as you progress through the book. Then, in Chapter 14, after exploring ornamentation, blowing, phrasing, articulation, and the use of the breath, we will revisit the analogy.

VERY SIMILAR, BUT DIFFERENT

Of course, music and spoken language are different in some fundamental ways.

As mentioned above, words refer directly to things in the external world. Instrumental music refers to nothing outside itself. We often associate things of the outside world with instrumental music, for example by connecting a tune with its title. We may become inspired by the outside world to create instrumental music. But these external connections are not directly communicated by the music itself.

Almost all Irish music has a regular pulse and the durations of its notes are regular subdivisions of that pulse, lilt notwithstanding. The pitches of Irish music are discrete, contained in simple modes, and easily identifiable. Sometimes we slide into or out of a pitch or alter it in other ways, but these inflections and changes refer to known pitches.

In speech there is a feeling of rhythm but not a recurrent pulse, unless we are reciting verse or chanting. The durations of syllables are not necessarily proportional to each other, and the pitched inflections we use are not stable, discrete, and identifiable as part of any consistent pattern or musical scale.

Now let's look at some parallels.

KEEPING THE BIG PICTURE IN VIEW

One of the prime challenges for the novice musician is to elevate her focus from the small details of individual notes and the technical challenges of playing to a broader view in which she can hear and understand musical phrasing, structure, and meaning.

Compare individual notes to syllables. The articulation of a note is like the beginning consonant or vowel of a syllable: discrete, well-defined, and hard, or soft and smoothly connected to the previous syllable. Syllables link together to form longer words, just as three-note groupings in a jig might form a melodic "word." Several words join together to form a phrase, a complete thought. Note groupings connect to form a musical phrase, a structure that creates direction and motion.

Phrases join to form a sentence. Punctuation delineates the phrases, clarifies their relationships, and gives the sentence finality. "Question and answer" in speech are reflected by "anticipation and resolution" in music. Musical phrases form melodies that embody a complete musical statement, such as a complete A part or B part of a tune, which are punctuated by pauses, breathing, and cadence.

Sentences join to form paragraphs, or stanzas of poetry. A and B parts, sometimes more parts, form musical stanzas or paragraphs to make a complete musical poem or story. Medleys of tunes can be seen as longer, more complex story or poem structures.

To make sense of a poem or story, one cannot focus solely on the sounds of individual syllables. We are so thoroughly familiar with our native language that we scarcely notice such tiny things. We automatically focus foremost on the level of meaning in all its subtle shadings. Only by conscious decision do we examine the mechanics of consonants, vowels, and articulations.

This must be our goal in playing music: *to master the technical aspects to such an extent that we naturally enter into the playing experience at the level of meaning.* If you cannot do that yet as a player, you certainly can, and do, as a listener. Bring the depth and breadth of your listening to your playing. Don't get completely caught up in the details of what you are doing. As you do the necessary detail work, at the same time stand back and hear the poetry of the music. This will guide your technical work and keep you on course toward expressive, eloquent playing. Just as we function simultaneously on several levels in daily life (e.g. performing the complex physical, visual, auditory, and tactile tasks of driving a car while planning the next day's work and listening to music on the radio), so we must learn to give our attention to music at multiple levels at the same time.

A STRANGER IN A STRANGE LAND

If you did not grow up with this music, your experience is very much like learning to speak a foreign language in a foreign country. You are immersed in the language and eventually you reach a point where you can think in that language, no longer translating in your mind. You learn the grammar to a sufficient extent that you can begin to converse freely. You may not speak like a native right away. In fact you may spend years polishing your grammar, syntax, and vocabulary. But you have reached a critical point: you know the language well enough to eliminate the step of mental translation. This is the key to fluency—in language and in music.

BREATHING

When we speak, our breath, the flow of air through our bodies, is the medium for the sound of our voice. As whistle players, our breath is also the substance of the sound of our music. A fiddler breathes simply to get oxygen. We breathe for that purpose, but also to breathe life into our music.

As I noted in Chapter 1, the flute and whistle are the only instruments of traditional Irish music that are not suited to nonstop playing. We must interrupt the flow of sound in order to breathe, just as we do when speaking or singing.

When we speak in our native language, we have an intuitive, automatic sense of when it is appropriate to breathe. We do not disrupt meaning by breathing in the middle of a phrase. In fact, we use the necessity of breathing to shape our speech and enhance its clarity and meaning. We use breathing for punctuation. We know that pausing gives emphasis to the next words we speak.

The musician's use of space enhances musical meaning in very much the same ways. Many musicians forget to use space in these meaningful ways, but wind players and singers cannot avoid leaving spaces in their music. It is up to us to learn to use the necessary creation of these spaces in an articulate and eloquent way. That means learning to leave out notes, and shorten longer notes, in ways that *contribute* to our interpretation of the music. We will explore this subject in depth in Chapter 13, *Musical Breathing.*

TONGUING

In speech, we use our tongue to produce a vast spectrum of consonant sounds and to color and shape our vowel sounds. The tongue is capable of amazingly fine nuance. In playing the whistle we can use our tongues to produce a similarly wide array of articulations and tone colors with seemingly endless gradations of quality. I explore this subject in Chapter 12, *Tonguing,* and in even more depth in my book *The Essential Guide to Irish Flute and Tin Whistle.*

A SINGLE, LINEAR VOICE

When we speak, we have only one voice. We cannot speak in "harmony" with ourselves, expressing several different ideas at the same time, the way a pianist can harmonize her own melodies.

The same is true of whistle playing. We play one note at a time. We have a single voice. This is also the intrinsic nature of traditional Irish music. A tune is complete in itself as a single, unaccompanied melody.

A COMMON VOCABULARY

Music and language share a common vocabulary. Think of how the following words have meaning in describing both speech and music: intonation, inflection, delivery, attack, rhythm, tone, nuance, phrasing, accent, cadence, expression, lilt; eloquent, articulate, melodious, singsong, muted, brash. The personality of a speaker, and a musician, are revealed as much through these aspects of speaking and playing as through verbal or musical content.

CROSS-FERTILIZATION AND INSPIRATION

Instrumentalists the world over draw inspiration from the expressiveness of singers, who use the most natural of all instruments, the human voice. In Irish instrumental music this emulation finds its highest form in the playing of slow airs. When playing slow airs, instrumentalists ideally know the lyrics of the air intimately and are guided by them in their musical expression and interpretation. You can read about playing slow airs in *The Essential Guide to Irish Flute and Tin Whistle.*

Singers also are inspired to imitate instruments. In Irish vocal music this finds its highest form in the art of lilting, the singing of instrumental tunes using the texture of improvised syllables to evoke the articulations, ornamentation, and rhythms of instruments. Traditionally, singers lilt tunes for dancing when instrumentalists cannot be present.

❖ SECTION 2 ❖

ORNAMENTATION

Introduction to Ornamentation

Traditional Irish music is a living aural tradition, one that is continually evolving. Styles and techniques of ornamentation among Irish whistle players are very diverse. It would be a mistake to think that anyone can reduce them to a uniform catalog of rules.

In your exploration and study of ornamentation, and during the development of your own ornamentation style, it is essential that you do a great deal of listening to excellent players, in person when possible. Establish this habit early. This book will allow you to better understand what you hear and see in their playing.

I find that the closer I look at the details of ornamentation in my own playing, and in the playing of people who have styles different from mine, the more I realize that there are subtle differences of approach in many aspects of ornamentation and articulation that happily coexist within the living tradition. This stylistic diversity is part of what makes Irish music so vital. Yet there is a common ground amid the diversity, and that is where one should start one's study. A full understanding of the art of ornamentation, and the development of one's own ornamentation style, requires years of playing and attentive listening.

Since beginning to play the whistle in the early 1970s I have formed some clear opinions on how best to think of and execute the building blocks of whistle ornamentation, as well as its more complex structures. In this book I take quite a bit of time and care to present these building blocks and two of these complex structures (i.e. the long roll and short roll), as clearly and comprehensively as I can, for this is an area where the available teaching materials have proven inadequate and where there is a great need for completeness and clarity.

You Will Find Much More on Advanced Ornamentation Techniques in *The Essential Guide to Irish Flute and Tin Whistle*

If you wish to explore ornamentation further, my book *The Essential Guide to Irish Flute and Tin Whistle* continues that study where this book leaves off, exploring the rest of the complex ornamentation structures in seven more chapters: *Condensed Long Rolls, Condensed Short Rolls, Double-Cut Rolls, Cranns, Rolls in Tunes with Overtly Uneven Subdivisions of the Beat, Other Multi-Note Ornaments*, and *Ornamentation through Melodic Variation*.

Many styles and approaches to ornamentation are documented and discussed in Section 8 of *The Essential Guide to Irish Flute and Tin Whistle*, where I present in-depth transcriptions of 27 commercial recordings of flute and tin whistle performances dating from 1926 to 2001. The twenty-two players included, representing a wide variety of playing styles and approaches to ornamentation, are: John McKenna, Tom Morrison, William Cummins, Séamus Ennis, Willie Clancy, Paddy Taylor, Paddy Carty, Josie McDermott, Matt Molloy, Cathal McConnell, Mary Bergin, Donncha Ó Briain, Desi Wilkinson, Breda Smyth, Seán Ryan, Conal Ó Gráda, Micho Russell, Joanie Madden, Kevin Crawford, Catherine McEvoy, Seamus Egan, and me.

Whistle and Flute Ornamentation are the Same

You should know that Irish tin whistle and Irish flute ornamentation are the same, and both are very similar to, and derived from, uilleann pipes ornamentation. How whistle and flute players use ornaments may differ slightly, and adapting this ornamentation to the modern, Boehm-system flute requires modification of some fingerings and techniques.

You can transfer the ornamentation techniques you learn on the tin whistle directly to the simple-system, Irish flute. The whistle and the simple-system flute share the same fingering system.

Above All, an Aural Tradition

Traditional Irish music has always been passed along and learned by ear. It is therefore understandable that no clear consensus has emerged on how to conceptualize ornamentation techniques so that they can be clearly conveyed in words and in music notation. I hope that my innovations with the concepts and notation of these techniques will bring us closer to such a consensus.

But amid all of this ink on paper, let us never forget the central and critical importance of learning and passing along this music by ear. Music notation is an excellent servant, a very elegant box of tools, and I encourage everyone to learn to use it. But it was never meant to become our master. Beware of becoming dependent upon music notation. (For more on this see Chapter 1.)

Too Much Borrowing from Classical Music

Most writers who have attempted to describe traditional Irish whistle playing have borrowed concepts and notation practices from classical music. This works fairly well in some areas, and not well at all in others.

Ornamentation is an area where this borrowing has not served us well. In many years of teaching, I have encountered a great many players who are mystified by ornamentation techniques. Most of them have not had personal access to good players. Struck by the beauty of what they hear on recordings but missing important knowledge, they often turn to books in their search for insight. The more or less foggy and incomplete explanations that these books provide offer some help, but unfortunately many of them also create and perpetuate misunderstandings about Irish whistle ornamentation.

Most of this confusion has arisen from the vague and liberal use in these books of the *grace note,* as a term, as a concept, and as a notation practice. I feel that such use of grace notes has limited our thinking and is the single biggest factor in constraining many people's understanding of ornamentation to what I feel is a fairly primitive level. In the following chapters, I bring to light the confusions that this has caused and lay out a new and accurate way to understand and notate Irish whistle ornamentation. The concept of the *articulation* is a key that opens doors to better understanding and deeper exploration.

What is Ornamentation?

When I speak of ornamentation in traditional Irish music I am referring to ways of altering or embellishing small pieces or cells of a melody that are between one and three eighth-note beats long. These alterations and embellishments are created mainly through the use of special fingered articulations and inflections, not through the addition of extra, ornamental or grace notes.

The modern classical musician's view of ornamentation is quite different. *Ornamentation, A Question & Answer Manual,* a book written to help classical musicians understand ornamentation from the baroque era through the present, offers this definition: "Ornamentation is the practice of adding notes to a melody to allow music to be more expressive."[i]

Classical musicians naturally tend to carry this kind of thinking with them as newcomers to traditional Irish music. However, as long as they overlay the "added note" concept onto Irish ornamentation, they will be unable to gain fluency in the language of Irish music.

More than "Ornamental"

The word ornament implies a musical element that could just as well be left out, leaving the essence of the music perfectly intact. Many ornaments used in Irish music do fit that description, but there are others that do not, that are essential or intrinsic to the life of the tune. Stated another way, there are places in many tunes that do not sound "right" without the use of ornamentation.

Ornaments are among the tools we use in the larger pursuits of variation and interpretation. Returning to the language analogy I introduced in Chapter 6, *ornamentation* corresponds to the many ways you can enunciate, pronounce, and deliver individual syllables and words. *Variation* corresponds to the particular ways that you choose to combine words into phrases and use idioms and slang. *Interpretation* corresponds to how you combine phrases into sentences and paragraphs, how you reveal and express your personality, your soul, and your view of the world through your command of language.

Ornamentation techniques join together with the air-management techniques of tonguing, slurring, and breath control to give the player a vast variety of tools for musical expression.

HATS OFF TO THE PIPES

As stated in Chapter 1, Irish tin whistle ornamentation techniques have their origins in the tradition of the uilleann pipes, the current bellows-blown bagpipe of Ireland, whose music developed out of the older pastoral bagpipe and *píob mór* traditions. The nature of the playing capabilities of these antecedent bagpipes sheds important light upon why many uilleann pipe, tin whistle, and Irish flute techniques have evolved as they have. With these older bagpipes, in order to articulate or separate notes of the same pitch, it was necessary to use fingered articulations. These articulations have come down to us in the form of the *cut,* the *strike,* and the multi-note ornaments that make use of cuts and strikes.

Of course Irish flute and tin whistle traditions have also developed independently of piping, so the differences between the uilleann pipes and our mouth-blown flutes and whistles are very important as well.

ARTICULATION OR ORNAMENTATION?

Many Irish flute players, but very few whistle players, use glottal and diaphragm techniques in place of tonguing. From here forward, for simplicity's sake, I will group these glottal and diaphragm techniques together under the term *throating.*

Tonguing and throating are usually grouped under the moniker of **articulation.** For our purposes I identify an articulation as *that extremely brief sound component of a note that defines its beginning or attack.*

So far, I have been freely using the term articulation as if it were a part of a vocabulary that is commonly accepted for describing Irish music. But in fact, this has not been so. I hope that will change.

Cuts and strikes, the fingered articulations referred to above, are referred to by nearly all Irish musicians as "ornaments". I acknowledge that common practice. But I feel it is more accurate to describe cuts and strikes as articulations. They are very brief sounds that define the attacks of notes. Since cuts and strikes are so central to tin whistle ornamentation, the ramifications of choosing to look upon them as articulations are quite far-reaching.

Cuts and strikes are special articulations that have their own pitch element. One could accurately call them *pitched articulations.* They sound ornamental to our ear because of their pitch element. Other articulations that do not have a pitch element, such as tonguing and throating, do not sound ornamental to our ears.

ORNAMENT CATEGORIES

I divide ornaments into two groups: *single-note ornaments* and *multi-note ornaments.*

The single-note ornaments are the pitched articulations (the cut and the strike) and the pitch inflections called *slides.*

Multi-note ornaments include *rolls, cranns, trills, finger vibrato,* and a few others. There are many varieties of rolls and cranns. In this book we will work with short and long rolls, but not with other kinds of rolls and not with cranns. As stated above, these are advanced techniques that I explore in depth in my book *The Essential Guide to Irish Flute and Tin Whistle.*

I strongly recommend that you progress sequentially through the five chapters in this section of the book, for the information in later chapters is built upon that of the earlier ones.

FIRST WE WILL EXPLORE SINGLE-NOTE ORNAMENTS

The single-note ornaments are **cuts, strikes,** and **slides.** Cuts and strikes are *pitched articulations* while tonguing and throating are *non-pitched articulations.* The slide is an *inflection.* It has too long a duration to be considered an articulation in my view, though you can certainly play very quick and subtle slides.

Single-note ornaments and articulations can be utilized alone, and some can be combined and played simultaneously, or "stacked," in a variety of ways to give the player a very wide palette of ways to express a single note.

---

[i] Valery Lloyd and Carol L. Bigler, *Ornamentation, A Question & Answer Manual,* (Van Nuys, Calofornia: Alfred Publishing Co., 1995) p.8.

chapter 7: cuts

The first and most important single-note ornament to learn is the **cut**. The cut is by far the most-used ornament in this music and we will spend quite a bit of time exploring the many contexts in which we can employ it. Other names sometimes heard for the cut are *chip, grace, grace note,* and *upper grace note.*

The movement of the cut is a very small and quick lift of a finger completely off its hole and the immediate replacement of that finger. When executed well the movement of the cut can be almost invisible. The finger barely needs to lift from the hole, though it does completely uncover it. It is very important to keep your hands relaxed when learning and using cuts. Don't fall prey to the temptation to tense up while trying to make your cuts quick and crisp.

> The sound of the well-executed cut is extremely brief, so brief that a listener does not perceive it as having an identifiable pitch, duration, or rhythmic identity. The well-played cut is therefore not perceived as a *note* but as an *articulation.*

The cut forms the attack of a note and gives that note emphasis. I call the note that it articulates its *parent note.* Though a well-played cut doesn't seem to have a pitch, in fact it does, and that pitch is always higher than that of its parent note. This higher pitch is part of what gives the cut its unique qualitative identity.

A cut is a *pitched articulation.*

A cut can range from being very subtle to very emphatic, depending upon the melodic context, the quality of the breath used, and whether or not (or how) you tongue and/or slide at the same time that you cut. (Slides are addressed in Chapter 9.)

CORRECTING A MAJOR MISCONCEPTION

Unfortunately, everything I have seen in print regarding cuts supports the idea that they are to be thought of and perceived as notes unto themselves. However, this notion doesn't fit with what one hears when listening to a good whistle player using cuts.

Though it may seem like a small or subtle distinction at first, regarding cuts as articulations leads to a completely different and more accurate understanding of their nature and function. It is well worth the time and effort to delve deeply into this matter and understand it thoroughly since the cut is such a critical element of the language of traditional Irish music, and since the way we think about music has a tremendous impact on how we play it. Often with Irish music it is very important to pay close attention to the details. The cut is a tiny thing, yet it can convey a great deal in energy and expression when it is executed well.

TRY SOME CUTS

First, try some cuts. Play a low G. (Later on you can do this same exercise on high G.) While holding a long low G, and without tonguing at all, try to create little "blips" in the sound by lifting and quickly replacing T2, keeping T3 down. Without tensing up, keep the finger lift as small and quick as you can. (For a key to these fingering indications see Figure 3-1 on p. 34.)

If cuts are new to you, your cuts probably do not sound very crisp at this point. That's perfectly fine. It is much more important to relax and avoid forming the bad habit of tensing up. Be content with your cuts as they are now. They will get better over time.

These "blips" you are creating have a pitch somewhere around B. The exact pitch will vary from whistle to whistle. It's just fine for it to be out of tune. Ultimately, when you're more experienced, your cuts will be so quick that the ear won't perceive them as having an identifiable pitch, and "out-of-tuneness" will become a non-issue.

Keep a steady, slow beat by setting a metronome at a comfortable tempo somewhere around 60 beats per minute, or by tapping your foot, and try to place the blips exactly on those beats, not before and not after.

This is not easy. As I said earlier, if you are new to this your blips are probably not very short. Most likely you can hear each one's beginning and ending and easily discern its pitch. So, which do you place on the beat, the beginning or end of the blip? For now, make sure the end is on the beat, and as you practice, keep drawing the beginning closer and closer into the beat. See Figures 7-1 through 7-4. (In these diagrams, the horizontal axis represents time while the vertical axis represents pitch.)

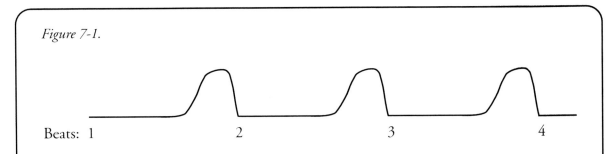

Figure 7-1.

Beats: 1   2   3   4

A beginner's cuts. The ends of the cuts are placed on the beat. At this stage, the blips are long and sound like notes. The beginnings of the blips anticipate the beat or pulse.

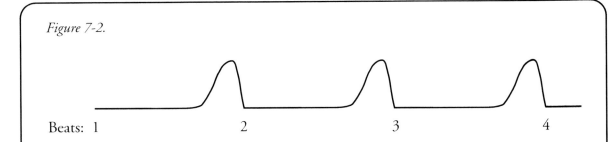

Figure 7-2.

Beats: 1   2   3   4

Making progress. The ends of the cuts are still placed on the beat but the beginnings are drawn in closer to the beats. The cuts still sound like notes.

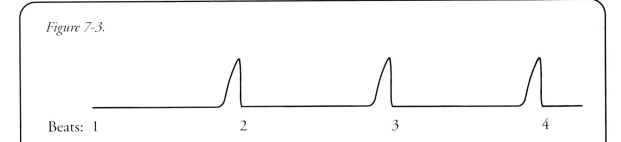

Figure 7-3.

Beats: 1   2   3   4

Further Progress. The cuts are getting shorter. The beginnings of the cuts are drawn in closer to the beats, and the cuts are sounding less like notes unto themselves.

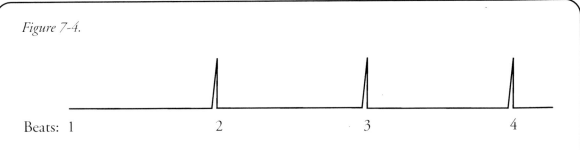

Figure 7-4.

Beats: 1   2   3   4

Well-played cuts. They are short enough that the brain does not perceive them as having beginnings and endings, duration, or pitch. They no longer anticipate the beat but are placed right on the beat. They sound like articulations.

If you're tapping your foot, don't speed up. Using a metronome is highly recommended. Make the blips as crisp and brief as you comfortably can.

Now, instead of hearing alternating G notes and blips, *adjust your thinking* and imagine that each blip forms the beginning of a G note. Each G note lasts one beat. Now you hear only a succession of G notes and each one is initiated by a blip. Thinking this way, these blips no longer have independent identities as *notes*. Each is merely the attack, the articulation of its parent G note.

Be patient! It will take a long time to gain the skill to play cuts well. Keep the ideal sound of well-played cuts in your mind's ear. (You will hear many examples of well-played cuts on the companion CD, for example, in Track 8.) That memorized ideal sound will guide your muscles and nervous system as they learn to do their jobs.

TAKE HEED!

I cannot overemphasize the importance of learning to place cuts (and strikes, described in the next chapter) precisely on a beat. Think about it: Since cuts and strikes are the articulations of their parent notes, I'm simply saying that it is of paramount importance to be able to place notes on their beats, in a good solid rhythm. As you advance in your skill you will not always want to place every note strictly on a beat or a subdivision of a beat, but you will always need to be able to, especially when playing tunes at fast speeds.

THE CUT IS *NOT* A NOTE

The well-played cut is not a note, for the simple reason that it is not *perceived* as a note.

A cut is more properly thought of as a verb than as a noun. When you cut a slice of bread from its loaf, you "articulate" that slice with the action of your knife. The cut can only be seen in its *effect:* that is, the new edge of the slice of bread. The cut does not exist independent of its slice of bread.

To cut is to articulate a note in a special way. To tongue is a different way to articulate a note. While it's true that every articulation does occupy a tiny bit of time, if that duration is brief enough, a listener will not perceive it as having a duration, and therefore will not hear it as being a note unto itself. The listener will also not perceive it as having an identifiable pitch. *These are the secrets of the cut and the strike.*

The cut and strike, the pitched articulations we use in this music, seem magical. Their musical qualities exist as they do because they are so brief that they fall below a certain threshold of human perception. It is these *perceptions* that are truly important, not the fact that these articulations do have tiny, measurable durations. If they fall below that duration perception threshold, then in effect they are not notes.

A BRIEF DIGRESSION – MOVIES AND HOUSEFLIES

As you may know, films are sequences of still photographs that race by at 24 frames per second. This speed surpasses a certain threshold of human visual perception and, as a result, like magic, we see wonderful, smooth, continuous motion. In effect, for us, there are no still photos zooming by.

I have heard it said, however, that to a housefly a film looks like a slide show, because the fly's visual perception thresholds are so different from ours. (Whether this is actually true or not is beside the point.)

If a housefly's audio perception thresholds are different from ours in a similar way, then perhaps even the most well-executed cut sounds like a bona fide note to a fly. If this is so, as I (in my blissful ignorance) suspect it is, then houseflies cannot truly appreciate traditional Irish music. That is a shame. Perhaps they would behave differently if they could.

Alright – back to the matter at hand.

A CUT'S LOCATION IN TIME

When the cut is understood simply as a way to articulate a note, it follows that the cut will fall exactly upon the location in time where its parent note is placed.

70

So it is in this music. When you cut a note, the cut does not come before the beginning of the note, it *is* the beginning of the note, it defines the leading edge of the note. It is of crucial importance that you understand this fact of perception. You will not be able to execute such brief and precise cuts at first, or perhaps for a long time, but as long as you are hearing that sound in your mind's ear and are striving for it, you will gradually come to master it.

Neither Is the Cut a Grace Note

Figure 7-5. The conventional, misleading way of notating a cut as a grace note.

In my experience, at the time of this writing, all who have written about Irish whistle ornamentation have defined the cut as a kind of *grace note*. Some don't even call it a cut, but just call it a *grace* or *grace note*. In addition to adopting this classical music term to define or name the cut, almost universally these writers have used grace notes to notate them.

For several reasons, the practice of equating cuts with grace notes, in both verbal description and musical notation, is very misleading. Cuts, when executed well, do not sound like grace notes.

Why Is It Misleading to Equate Cuts with Grace Notes?

Grace notes, as understood in classical music traditions from the baroque to the present, have a definite pitch and are meant to be heard as such. The notated pitch determines the fingering to be used for grace notes and they are expected to be "in tune."

A well-played cut, while it does have a pitch, is an event of such short duration that the listener should not be able to discern its actual pitch. The pitch of a cut is sometimes not in the mode of the melody or even in tune with any of the twelve pitches of the chromatic scale. A cut fingering should be chosen for its responsiveness, clarity, and its qualitative effect, not for the pitch it produces.

Grace note notation implies that the grace note is meant to be heard as distinct from the principal note.

The cut is an articulation. It should not be heard, or thought of, as an entity separable from its parent note.

Grace notes are understood to have a duration and must "steal time" from another note or rest. Due to the visual placement of the grace note before the principal note and before its beat, grace note notation implies that the grace note steals time from the note or beat preceding the principal note.[i]

The cut is a way to attack a note. It occurs right on a beat, not before it. It's best to think of it as having no duration. Think of the cut as the leading edge of the parent note, the beginning of the parent note's envelope, or the attack of the parent note.

Cut Fingerings: an Important Choice Is at Hand

In my opinion, a cut should almost always sound as well defined and crisp as possible. (I'll elaborate on this shortly.) Using the optimum fingerings is a great help in achieving this. To this end I use fingerings that are somewhat different from those that most players use. There is actually quite a bit of variance among players in their choice of cut fingerings.

In my method, for each of the notes D, E, F-sharp, G, and A, in both registers, the lowest covered hole remains covered (i.e. the covered hole that is furthest from the mouthpiece). You perform the cut by quickly uncovering and recovering the next hole up. Therefore D is cut with B2, E with B1, F-sharp with T3, G with T2, and A with T1. The exception to this rule occurs when cutting B. You cut B with T1, as this is the only finger available for the job.

Why do I prefer cutting with the finger above the lowest covered hole? Cutting on the lowest covered hole, while achieving a good quick response, produces a cut that is very close in pitch to that of its parent note. This closeness of pitch lessens the definition of the cut note's attack.

I feel that it is almost always better to maximize the clarity and definition of that attack. But there may be times when you would like to use a gentler sounding cut. At those times you might choose to cut with the finger on the lowest covered hole.

Note however that *you cannot cut on the lowest covered hole when you are descending to a cut note.* In such cases, that hole must be covered just to *arrive* at the lower note. For example, when descending from G to F-sharp and cutting the F-sharp, you cannot perform the cut with B1 because B1 must cover its hole just to get you to the F-sharp. B1 cannot do both jobs because the arrival at the note and its cut occur simultaneously. If you form the habit of cutting with the finger on the lowest covered hole (such as B1 in the case of F-sharp), you may unconsciously become disinclined to cut when descending to a note. It would be a great shame to limit yourself in this way. (If these matters are hard to understand now, they will become more clear as you work through this chapter.)

You may wish to explore other cut fingerings to hear their qualitative effects. Feel free to do so but beware of the sluggish response that many of them have. This is more of a hazard with the flute and the larger whistles than on the smaller whistles, and the high register of the flute and larger whistles are particularly prone to this problem. But it is a problem with the high register of any whistle, and on some whistles with the low register as well. Uilleann pipers have more options because their instrument is exquisitely responsive to nearly all cut fingerings.

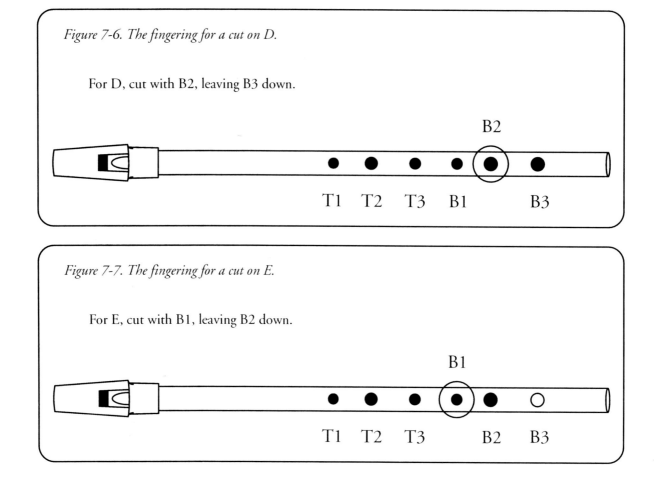

Figure 7-6. The fingering for a cut on D.

For D, cut with B2, leaving B3 down.

Figure 7-7. The fingering for a cut on E.

For E, cut with B1, leaving B2 down.

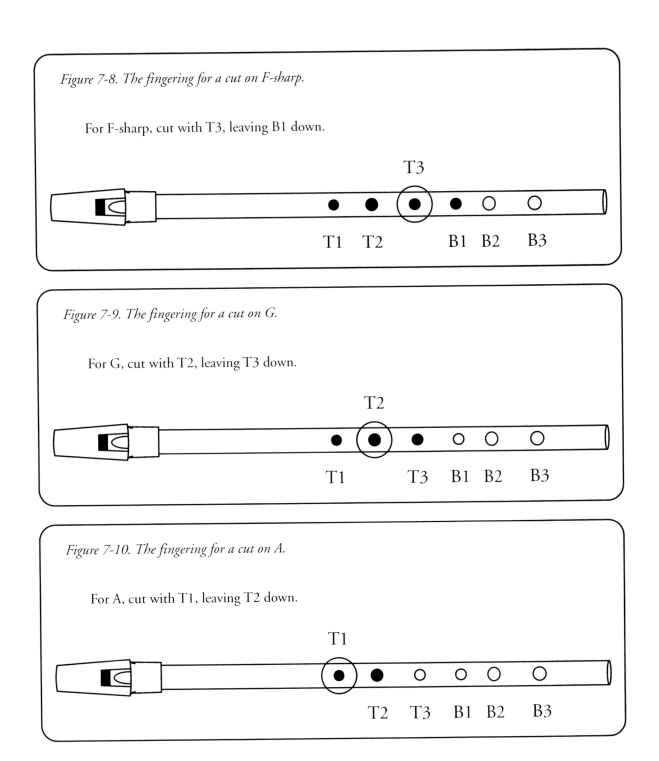

Figure 7-8. The fingering for a cut on F-sharp.

For F-sharp, cut with T3, leaving B1 down.

Figure 7-9. The fingering for a cut on G.

For G, cut with T2, leaving T3 down.

Figure 7-10. The fingering for a cut on A.

For A, cut with T1, leaving T2 down.

The exception to the rule is that for the note B you have no choice but to cut with T1, leaving no finger down.

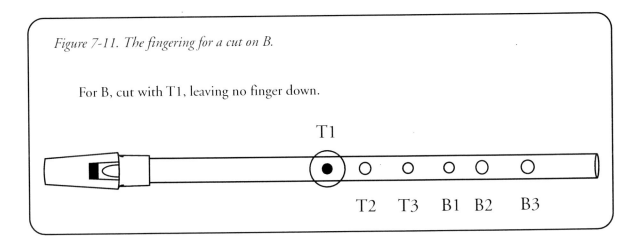

Figure 7-11. The fingering for a cut on B.

For B, cut with T1, leaving no finger down.

There are some instances when one needs to use different cut fingerings. We'll grapple with that later in the chapter, in the section called *Cuts on Notes that Descend by an Interval Larger than a Major Second* on p. 88.

There are ways to play or simulate cuts on low C and C-sharp, though not many players use them. For C there is a strike fingering that simulates the sound of a cut (see Figure 8-8 on p. 100 in the next chapter).

For low C-sharp there is a cut fingering that seems to work on some whistles but not on others. This fingering is shown below.

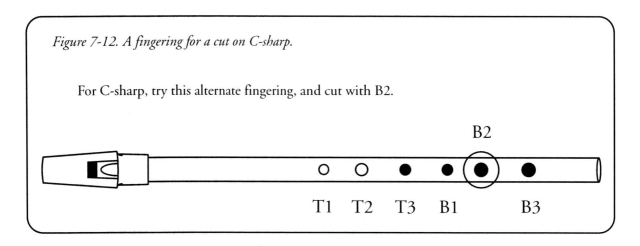

Figure 7-12. A fingering for a cut on C-sharp.

For C-sharp, try this alternate fingering, and cut with B2.

THE CUT FINGERINGS MOST COMMONLY USED

Many, if not most players use another approach to cut fingerings, shown below, and this is what you will encounter in most other instruction books.

For D, E, F-sharp, and G they cut with T3.

For A and B they cut with T1.

The attraction of this approach is that you need only learn to cut with two fingers, T1 and T3. (For the notes F-sharp, A, and B, note that these are the same as my recommended cut fingerings.)

However, note well this rule: **the farther removed the cutting finger is from the lowest covered hole, the less responsive and more sluggish is the cut.**

This holds true for the small D whistle, but even more so for the larger whistles and for flutes, with their more voluminous air columns. You'll usually find that sluggish cut fingerings respond even more sluggishly in the high register of both flutes and whistles.

The particulars of the various cut fingerings and the sounds they produce will vary somewhat from instrument to instrument, but the above rule holds true overall.

DON'T BE FOOLED!

Be careful in your choice of cut fingerings! Until you have gained the ability to execute short, crisp cuts you may well have trouble hearing the relative sluggishness of certain fingering options. Also, you may be playing relatively slowly now and not realize that the faster you play the more important it will be to have crisp, clean, responsive cuts. The extra work you put in now to learn these recommended cut fingerings will pay off a great deal in the future. It's even worth it to re-learn this method if you have already learned another. That's what I did.

A word of caution: With the small D whistle you may feel that the difference in clarity and responsiveness is not a big enough one to justify the extra work entailed in learning to cut with these fingerings. However, if you think you may someday wish to play the flute, or the larger, lower whistles, I suggest that you learn this method now so that you can avoid re-learning cut fingerings later.

A New Cut Notation

Since a cut is an articulation, I notate it as a slash placed over its parent note.

Figure 7-13. A new symbol for a cut.

This is a simple, clean notation that reflects the reality of the cut's sound and function. There is only one note here, not two. There is no indication or implication of pitch or duration for the cut. The notation is similar visually to other markings, such as staccato markings or accents, which are placed above the note they affect.

The Simplest Use of a Cut: Articulating a Repeated Note

As stated in Chapter 1, much of the foundation of whistle ornamentation technique and style came to us through the traditions of the uilleann pipes and its antecedents, the pastoral bagpipe and the *píob mór*. With these older bagpipes there was a constant flow of air through the chanter.

When two notes of the same pitch are played, the second one must be articulated in some way. Since these pipers had nothing analogous to tonguing or throating, i.e. the techniques with mouth-blown wind instruments of stopping and re-initiating the air flow with the tongue or in the throat (see Chapter 12), they had to use a finger articulation, such as a cut, to articulate the second note.

With the whistle we have several choices in this situation. We can cut, tongue, or both cut *and* tongue. (Another ornament called a *strike* can also be used like a cut in this situation, though cuts are more commonly used. This subject is addressed in the next chapter.) Until you have a good handle on cuts, I recommend that you mainly cut *without* also articulating the note with tonguing. Tonguing your cuts at this point may mislead you into thinking that you have more precise control of your cuts than you actually have.

Now let's try using cuts to articulate notes of the same pitch (i.e. repeated notes).

Exercise 7-1. *Practicing cuts on repeated Ds.*

Track 8, Index 1

Play a series of Ds. Tongue only the first one. Without interrupting the flow of air, articulate the rest of them only by cutting them with B2. Keep a steady, slow beat by setting a metronome at a comfortable tempo somewhere around 60 beats per minute, or by tapping your foot. Each beat of the metronome, or foot tap, represents an eighth note, as notated above. Try to place the cuts right on the beat. Note that if you are playing D in the second register (an octave above the low D) and you are venting the note by uncovering the T1 hole, the cut will produce a pitch that is lower than its parent note. Try these exercises in both octaves.

Exercise 7-2. *Play a series of Es.* Proceed as in Exercise 7-1, cutting with B1.

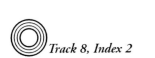
Track 8, Index 2

Exercise 7-3. *Play a series of F-sharps.* Proceed as in Exercise 7-1, cutting with T3.

Track 8, Index 3

Exercise 7-4. *Play a series of Gs.* Proceed as in Exercise 7-1, cutting with T2.

Track 8, Index 4

Exercise 7-5. *Play a series of As.* Proceed as in Exercise 7-1, cutting with T1.

Track 8, Index 5

Exercise 7-6. *Play a series of Bs.* Proceed as in Exercise 7-1, cutting with T1.

Track 8, Index 6

Here are eight more exercises for practicing cuts on repeated notes. With this group of exercises we begin to use such cuts in the context of ascending and descending notes. Beneath each cut note you will find the recommended cut fingering.

Exercise 7-7. *Cuts on repeated notes in the context of a stepwise descending melody.*

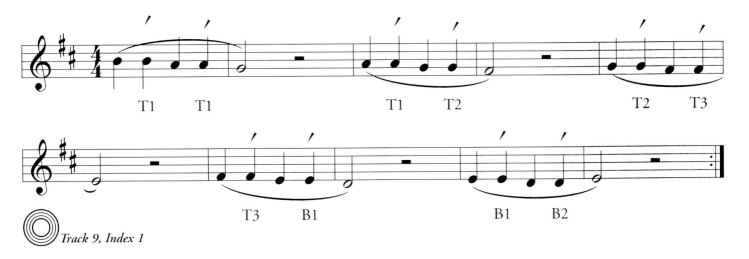

Track 9, Index 1

Exercise 7-8. *Cuts on repeated notes in the context of a stepwise ascending melody.*

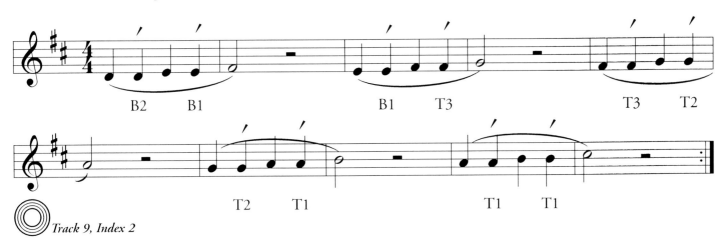

Track 9, Index 2

Exercise 7-9. *Cuts on repeated notes in the context of descending thirds.*

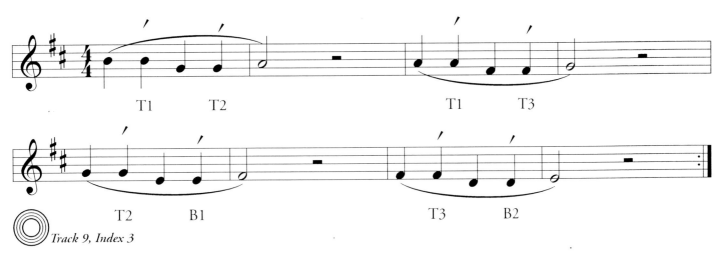

Track 9, Index 3

Exercise 7-10. *Cuts on repeated notes in the context of ascending thirds.*

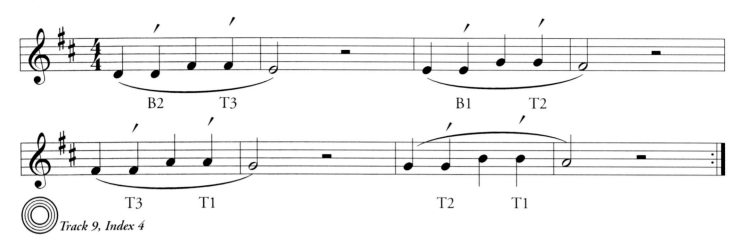

Track 9, Index 4

Exercise 7-11. *Cuts on repeated notes in the context of ascending and descending fourths.*

Track 9, Index 5

Exercise 7-12. *Cuts on repeated notes on the second subdivision of the pulse in a jig.*

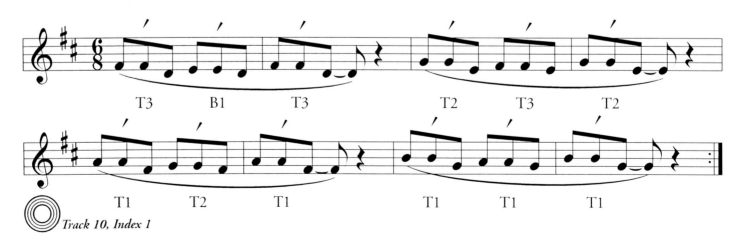

Track 10, Index 1

Exercise 7-13. *Cuts on repeated notes on the third subdivision of the pulse in a jig.*

Track 10, Index 2

Exercise 7-14. *Cuts on repeated notes on the first and second subdivisions of the pulse in a jig.*

Track 10, Index 3

If the cut seems like a fairly simple thing at this point, that's good. However, cuts are used in some other melodic contexts which make their use more challenging.

THE NEXT CHALLENGE: CUTS ON STEPWISE ASCENDING NOTES

You will often want to use a cut to draw attention to a note, to make your phrasing ideas more clear, not just to separate repeated notes. Let's say you want to cut a G that comes right after an F-sharp.

Figure 7-14. Ascending from F-sharp to G and cutting the G.

The movement from F-sharp to G is called *stepwise* because it is the smallest distance we can move within the natural whistle scale, i.e. one step up or down the ladder of pitches. In this case the length of that "step" is the interval of a semitone. In the case of D to E the length of the step is the interval of a whole-tone, or two semitones.

Getting back to our example, to move from F-sharp to G while cutting the G you have to do two very different things *simultaneously*. You lift B1 off its hole to change notes. At the same time you cut the G with T2. T3 stays on its hole the entire time.

Stated another way, you lift both T2 and B1 *at exactly the same moment*, i.e. right on the beat, while leaving T3 down. But you replace the cutting finger, T2, immediately while you leave B1 off its hole.

Remember that the cut is an articulation. It initiates the G and therefore defines the location of the note and the beat. It is not a note or grace note that comes before or after the beat.

Musical Alchemy: Turning Three Notes into Two

Let's break this down. Try the following slow-motion exercise and don't worry for the moment about the fact that at first the cut won't sound like a cut.

Play an F-sharp. Without tonguing, lift B1 and T2 simultaneously and hold them both off the finger holes for a moment while you continue to blow. This will produce a B-ish sort of note. Don't worry if it's out of tune. Still blowing, and without tonguing, replace T2. Do all this on a single breath and without tonguing. Do this repeatedly, making sure to lift B1 and T2 *simultaneously*. That simultaneous lift is the crux of this exercise.

Played this way the cut is elongated, and so it doesn't sound like an articulation. What you hear as you play this exercise is three notes: F-sharp, a B-ish note (the cut stretched out in time), and G.

Once you get comfortable with this exercise start replacing T2 a little bit sooner each time. Soon it will begin to sound like you are playing only two notes instead of three. Recognize that you are cutting the G now, instead of playing a B-ish note between the F-sharp and G. You are placing this cut right on a beat. You are using it to articulate the G. You could have tongued the G, but instead you are using a finger ornament, the cut, to articulate it. As you repeat this, begin to feel a rhythmic pulse and place the cut note right on a beat. Try it in both octaves.

Exercise 7-15. *F-sharp to a cut G.*

Track 11, Index 1

Now you see that although cutting is fairly simple, combining the cut with another simultaneous finger movement is not so simple, at least at first. Eventually, with practice, you will be able to cut notes in any context without giving it a thought.

Stretching the Brain a Bit Further

When doing this exercise with F-sharp and G you are dividing the fingering labor between your two hands. When doing many of the exercises that follow, the work is done with only one hand. Some people find that to be a little more challenging.

Do the following exercises in the same manner. Start in slow motion, out of rhythm. Gradually replace the cutting finger a bit sooner each time until you begin to hear two notes instead of three. Then find a pulse and place the cut note right on the beat. Try these exercises in both octaves.

Exercise 7-16. *D to a cut E.* This exercise is just like Exercise 7-15, but it is done with the notes D and E. Play D. Simultaneously lift B3 and B1. Replace B1. All the labor is in the bottom hand.

Track 11, Index 2

Exercise 7-17. *E to a cut F-sharp.* Play E. Simultaneously lift B2 and T3. Replace T3. Here we get to divide the labor between the two hands again, as in exercise 7-15.

Track 11, Index 3

Exercise 7-18. *G to a cut A.* Play G. Simultaneously lift T3 and T1. Replace T1. All the labor is in the top hand.

Track 11, Index 4

Exercise 7-19. *A to a cut B.* Play A. Simultaneously lift T2 and T1. Replace T1. All the labor is in the top hand. This situation feels different because there is no intervening finger between the two moving fingers. You must cut B with T1.

Track 11, Index 5

THREE EXERCISES FOR CUTS ON STEPWISE ASCENDING NOTES

Exercise 7-20. *Cuts on stepwise ascending notes on the secondary pulse in a reel.*

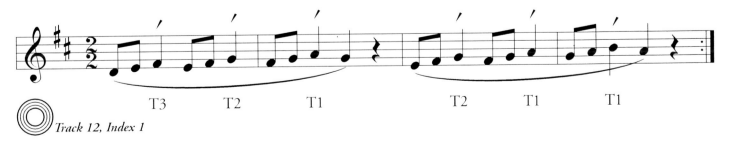

Track 12, Index 1

81

Exercise 7-21. *Cuts on stepwise ascending notes on the primary pulse in a reel.*

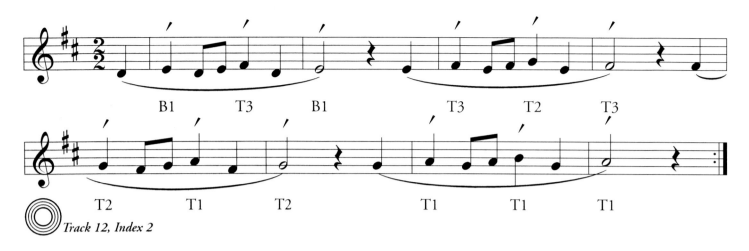

Track 12, Index 2

Exercise 7-22. *Cuts on stepwise ascending notes on the secondary pulse in a reel.*

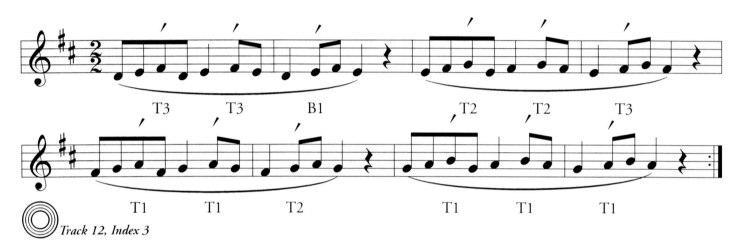

Track 12, Index 3

WHERE TO BREATHE?

At this point I need to briefly address an issue that we will explore in more depth later, as the subject of Chapter 13, *Musical Breathing.*

Traditional Irish dance tunes have no breathing places built into them for whistle players. We have to create breathing places ourselves by omitting eighth notes, or shortening longer notes. Learning which notes to omit or shorten is a subject of utmost importance, but it is one I have chosen to address in depth after fully exploring ornamentation. Why I have done so will become apparent later.

Up until this point in the book, I have been presenting exercises that have breathing places built into them. But starting now, we will also begin to work with actual tunes, which have no built-in breathing places.

I will indicate potential breathing places in tunes by placing a comma above an eighth note, above the second half of a quarter note, or above the third third of a dotted quarter note. These are places where you can create a space for breathing that has a duration of one eighth note. Why I choose these particular potential breathing places will become clear in Chapter 13, but for now, note that none of them fall on the *pulse* of the music, the beats where you would be inclined to tap your foot. *Never create a breathing spot that falls on a pulse.*

82

You don't have to breathe at all of these potential breathing spots. Just use the ones you need. There is no need to choose breathing places and use those same ones consistenly. Let this be a fluid, changeable choice, one that is determined by your air supply at the moment.

You'll probably find that some of these breathing spots produce a result that is musically satisfying, while others may seem a bit disruptive of the melody. Choosing breathing spots that work for you is an important aspect of your own musical interpretation. You may also find others that I have not marked.

If you are playing very slowly (which is often an excellent thing to do), you may indeed need to use all of these breathing spots. That's fine for now.

TRY USING SOME CUTS IN A TUNE

Before we explore some different contexts for cuts, let's put to practical use the cuts we have just been practicing, that is cuts on repeated notes and cuts on stepwise ascending notes. Figure 7-15 (below) shows a version of *The Lonesome Jig* (also known as *The Rolling Waves, McGuire's March,* or *Maguire's Kick*) which makes use of only these types of cuts. Try playing through it, playing the cuts that are indicated. For now, do not tongue at the same time that you cut.

Next, play the tune through with no cuts. This will show you how even the use of fairly simple cuts goes a long way in bringing a traditional sound to your playing.

Figure 7-15. A version of **The Lonesome Jig** which makes use of cuts only on repeated notes and stepwise ascending notes. Potential breathing spots are indicated with commas above the staff.

 Track 13

In the above tune setting, cuts occur only on strong beats or pulses. As you will see soon, that is not always the case.

Now let's continue exploring other contexts for using cuts.

CUTS ON NOTES THAT ASCEND BY AN INTERVAL LARGER THAN A MAJOR SECOND

Of course you will encounter melodies in which you will want to cut a note that ascends by an interval larger than a major second, not stepwise but "leapwise." Try the cuts shown below. With almost all of them you will once again be dividing the labor between the two hands, but now there are more fingers to lift simultaneously. Try these in both registers.

Exercise 7-23. *Move from D to F-sharp, cutting the F-sharp.* Simultaneously lift B3, B2, and T3, leaving B1 down. Replace T3.

 *Track 14, Index 1*

Exercise 7-24. *Move from D to G, cutting the G.* Simultaneously lift B3, B2, B1, and T2, leaving T3 down. Replace T2.

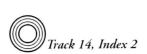 *Track 14, Index 2*

Exercise 7-25. *Move from D to A, cutting the A.* Simultaneously lift B3, B2, B1, T3, and T1, leaving T2 down. Replace T1.

 *Track 14, Index 3*

Exercise 7-26. *Move from D to B, cutting the B.* Simultaneously lift all six fingers. Replace T1.

 *Track 14, Index 4*

Exercise 7-27. *Move from E to G, cutting the G.* Simultaneously lift B2, B1, and T2, leaving T3 down. Replace T2.

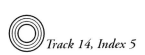 *Track 14, Index 5*

Exercise 7-28. *Move from E to A, cutting the A.* Simultaneously lift B2, B1, T3, and T1, leaving T2 down. Replace T1.

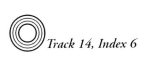 *Track 14, Index 6*

Exercise 7-29. *Move from E to B, cutting the B.* Simultaneously lift all five fingers. Replace T1.

 *Track 14, Index 7*

Exercise 7-30. *Move from F-sharp to A, cutting the A.* Simultaneously lift B1, T3, and T1, leaving T2 down. Replace T1.

 *Track 14, Index 8*

Exercise 7-31. *Move from F-sharp to B, cutting the B.* Simultaneously lift all four fingers. Replace T1.

 *Track 14, Index 9*

Exercise 7-32. *Move from G to B, cutting the B.* Simultaneously lift all three fingers. Replace T1.

Track 14, Index 10

Exercise 7-33. *Practicing a variety of cuts on notes that ascend by intervals larger than a major second (i.e. leapwise).*

Track 15

THE NEXT CUTTING CHALLENGE: CUTS ON STEPWISE DESCENDING NOTES

Let's say you're moving from G to F-sharp and you want to cut the F-sharp. Cutting a stepwise descending note like this presents a different challenge. Once again you need to perform two different finger movements simultaneously. But this time you'll be cutting while putting down another finger.

Exercise 7-34. *Move from G down to F-sharp, cutting the F-sharp.*

Track 16 Index 1

Place B1 onto its hole to change from G to F-sharp and, at exactly the same moment, i.e. right on the beat, lift the cutting finger, T3, and then immediately replace it on its hole.

As before, it is very useful to break this down into a slow motion exercise. The cut will be elongated and won't sound like a cut at first. Again, you may find it helpful to do this in front of a mirror so you can see your fingering clearly.

Play a G. Without tonguing, place B1 down on its hole and simultaneously lift T3 off its hole. This will produce an A-ish note. (If you hear a short F-sharp between the G and the A-ish note, then you are lifting T3 a little late.) Next, replace T3 on its hole to complete the cut. Do all this on a single breath and without stopping the air. As you play this exercise you hear three notes: G, an A-ish note (the cut stretched out in time), and F-sharp.

Play this repeatedly. Once you get comfortable with this exercise start replacing T3 a little bit sooner each time. As before it will begin to sound like you are playing only two notes instead of three. Recognize that you are cutting the F-sharp now, instead of playing an A-ish note between the G and F-sharp. You are placing this cut right on a beat, using it to articulate the F-sharp. As you repeat this, begin to feel a pulse and place the cut F-sharp right on a beat. Try it in both octaves.

Strikes Can Be Used in Place of Cuts on Descending Notes, But Beware

I will note briefly here that strikes can be used in place of cuts on descending notes. The next chapter is devoted to strikes and I address this topic there. However, I want to caution you now not to neglect learning cuts on descending notes. They sound very different from strikes and I feel they often sound better. I also observe that most traditional players use cuts more often than strikes in these situations. You should have both techniques at your command.

Continuing to Learn Cuts on Stepwise Descending Notes

Here are some more descending stepwise cut exercises. Do these in the same manner that we just did Exercise 7-34. Start in slow motion, out of rhythm. Gradually replace the cutting finger a bit sooner each time until you begin to hear two notes instead of three. Then find a pulse and place the cut note right on the beat. Try both octaves.

Exercise 7-35. *Move from E down to D, cutting the D.* Simultaneously put down B3 and lift B2. Replace B2. All the labor is in the bottom hand.

 *Track 16 Index 2*

Exercise 7-36. *Move from F-sharp down to E, cutting the E.* Play F-sharp. Simultaneously put down B2 and lift B1. Replace B1. All the labor is in the bottom hand.

 *Track 16 Index 3*

Exercise 7-37. *Move from A down to G, cutting the G.* Play A. Simultaneously put down T3 and lift T2. Replace T2. All the labor is in the top hand.

 *Track 16 Index 4*

Exercise 7-38. *Move from B down to A, cutting the A.* Play B. Simultaneously put down T2 and lift T1. Replace T1. All the labor is in the top hand.

Track 16 Index 5

Exercise 7-39. *Practicing a variety of cuts on notes that descend by one step (i. e. stepwise).*

Track 17

CUTS ON NOTES THAT DESCEND BY AN INTERVAL LARGER THAN A MAJOR SECOND

Here we come to a category of cuts in which it is necessary to use cut fingerings different from the ones we have been learning. This is necessary when descending to a cut note by an interval larger than a major second, but *only* when both notes are in the same octave, or register, of the whistle. When descending from a note in the second octave to a note in the first octave, and cutting the lower note, the standard cut fingerings can and should be used.

Let's look first at the example of going from F-sharp down to D and cutting the D.

Exercise 7-40. *Move from F-sharp down to D, cutting the D.*

Track 18, Index 1

Normally we would cut D with B2. But, just to get from F-sharp to D you have to put down B2 and B3. Clearly it is impossible to do that and simultaneously cut with B2. So you must cut with a different finger. The next best option, yielding the best sounding available cut, is to cut the D with B1, the lowest finger available for the job. Note that when playing F-sharp, the note preceding the cut, B1 is the lowest finger covering a hole.

A GENERAL RULE

This is the general rule for getting the best cuts in all such situations (i.e. when descending to a cut note by an interval larger than a major second when both notes are in the same octave): *cut with the lowest available finger.* This will always be the lowest finger covering a hole when playing the higher of the two notes.

For the sake of completeness, in the following exercises you will find each of these cuts described. In practice some of these cuts are awkward or do not speak well (especially in the second octave) and are not often played. Generally, the larger the descending interval, the less useful the cut.

AN ALTERNATE APPROACH

It is worth mentioning, before proceeding to work through these special cuts, that there is another option in performing cuts of this kind. You may want to use it especially on some of the more awkward cuts that you will encounter in the following exercises, and it is really the only way to effectively cut a note when descending from C-sharp. If you make the higher note short, by stopping the air with your tongue, during the brief silence thus created you can put down the fingers required to play the lower note and *then* cut it as you tongue it, using the normal cut fingering.

For example, let's say you are moving from low B down to low E and cutting the low E. You would play the B, make it short, then during the brief silence thus created you would put down T2, T3, B1, and B2, i.e. the fingers needed to play low E. Then, on the next beat, you would articulate the E with your tongue, and, *at the same time,* cut it with B1. Making a note very short like this is conspicuous, so be sure that it is musically appropriate.

If you are very clever, during the brief silence described above you could put down T2, T3, B2, and not B1, waiting to put down B1 until you articulate the E with your tongue. This achieves the same effect with slightly less effort, as you are putting down B1 only once, i.e. to execute the cut.

Now we'll proceed with the exercises.

Exercise 7-41. *Move from G down to D, cutting the D.* Play G. Simultaneously put down B1, B2, and B3 and lift T3. Replace T3. Playing both notes in the upper register, you will want to vent the D (i.e. lift T1) as you cut it.

Track 18, Index 2

Exercise 7-42. *Move from A down to D, cutting the D.* Play A. Simultaneously put down T3, B1, B2, and B3 and lift T2. Replace T2. Playing both notes in the upper register, you will want to vent the D (i.e. lift T1) as you cut it.

Track 18, Index 3

Exercise 7-43. *Move from B down to D, cutting the D.* Play B. Simultaneously put down T2, T3, B1, B2, and B3 and lift T1. Replace T1. This is a fairly impractical cut which may not work well on some instruments, especially in the second octave. Playing both notes in the upper register, you cannot vent the D (i.e. lift T1) because you need this finger to perform the cut.

 *Track 18, Index 4*

Exercise 7-44. *Move from C-natural down to D, cutting the D.* Play C-natural. On most whistles, finger this by covering holes with T2 and T3. Simultaneously put down T1, B1, B2, and B3 and lift T3. Replace T3. (If you need to add lower fingers to get the C-natural in tune this cut will still work.)

 *Track 18, Index 5*

Exercise 7-45. *Move from G down to E, cutting the E.* Play G. Simultaneously put down B1 and B2 and lift T3. Replace T3. Try both registers.

 *Track 18, Index 6*

Exercise 7-46. *Move from A down to E, cutting the E.* Play A. Simultaneously put down T3, B1, and B2 and lift T2. Replace T2. Try both registers.

 *Track 18, Index 7*

Exercise 7-47. *Move from B down to E, cutting the E.* Play B. Simultaneously put down T2, T3, B1, and B2 and lift T1. Replace T1. This may not work well on some instruments, especially in the upper register.

Track 18, Index 8

Exercise 7-48. *Move from C-natural down to E, cutting the E.* Play C-natural. On most whistles, finger this by covering holes with T2 and T3. Simultaneously put down T1, B1, and B2 and lift T3. Replace T3. (If you need to add B1 and/or B2 to get the C-natural in tune this cut will still work. If you need to add B3 you will have to lift it simultaneous with the cut.)

Track 18, Index 9

Exercise 7-49. *Move from A down to F-sharp, cutting the F-sharp.* Play A. Simultaneously put down T3 and B1 and lift T2. Replace T2. Try both registers.

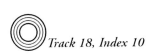
Track 18, Index 10

Exercise 7-50. *Move from B down to F-sharp, cutting the F-sharp.* Play B. Simultaneously put down T2, T3, and B1 and lift T1. Replace T1. This may not work well on some instruments in the upper register.

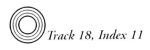
Track 18, Index 11

Exercise 7-51. *Move from C-natural down to F-sharp, cutting the F-sharp.* Play C-natural. On most whistles, finger this by covering holes with T2 and T3. Simultaneously put down T1 and B1 and lift T3. Replace T3. (If you need to add B1 to get the C-natural in tune this cut will still work. If you need to add B2 or B3 you will have to lift them simultaneous with the cut.)

Track 18, Index 12

Exercise 7-52. *Move from B down to G, cutting the G.* Play B. Simultaneously put down T2 and T3 and lift T1. Replace T1. This may not work well on some instruments in the upper register.

Track 18, Index 13

Exercise 7-53. *Move from C-natural down to G, cutting the G.* Play low C-natural. On most whistles, finger this by covering holes with T2 and T3. Simultaneously put down T1 and lift T3. Replace T3. (If you need to add B1, B2, or B3 to bring the C-natural into tune you will have to lift them simultaneously with the cut).

Track 18, Index 14

Exercise 7-54. *Cutting D while descending to it leapwise from various notes.* Exercises 7-54 through 7-57 assume the use of the T2 and T3 cross-fingering for C-natural.

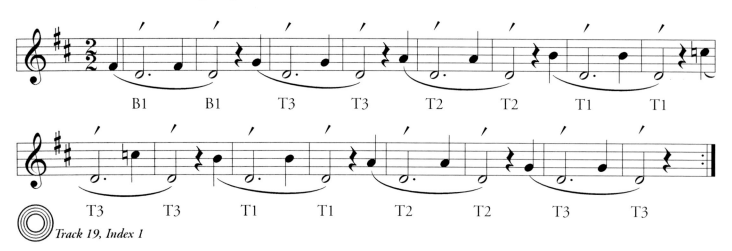

Track 19, Index 1

92

Exercise 7-55. *Cutting E while descending to it leapwise from various notes.*

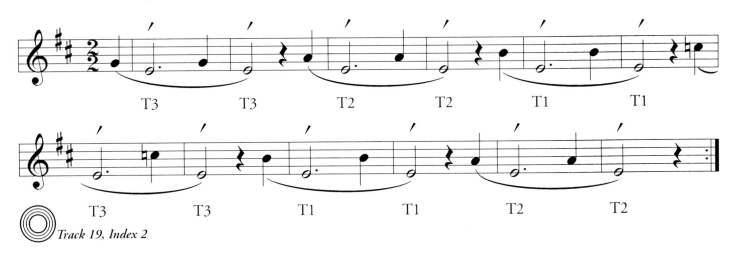

Track 19, Index 2

Exercise 7-56. *Cutting F-sharp while descending to it leapwise from various notes.*

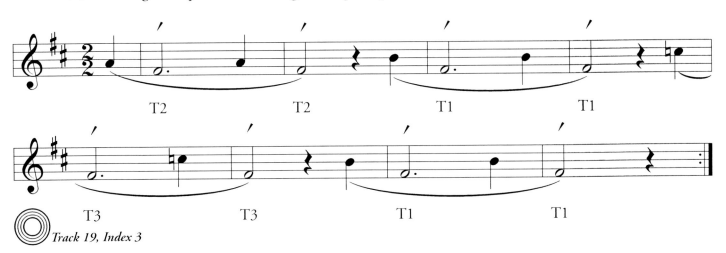

Track 19, Index 3

Exercise 7-57. *Cutting G while descending to it leapwise from various notes.* Descending from C-natural, G is cut with T2, the normal cutting finger for G.

Track 19, Index 4

TRY USING ALL TYPES OF CUTS IN A TUNE

Now that we have worked through all of the different classes of cuts let's put them to use in a tune. Figure 7-16 shows a version of the slip jig *The Boys of Ballisodare* that makes use of them all. You should try following the phrasing I have indicated for the purpose of practice. For example, the second slur in measure 4 forces you to cut the E, and the D in the next measure, with T3 instead of the normal cutting fingers. Similar cuts occur in measures 8, 12, and 16.

93

Also, in measures 4 and 12 we encounter a situation we haven't yet discussed. We will touch on it here but will discuss it in more depth in the next section, *Cutting and Tonguing at the Same Time.* A C-natural is followed by a cut B. In cutting the B, all fingers are momentarily off the instrument. The cut sounds more clear and distinct if you make the C-natural short, by stopping the air with the tongue, and then tongue the cut B. The dot above the C-natural is called a *staccato* marking, a symbol used in classical music to indicate that you should separate the indicated note from the next note. (For more information on this term, see p. 164 in Chapter 12.)

Try the B cut with and without articulation and see what you think. It can be played both ways, but I think you'll find that tonguing the cut B makes the fingering sequence a bit easier to execute as well as making the cut B more distinct.

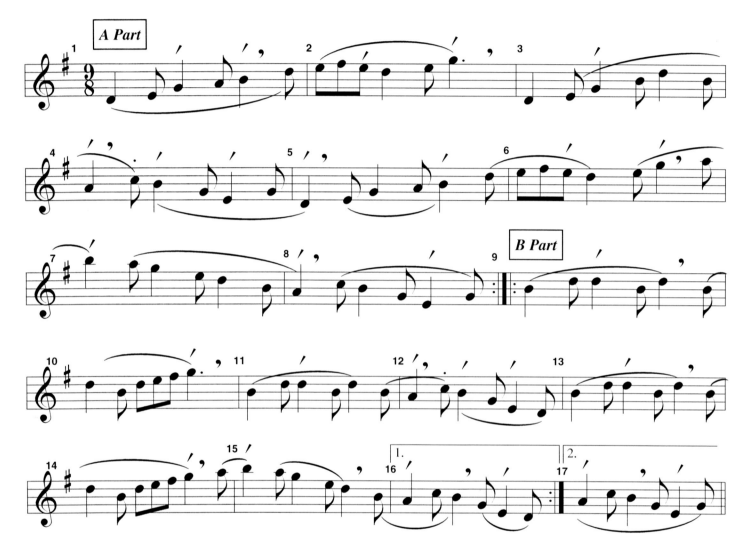

*Figure 7-16. A version of the slip jig **The Boys of Ballisodare** that makes use of examples of every class of cuts.*

Track 20

CUTTING AND TONGUING AT THE SAME TIME

A cut gives special emphasis to a note. The cut seems to command more attention than a tongue articulation. Perhaps this is because of the pitched element of the cut.

It follows that tonguing *and* cutting a note will give that note more emphasis than either articulation would bring to it when used alone. Be careful when you try this—good timing is critical. Remember that when you cut and tongue at the same time, your cutting finger needs to be in the air, not still on the instrument, at the instant that you tongue. If you cut slightly after you tongue you will hear the cut an instant late and the result will be a kind of double articulation.

94

A word of caution here: If you do not have a good handle on the accurate timing of your cuts, tonguing them may hide that fact from you. For example, if you tend to cut late, as many novices do, you will hear (if you are *not* tonguing, and if you are paying attention) the start of the parent note and *then* the cut. When your cut timing is good, these two things will coincide.

If your cut is late, the problem will be especially apparent when you are approaching the cut note from a pitch above or below. If you are tonguing that same cut, however, you are momentarily stopping the sound and introducing another rhythmic factor into the equation. That can obscure your perception of what you are actually doing. Stated another way, if you tend to cut slightly late and that late lift of the cutting finger happens during the brief silence introduced by tonguing, you will not hear the effect of the lateness of the cut.

BREATH IS LIKE A FIDDLE BOW

There are other factors as well that play into the effect of articulations and combined articulations. Primary among these is the quality of the breath one uses. One can, with great subtlety, "lean into" and "back off of" the breath, much as a fiddler can add or release pressure from her bow stroke. Much more is possible with this technique on the flute than on the whistle, though good handmade whistles offer more in this regard than most of the mass-produced ones.

You can begin to see why the possibilities here are vast for the expressive musician. We will discuss such subjects in more depth later.

DELAYING THE CUT, OR CUTTING IN THE MIDST OF A NOTE

Once you have mastered your articulations you may on occasion want to play around with their timing for expressive effect. For example you may sometimes choose to cut not at the start of note but in the midst of it.

In slow airs the sense of pulse can be highly changeable, elastic, or even nonexistent. This is a form of music in which the player emulates *sean-nós* (old-style) singing. In slow airs, cuts and other articulations may be used mid-note without regard to any underlying pulse. The playing of slow airs is addressed in my book *The Essential Guide to Irish Flute and Tin Whistle*.

DELAYING THE CUT BY PLACING IT ON A SUBDIVISION OF THE PULSE

In tunes other than slow airs, i.e. tunes with a regular pulse, players almost always apply this technique by cutting halfway through the duration of the note in question, or at least on some regular subdivision of the beat. That way they don't disturb the underlying rhythms of the music that are so essential to its forward motion.

For an example of this, look at the first measure of the slip jig *Hardiman the Fiddler.* In Figure 7-17 note that there is a cut defining the attack of the first note, a quarter note A.

Figure 7-17. The first two measures of the slip jig **Hardiman the Fiddler** *with a cut placed at the onset of the first note.*

 Track 21

This is the way we have been learning to apply cuts.

One could, instead, place a cut halfway through the duration of the first note. I have shown this in Figure 7-18 by re-writing the quarter note A as two eighth notes tied together and placing the cut on the second eighth note.

*Figure 7-18. The first two measures of the slip jig **Hardiman the Fiddler**. The first note, which had been notated as a quarter note A, is now notated as two tied eighth notes. The second of these eighth notes is articulated with a cut.*

By viewing the situation this way we can see that this is still the way we have been learning to apply cuts. The cut still forms the articulation, the attack, of a note. In this case it is simply the second of two eighth notes instead of the first.

Most musicians, however, will still think of this cut as coming in the middle of a quarter note. After all, if they were to play this passage without using a cut they would most likely play a quarter note, not two eighth notes. For that reason I prefer to use the notation shown in Figure 7-19 in this kind of situation

Figure 7-19. The clearest way to notate what is played in Figure 7-18.

Track 22

Here the quarter-note notation is restored, since this is the way most musicians think of the tune, and the cut symbol is placed halfway between the start of the quarter note and the following eighth note, showing where the cut happens in time. When you encounter this kind of cut notation remember that the cut is meant to be placed on a subdivision of the beat.

TINY DELAYS OF THE CUT

On occasion a player will place a cut just a very tiny bit after the attack of a note, but not nearly late enough to suggest any rhythmic subdivision of the note. The cut still sounds like it belongs to the beginning of the note, but there is something just a little "different" about it, something more "ornate" or rhythmically florid in it. This kind of delay can of course happen as the result of sloppy fingering. But you can hear it sparingly and effectively used in the music of such great players as Matt Molloy and Séamus Egan. When you listen very closely to this (especially if you are able to play a recording at slower than normal speed) you can hear the arrival of the parent note just an instant before the cut.

"DOUBLE GRACES" AND THE *CASADH*

I think that these two special applications of delaying the cut are what some authors are actually referring to when they vaguely describe "double graces" or "double grace notes." Afterall, if you are thinking of cuts as grace notes, then a cut that comes just slightly after the arrival of its parent note might seem like the *second* of two grace notes: the very brief piece of the parent note (the first grace note), followed by the cut (the second grace note), then the rest of the parent note.

I think this is what Geraldine Cotter calls the *casadh* (an Irish word for *twist* or *turn*) in her book *Geraldine Cotter's Traditional Irish Tin Whistle Tutor*.[ii] I have not been able to find any other mention of the term *casadh* in the literature.

A VARIANT: ELONGATING THE CUT

Sometimes, when cutting a repeated note, it is pleasing to elongate the cut such that in effect it becomes a new melody note.

Here are the first two measures of the second part of the reel *The Gravel Walk*. Notice the first two notes: two A eighth notes, the second of which is cut.

*Figure 7-20. The first two measures of the second part of the reel **The Gravel Walk** using a normal cut.*

Track 23

If you now elongate the cut enough, it in effect becomes a sixteenth note in its own right, as shown below. Note that the cut is stretched so that its beginning now comes earlier. The end of the elongated cut now falls where the entire cut used to be, i.e. on the beat that defines the attack of the second A.

The cut fingering is still being used, not the normal fingering for C-natural. The C-natural produced this way may be a bit sharp. (This sharper C-natural is sometimes referred to as the "piping C". For more on this, see *Outside the Modal Boundaries* on pp. 20-21 in Chapter 1.) It would be difficult to play such a brief C-natural using the normal cross-fingering.

*Figure 7-21. A variation on the first two measures of the second part of the reel **The Gravel Walk** created by elongating a cut.*

Track 24

Since the normal cut and the variation produced by elongating the cut are so similar physically (with both you move the same finger, just with a slightly different timing), the "decision" to elongate the cut can be made very spontaneously. I put "decision" in quotes because this kind of action is not normally the result of conscious planning but rather improvisation that occurs on an intuitive level.

For a beautiful example of elongated cuts listen to Matt Molloy's recording of the reel *Griffin from the Bridge*.[iii] You will a find a transcription of Molloy's recorded rendition of this tune in my book *The Essential Guide to Irish Flute and Tin Whistle*.

---

[i] In the Baroque and Classical periods, grace notes, more properly termed *appogiaturas* or *accaciaturas*, were played on the beat, stealing time from the principal note. During the Romantic period, grace notes sometimes came to be played before the beat of the principal note. Classical musicians today, if they are not well acquainted with the performance practices of the period of the piece at hand, may be found to play grace notes either on the beat or before the beat. For more on this subject, see the book *Ornamentation, A Question and Answer Manual* (Van Nuys, California: Alfred Publishing Co., 1995).

[ii] Geraldine Cotter, *Geraldine Cotter's Traditional Irish Tin Whistle Tutor*, 2nd ed. (Cork: Ossian Publications, 1989).

[iii] This is on Matt Molloy's 1987 recording, *Stony Steps*, Green Linnet GLDC 3041.

chapter 8: strikes

The second single-note ornament to learn is the **strike**. It is sometimes known by the names *tip, tap, pat, slap, lower grace,* or *lower grace note.*

The strike is just like the cut in several important ways. The strike is a pitched articulation, *not* a note or a grace note. It is a way to attack a note and give it emphasis. Therefore, it follows that the strike, like the cut, will fall exactly upon the beat where its parent note itself is placed. Its duration is so brief that we don't hear it as having an identifiable pitch or duration.

Unlike the cut, a strike's pitch is lower than that of its parent note. When it is played well, we can't identify its pitch, but qualitatively it feels different from the cut because of its lower pitch and the particular quality of its attack. And while the strike produces a sound very similar to that of the cut, the physical motions required to produce these two articulations could hardly be more different.

The Physical Movements and Fingerings of the Strike

The strike is well named, for its crisp sound is due to its percussive nature. In performing a strike one "throws" one's finger at its tone hole so that it hits the instrument at a high velocity. Due to that velocity, the finger bounces back of its own accord. As with the cut, your fingers must be relaxed, though not limp.

Unlike cut fingerings, strike fingerings seem to be universally agreed upon. As a rule, and this one has no exceptions, a strike on any given note is performed on the open tone hole closest to the mouthpiece. For example, on the note E a strike is performed with B3. For F-sharp, you strike with B2, for G with B1, for A with T3, for B with T2, for C-natural (using the normal cross fingering) with T1, and for C-sharp also with T1. You cannot do a strike on D.

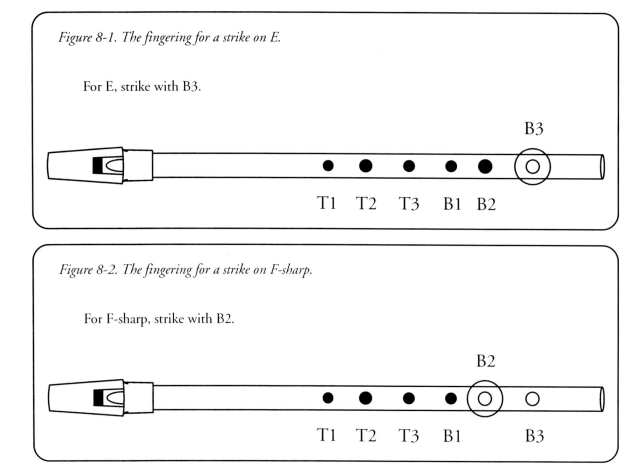

Figure 8-1. The fingering for a strike on E.

For E, strike with B3.

B3

T1 T2 T3 B1 B2

Figure 8-2. The fingering for a strike on F-sharp.

For F-sharp, strike with B2.

B2

T1 T2 T3 B1 B3

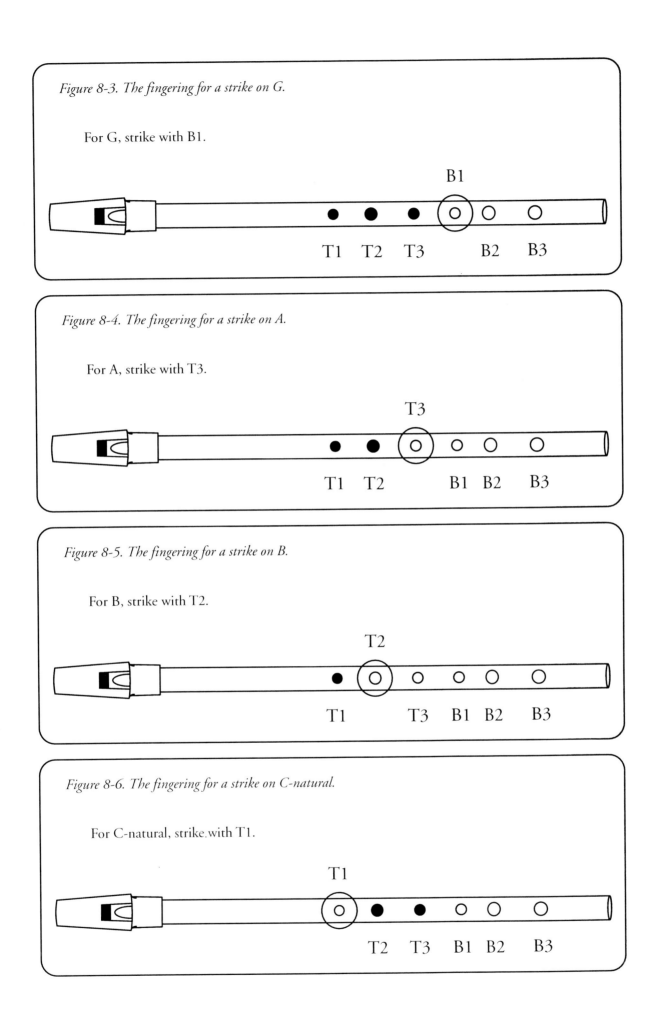

Figure 8-3. The fingering for a strike on G.

For G, strike with B1.

B1

T1   T2   T3   B2   B3

Figure 8-4. The fingering for a strike on A.

For A, strike with T3.

T3

T1   T2   B1   B2   B3

Figure 8-5. The fingering for a strike on B.

For B, strike with T2.

T2

T1   T3   B1   B2   B3

Figure 8-6. The fingering for a strike on C-natural.

For C-natural, strike.with T1.

T1

T2   T3   B1   B2   B3

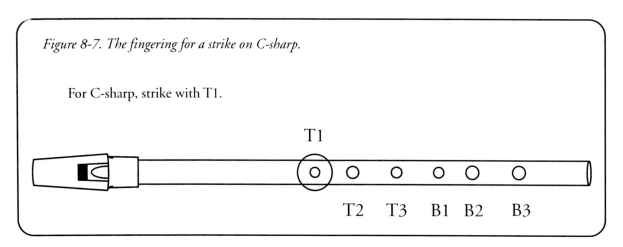

Figure 8-7. The fingering for a strike on C-sharp.

For C-sharp, strike with T1.

T1

T2   T3   B1   B2   B3

Using an alternate fingering one can perform a strike on C in the low register that produces a pitch higher than that of its parent note, making the strike sound much like a cut. This, in fact, is the way to simulate a cut on C-natural, as shown in Figure 8-8 below.

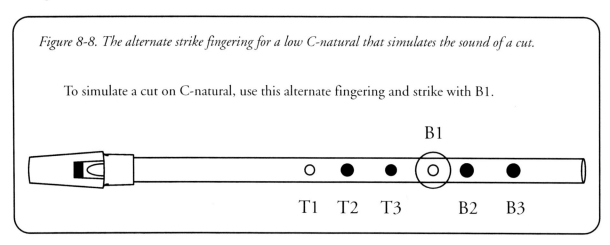

Figure 8-8. The alternate strike fingering for a low C-natural that simulates the sound of a cut.

To simulate a cut on C-natural, use this alternate fingering and strike with B1.

B1

T1   T2   T3   B2   B3

THE THREE PHASES OF THE STRIKE

The strike has a large, conspicuous motion, unlike the cut. That motion has three phases and each phase merges seamlessly into the next. This may make you suspect that the strike is hard to learn, but for many people it is easier to master than the cut.

RESTING POSITION

To understand the three phases of the strike you must first understand the idea of *resting position*.

When any of your fingers are not covering their respective tone holes they should be relaxed, resting approximately a quarter of an inch above the holes.

Figure 8-9. The bottom hand's fingers in resting position.

Often novices hold their fingers too high in the air, which indicates unnecessary muscle tension. With any instrument, it should be your goal to continually fine-tune your physical relationship with it so that you gradually eliminate any unproductive muscle tension in your body.

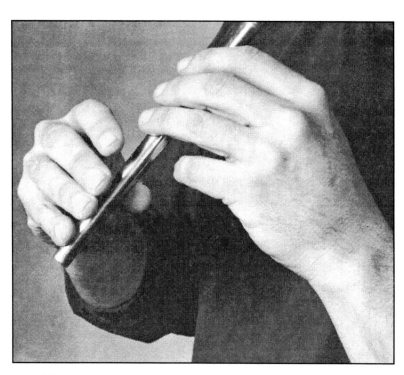

100

Before beginning a strike, make sure that all fingers not currently covering holes are in resting position.

1. The first phase is the preparation. As the time for the impact of the strike approaches you raise the striking finger high into the air.

As you are learning this, go ahead and raise the finger quite high. Once you have mastered the strike you may refine this to a somewhat smaller, more efficient motion.

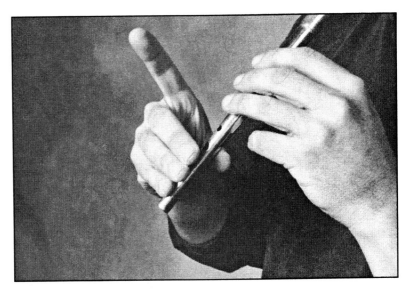

Figure 8-10. B1 raised in preparation for a strike on G.

2. The second phase is the velocity phase in which you propel your finger towards its impact, right on the beat, with its tone hole. This impact creates the attack, the beginning of the strike's parent note.

3. Phase three is the recovery phase. Your finger bounces back of its own accord. You have no need to lift it. In recovery, it normally rebounds a bit past resting position and then naturally returns to it, ready for its next task.

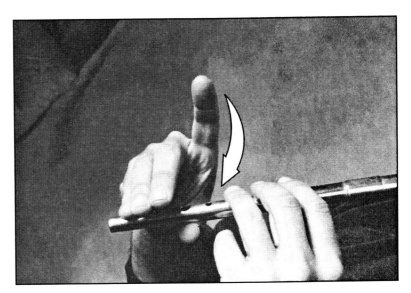

Figure 8-11. B1 in the velocity phase of the strike. The arrow indicates the movement, straight down onto the hole.

A New Strike Notation

Since a strike is an articulation, I notate it by placing a V over its parent note.

Figure 8-12. The symbol for a strike.

This symbol graphically illustrates the downward velocity, impact, and rebound of the strike. This is a simple, clean notation that reflects the reality of the strike's sound and function. Neither pitch nor duration are indicated or implied. There is only one note here, not two. Just like the cut, and for the same reasons (see p. 71 in the previous chapter), the strike is not a grace note. (Don't confuse this symbol with the *upbow* indication for bowed string instruments.)

101

WORTH REPEATING...

I said it in the last chapter and I'll say it again because it is so important: **you must learn to place strikes and cuts precisely on the beat.** You will not always want to articulate every note strictly on a beat or one of its subdivisions, but you will always need to be able to, especially when playing tunes at fast tempos.

A metronome is an invaluable tool in raising your awareness of how you are really faring in this regard—that is if you listen to it! You'd be surprised how often I have seen a student turn on her metronome and then blithely play away, unaware that she is completely out of synch with it. It won't adjust to you—that's why it is so enlightening to use.

THE SIMPLEST AND MOST COMMON USE OF A STRIKE: ARTICULATING A REPEATED NOTE

Set your metronome at a comfortable tempo somewhere around 120 beats per minute. You will play along with the metronome in a cycle (or meter) of four quarter-note beats, placing strikes on beat one of all but the first group of four. Count out the four-beat pattern until you are comfortable with it. Then, on beat one, start playing a G (low or high register). Don't tongue or interrupt the flow of air until you need to breathe.

Fingers B1, B2, and B3 should be in resting position. On beat four, begin the preparation phase of the strike (for the purpose of this exercise). The velocity phase of the strike begins just a hair before beat one so that the impact occurs exactly *on* beat one. With that impact you have just defined the beginning of the next four-beat G note.

Proceed this way, articulating each four-beat G note with a strike, until you need to breathe.

Exercise 8-1. *Practicing repeated strikes on G.* Strike with B3.

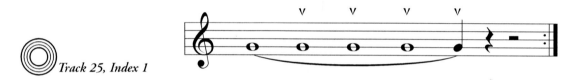

Track 25, Index 1

Take a breath, all the while maintaining your four beat count, and, catching the next beat number one, begin again. Pay attention! Are your strikes on the beat? If you're like most people you will tend to be early. If so, that's alright. Just notice it and try to place the next one more precisely. Effective practice is at least 90% attention and focus.

This and the following exercises can be done in both the low and high registers.

Exercise 8-2. *Practicing repeated strikes on F-sharp.* Strike with B2.

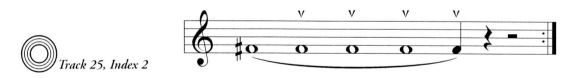

Track 25, Index 2

Exercise 8-3. *Practicing repeated strikes on E.* Strike with B3.

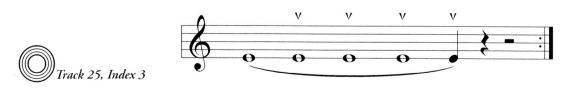

Track 25, Index 3

Striking on E is the only occasion when it is necessary to lift the anchoring pinky of your bottom hand off your instrument. Due to our anatomy, most of us simply can't move our B3 finger in the way required without also lifting the pinky. Lift the pinky at the same time that you lift B3, moving both as a unit.

I recommend that you also bring the pinky down with the striking B3, both fingers again moving as a unit. The pinky then remains on the instrument while B3 hits the instrument, rebounds from it and settles back to its resting position.

This works well for two reasons. First, B3 can move more freely when the pinky moves with it, and second, the pinky returns to its anchoring spot immediately, not as a later and unnecessary step in the sequence of finger movements.

Exercise 8-4. *Practicing repeated strikes on A.* Strike with T3.

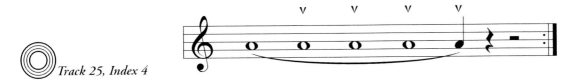

Track 25, Index 4

Exercise 8-5. *Practicing repeated strikes on B.* Strike with T2.

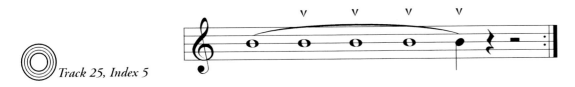

Track 25, Index 5

Exercise 8-6. *Practicing repeated strikes on C-natural.* Strike with T1.

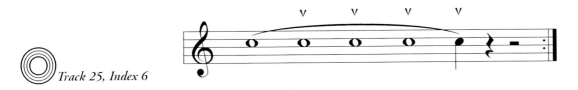

Track 25, Index 6

Exercise 8-7. *Practicing repeated strikes on C-sharp.* Again, strike with T1.

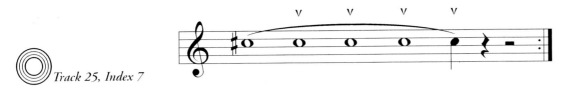

Track 25, Index 7

Exercise 8-8. *Practicing strikes on repeated notes in the context of a descending melody.*

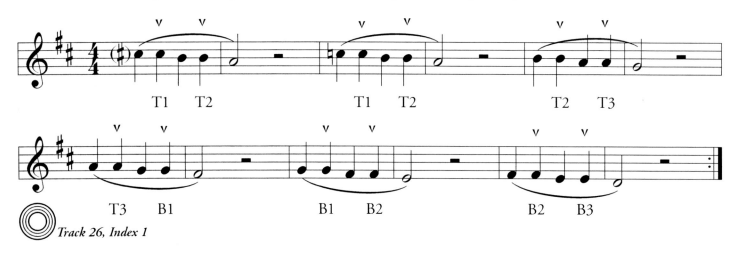

Track 26, Index 1

Exercise 8-9. *Practicing strikes on repeated notes in the context of an ascending melody.*

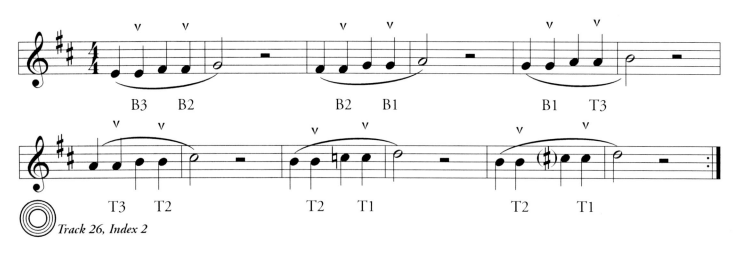

Track 26, Index 2

Exercise 8-10. *Practicing strikes on repeated notes in the context of descending thirds.*

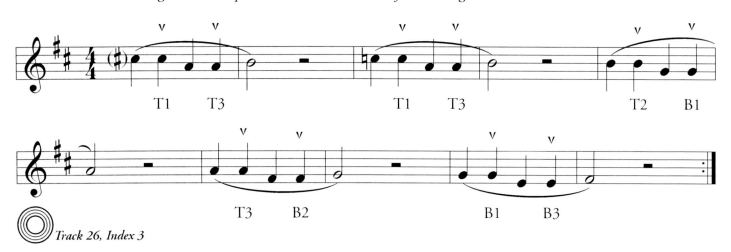

Track 26, Index 3

Exercise 8-11. *Practicing strikes on repeated notes in the context of ascending thirds.*

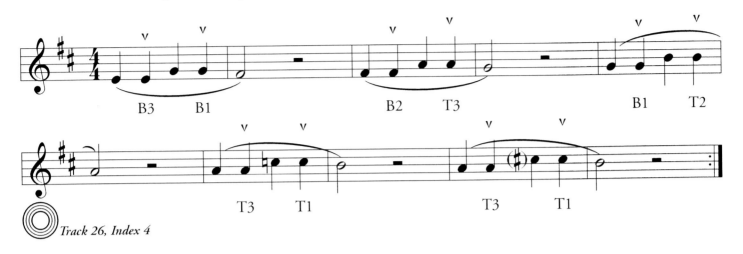

Track 26, Index 4

Exercise 8-12. *Practicing strikes on repeated notes in the context of ascending and descending fourths.*

Track 26, Index 5

105

Exercise 8-13. *Practicing strikes on repeated notes on the second subdivision of the pulse in a jig.*

Track 26, Index 6

Exercise 8-14. *Practicing strikes on repeated notes on the third subdivision of the pulse in a jig.*

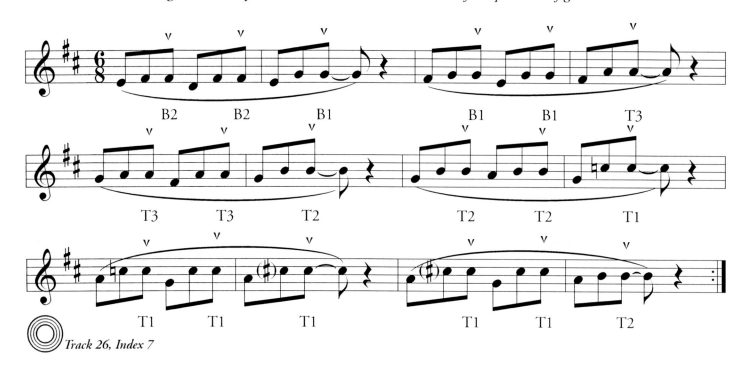

Track 26, Index 7

106

THE USES AND LIMITATIONS OF THE STRIKE

The strike is sometimes used as an ornamental articulation of single notes, but most of the time the cut is chosen for that purpose instead. I suspect this is the case because the cut is more versatile than the strike. One cannot strike a note when ascending to it if the preceding note is in the same register (low or high).

You can strike some notes when ascending to them across the register break. These are shown below in Figure 8-13.

Figure 8-13. The possible ascending strikes.

Strikes can be useful for articulating certain notes that cannot be cut. As shown on p. 100 in Figure 8-8, you can simulate a C-natural cut with a strike. On a few instruments it is possible to cut a C-sharp, as shown on p. 74 in Figure 7-12, but a C-sharp strike can be done on all whistles.

You can strike when descending, and of course on repeated notes. As noted earlier, you cannot strike a D.

By far the most important and common use of the strike is as an essential ingredient of a multi-note class of ornaments called *rolls*. We will examine rolls in Chapters 10 and 11.

Still, one can use the strike on its own to lovely effect in various contexts and you should have the technique at your disposal. Cathal McConnell is a flute and whistle player from Co. Fermanagh who makes use of strikes in a wide and intriguing variety of ways. For more on this, see the transcriptions of his playing of *Peter Flanagan's* and *The Long Slender Sally* in my book *The Essential Guide to Irish Flute and Tin Whistle*. Another example of the use of strikes to articulate notes that are not parts of rolls can be seen in the transcription of Desi Wilkinson's recording of the highland *Bidh Eoin* in the same book.

STRIKES ON STEPWISE DESCENDING NOTES

Let's say you're moving down from G to F-sharp (low or high register) and you want to strike the F-sharp. To do so, you need to perform two different finger movements simultaneously. To move from G to F-sharp you will place B1 on its hole. At the same time, right on the beat, you will strike with B2. Both B1 and B2 will contact the instrument at the same moment but B2 will rebound off while B1 stays down. If your strike is late you will hear two distinctly articulated F-sharps.

I think you'll find that this is not as hard as performing stepwise descending cuts. With all stepwise descending strikes, both fingers that are moving are moving in the same direction, coming down onto the instrument, and they are always adjacent fingers.

Play Exercise 8-15 along with the metronome. Set your metronome at 60, or slower. You are going to play along with it in a cycle (or meter) of four beats, placing the strikes on beat two of each group of four.

Count out the four beat pattern until you are comfortable with it. Then, on beat one, play a low G for one beat. Without tonguing or interrupting the air flow in any way, move to F-sharp, attacking it with a strike, on beat two. Hold the F-sharp for beats two and three. Then take a breath on beat four. Resume the same pattern again on beat one.

Exercise 8-15. *Practicing strikes on F-sharp when descending from G.*

Track 27, Index 1

Try this in the high register too. Do Exercises 8-16 through 8-19 in the same manner.

Next, move from F-sharp to E while striking the E. Play F-sharp. Place B2 on its hole and at the same moment, right on the beat, you will strike with B3.

Exercise 8-16. *Practicing strikes on E when descending from F-sharp.*

Track 27, Index 2

Next, move from A to G while striking the G. Play A. Place T3 on its hole and, at the same moment, strike with B1. Interestingly, traditional players often strike G with B1 and B2 simultaneously. Try it—it does feel good.

Exercise 8-17. *Practicing strikes on G when descending from A.*

Track 27, Index 3

Next, move from B to A while striking the A. Play B. Place T2 on its hole and, at the same moment, strike with T3.

Exercise 8-18. *Practicing strikes on A when descending from B.*

Track 27, Index 4

Next, move from C-sharp to B while striking the B. Play C-sharp. Place T1 on its hole and, at the same moment, strike with T2.

Exercise 8-19. *Practicing strikes on B when descending from C-sharp.*

Track 27, Index 5

Exercise 8-20. *Practicing strikes on stepwise descending notes.*

Track 28

Note that there are examples of ascending strikes in Figure 8-13 (p. 107) that use the same fingerings as some of the descending strikes given in Exercises 8-15 through 8-19. For example, Exercise 8-16 describes descending from F-

109

sharp to a struck E (low or high register). These same fingerings work for the second example in Figure 8-13, ascending from a low F-sharp to a struck *high* E. The only differences are in how you blow.

By the way, you'll find that it is impractical to strike a B when moving down to it from C-natural.

TRY USING SOME STRIKES IN A TUNE

Before we explore more contexts for strikes, let's put to use the strikes we have just been practicing, that is, strikes on repeated notes and strikes on stepwise descending notes.

Figure 8-14 below shows a version of the hornpipe *Bantry Bay* that makes use of only these types of strikes, as well as a variety of cuts. Play through it, with the strikes, cuts, and phrasing as indicated. Afterwards, play the tune through without strikes and cuts and see how different the music feels. Potential breathing spots are indicated with commas above the staff.

*Figure 8-14. A version of the hornpipe **Bantry Bay** using a variety of cuts, and strikes which articulate only repeated notes and descending stepwise notes. Potential breathing spots are indicated by commas above the staff.*

 Track 29

110

To complete our strike explorations, try the following exercises.

STRIKES ON NOTES THAT DESCEND BY AN INTERVAL LARGER THAN A MAJOR SECOND

Let's try striking E when descending from G. To move from G down to E, you put down B1 and B2. At the same moment strike with B3. All three fingers of the bottom hand will contact the instrument at the same moment but B3 will rebound off while the others stay down. Do this and the following exercises in the same manner as Exercises 8-15 through 8-19.

Exercise 8-21. *Practicing strikes on E when descending from G.*

Track 30, Index 1

Next, move from A to E while striking the E. Begin by playing A with T1 and T2 on their holes. Then move to E by placing T3, B1, and B2 on their holes and at the same time strike with B3.

Exercise 8-22. *Practicing strikes on E when descending from A.*

Track 30, Index 2

Next, move from B to E while striking the E. Begin by playing B with T1 on its hole. Then move to E by placing T2, T3, B1, and B2 on their holes and at the same time strike with B3.

Exercise 8-23. *Practicing strikes on E when descending from B.*

Track 30, Index 3

Next, move from C-natural to E while striking the E. Begin by playing C-natural with T2 and T3 on their holes. Then move to E by placing T1, B1, and B2 on their holes and at the same time strike with B3.

Exercise 8-24. *Practicing strikes on E when descending from C-natural.*

Track 30, Index 4

111

Next, move from C-sharp to E while striking the E. Begin by playing C-sharp with all holes open. Then move to E by placing T1, T2, T3. B1, and B2 on their holes and at the same time strike with B3.

Exercise 8-25. *Practicing strikes on E when descending from C-sharp.*

*Track 30, Index 5*

Next, move from A to F-sharp while striking the F-sharp. Begin by playing A with T1 and T2 on their holes. Then move to F-sharp by placing T3 and B1 on their holes and at the same time strike with B2.

Exercise 8-26. *Practicing strikes on F-sharp when descending from A.*

*Track 30, Index 6*

Next, move from B to F-sharp while striking the F-sharp. Begin by playing B with T1 on its hole. Then move to F-sharp by placing T2, T3, and B1 on their holes and at the same time strike with B2.

Exercise 8-27. *Practicing strikes on F-sharp when descending from B.*

*Track 30, Index 7*

Next, move from C-natural to F-sharp while striking the F-sharp. Begin by playing C-natural with T2 and T3 on their holes. Then move to F-sharp by placing T1 and B1 on their holes and at the same time strike with B2.

Exercise 8-28. *Practicing strikes on F-sharp when descending from C-natural.*

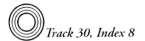*Track 30, Index 8*

Next, move from C-sharp to F-sharp while striking the F-sharp. Begin by playing C-sharp with all holes open. Then move to F-sharp by placing T1, T2, T3, and B1 on their holes and at the same time strike with B2.

Exercise 8-29. *Practicing strikes on F-sharp when descending from C-sharp.*

Track 30, Index 9

Next, move from B to G while striking the G. Begin by playing B with T1 on its hole. Then move to G by placing T2 and T3 on their holes and at the same time strike with B1.

Exercise 8-30. *Practicing strikes on G when descending from B.*

Track 30, Index 10

Next, move from C-natural to G while striking the G. Begin by playing C-natural with T2 and T3 on their holes. Then move to G by placing T1 on its hole and at the same time strike with B1.

Exercise 8-31. *Practicing strikes on G when descending from C-natural.*

Track 30, Index 11

Next, move from C-sharp to G while striking the G. Begin by playing C-sharp with all holes open. Then move to G by placing T1, T2, and T3 on their holes and at the same time strike with B1.

Exercise 8-32. *Practicing strikes on G when descending from C-sharp.*

Track 30, Index 12

Next, move from C-sharp to A while striking the A. Begin by playing C-sharp with all holes open. Then move to A by placing T1 and T2 on their holes and at the same time strike with T3.

Exercise 8-33. *Practicing strikes on A when descending from C-sharp.*

Track 30, Index 13

Exercise 8-34. *Practicing leapwise descending strikes on E.*

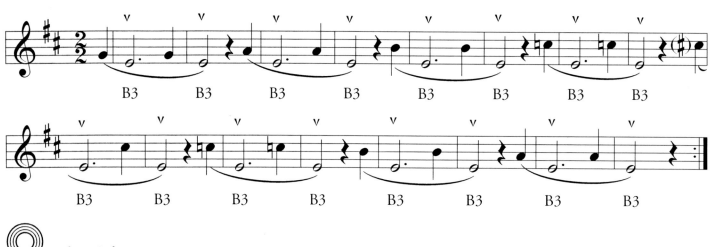

Track 31, Index 1

Exercise 8-35. *Practicing leapwise descending strikes on F-sharp.*

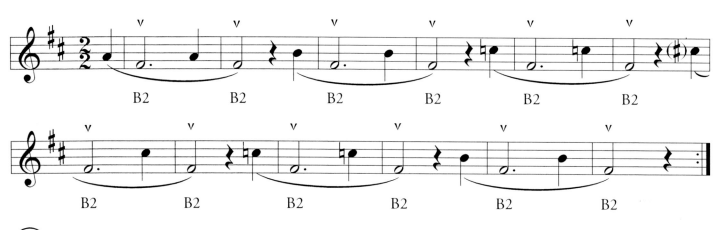

Track 31, Index 2

Exercise 8-36. *Practicing leapwise descending strikes on G.*

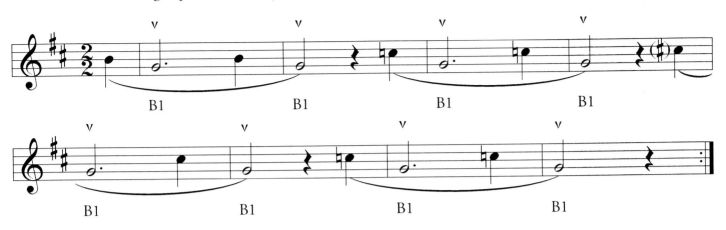

 *Track 31, Index 3*

BANTRY BAY, REVISITED

Now that we've practiced strikes on notes that descend by more than a major second, let's try out a version of *Bantry Bay* that incorporates some of them. This version is the same as the previous one with the addition of some strikes of this type as well as one strike on an ascending note that crosses the octave break.

*Figure 8-15. A version of the hornpipe **Bantry Bay** using cuts, and a variety of strikes.
Potential breathing spots are indicated by commas above the staff.*

 Track 32

ADDITIONAL STRIKE TECHNIQUES

Just as with cuts, one can strike and tongue at the same time. There are some examples of this in both of the versions of *Bantry Bay* presented above. See the discussion under *Cutting and Tonguing at the Same Time* on p. 94 of the previous chapter, which applies equally to strikes.

It is also possible to strike in the midst of a note. See the discussions under *Delaying the Cut, or Cutting in the Midst of a Note,* and *Delaying the Cut by Placing it on a Subdivision of the Pulse* on p. 95 of the previous chapter, which also apply to strikes.

chapter 9: slides

NOT AN ARTICULATION

The **slide** is quite different from the cut and strike in several ways. First, it is not an articulation. It is an *inflection*. It is not played or heard as an "instantaneous" event, as the cut and strike are. It is a continuous, moving alteration of a note's pitch. Some people refer to this as a *slur* or *smear*, but "slur" has another, more widely accepted meaning, as explained in Chapter 12. It is therefore best not to use the word slur for a slide. In the classical world, the slide is often referred to as a *portamento*.

For now, when I speak of the slide I am referring to a musical gesture that is accomplished using a finger technique. Note that pitch slides can also be accomplished by breath and embouchure technique. I'll get to that subject at the end of this chapter. Fingered slides, however, offer much more in speed and agility.

The cut and strike create the attacks of their parent notes and are therefore fixed in their temporal relationships to them. The slide exists independent of these considerations. The concept of a parent note is not always useful in regard to the slide. A slide can begin before the attack of a note, or after. It can be very brief or very long. It can be a way to move from one note to another and can therefore affect both notes. The slide is the free spirit of single-note ornaments and, as such, it can get carried away if you don't watch out, giving your playing a slurpy, even a drunken feeling.

Slides can rise or fall in pitch. Rising slides are used more often in Irish music than falling slides.

THE PHYSICAL MOVEMENT OF THE SLIDE

When you slide you are gradually, and sometimes only partially, covering or uncovering a finger hole in such a way that the pitch of the note you are playing at that moment smoothly rises or falls. By the way, the word *slide* refers to what happens to the *pitch* of the affected note or notes, not necessarily what the finger does to achieve that sound. Sometimes you do slide the finger, but other times you may tilt, rock, or roll it slightly instead.

Sliding is easy and natural on the tin whistle, simple-system flute and uilleann pipes since the fingers come into direct contact with the finger holes. Sliding is possible, but not as natural, on open-hole Boehm-system flutes because of the key mechanisms that intervene between the fingers and the tone holes themselves. Sliding is virtually impossible on the closed-hole Boehm-system flute. This difference is certainly one of the reasons why the simple-system flute is preferred by almost all Irish flute players.

AN ESSENTIAL PRINCIPLE

The finger movement of the slide should be one that leaves your hand in good playing position once the slide is complete. We will keep returning to that principle as we look at different kinds of slides.

TWO CLASSES OF SLIDES

Slides fall into two classes according to:

1. their relationship to the melody
2. the fingerings they require

The **simple slide** directly connects two consecutive notes in a melody, "filling in" the interval between them. Clearly, this kind of slide moves in the same direction as the melody. In sliding from one melody note to the next, the only finger or fingers moving are the same ones that, in normal playing, you would move to simply go from the first note to the second. For example, when moving from A up to B using a simple slide, one simply removes T2 *gradually* from its hole.

The **added-finger slide** requires the involvement of an *additional finger*, one that is not normally used in moving from the first melody note to the next. The pitch slide does not occur within the interval formed by the two melody notes, but *outside* of this interval, and it moves in the direction opposite to that of the melodic movement. For example, when moving from G down to E and using an added-finger slide, you put down B1 and B2 in a normal fashion to move from G to E, and, at the *same* time, B3 covers all or part of its hole and immediately moves smoothly off of it to produce a pitch slide up to E from below. The melodic movement from G to E is downward, but the movement of the pitch slide is upward, rising to E from below.

Both simple and added-finger slides can occur in rising and falling forms.

THE FIRST SLIDE: THE RISING STEPWISE SIMPLE SLIDE

Let's consider first the simplest and most natural application of the slide, the rising stepwise simple slide. By that I mean sliding from one note of a melody to the following note when that following note is higher by one step in the scale or mode. For example, see Figure 9-1.

Figure 9-1. Sliding up from E to F-sharp.

Track 33

In this slide, instead of simply lifting B2 off its hole, you gradually move B2 all the way off its hole, making the pitch gradually rise from E to F-sharp.

Do not draw B2 back toward your wrist. That would take your hand out of good playing position. Instead, scoop B2 up and away from your wrist and the hole, or putting it another way, simply straighten out B2, while keeping in contact with the instrument, so that it gradually uncovers the far edge of the hole first. See Figure 9-2.

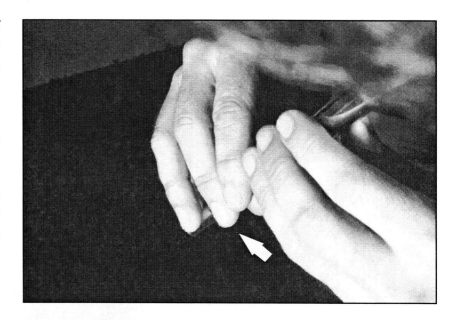

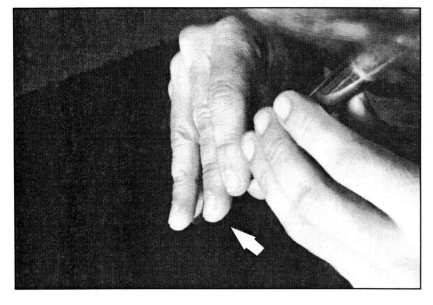

Figure 9-2. Upper: The fingers playing an E. Lower: B2 straightened out, having just completed a slide up to F-sharp. (The arrows identify the B2 finger.) Note that B3 may straighten as well, as it is naturally inclined to do, since it is not covering its hole.

As with all finger movements, it should be your goal to fine-tune the motion so that there is no unnecessary or wasted effort. Feel free to experiment with your own ways of executing slides. Differences in hand size and shape as well as instrument and finger-hole sizes will combine in various ways and you'll need to find what works best for you under various circumstances. Just take care not to draw your hand away from the instrument and out of good playing position.

A SLIDE NOTATION

In Figures 9-3 and 9-4, I show my slide notation symbols for rising and falling slides.

Figure 9-3. The symbol for a rising slide.

Figure 9-4. The symbol for a falling slide.

 Track 34

The horizontal placement of the symbol could be stretched out to illustrate where the slide begins and ends if you want to be that precise, for example if you are transcribing a particular performance. How and when one slides is a very personal element of one's style.

SLIDING TO A HALF-HOLE POSITION

Picking up on the example shown in Figures 9-1 and 9-3 above, let's say you now want to slide from E to F-natural.

Figure 9-5. Sliding up from E to F-natural.

 Track 35

In this case you do not slide or tilt B2 *all* the way off its hole, but just enough to get to F-natural, holding the finger there in that position as long as you need to sound the F-natural. This requires precision and practice.

Sliding from B to C-natural is another example of this same technique, one that is used quite a bit by whistle players. The typical C-natural fingering (covering holes with T2 and T3) sometimes yields an out of tune and/or a muted note, especially on mass-produced whistles. The half-hole fingering is often much more pleasing in tone and can be more in tune as long as your half-hole technique is good.

With some fingering sequences, it is impractical to half-hole the C-natural. But when ascending from B to C-natural the fingering is not difficult and the resultant slide can give a very pleasing effect. If the C-natural is followed immediately by another B, which is a fairly common occurrence, you can easily slide right back down to the B.

You can try both of these slides on the B–C-natural–B sequence that occurs in measures two and three of the jig *The Blarney Pilgrim,* shown below in Figure 9-6.

119

*Figure 9-6. The opening bars of **The Blarney Pilgrim**, with simple slides from B up to C-natural and back down to B.*

Track 36

THE FALLING STEPWISE SIMPLE SLIDE

As mentioned above, falling slides are not used as much in Irish music as rising ones. Falling slides are usually more challenging than rising ones. It is more difficult to gradually and smoothly add a finger from mid-air to cover a hole than it is to gradually and smoothly remove a finger that is already on the instrument. Most falling slides require a lot of practice.

Interestingly, while rising half-hole slides are more difficult than rising stepwise slides, many falling half-hole slides are easier than falling stepwise slides. If you are already using a half-hole fingering to play a note, all you have to do to play the falling slide is to ease your finger back to a position completely covering its hole. This is the kind of falling slide we encountered in Figure 9-6 (above).

For an example of a half-hole falling slide in a different context, let's look at the following excerpt from a variation on the beginning of the jig *The Cliffs of Moher.*

*Figure 9-7. An excerpt from a variation on the beginning of the jig **The Cliffs of Moher**.*

Track 37

Take a close look at measure three. Finger the first C-natural (the first note in the measure) in the normal way, using T2 and T3 to cover their holes. Finger the next C-natural by half-holing on the T1 hole. If you use your tongue to cut short the A that precedes this second C, thereby introducing a small silence before the second C, you can reach the half-hole fingering for C *during* that silence. Then you will not hear a slide up to the C. Now, to play the following B, simply ease T1 down to completely cover its hole, producing a falling half-hole slide. Try using the phrasing that I have indicated, at least in measure three.

SLIDES THAT RISE BY AN INTERVAL LARGER THAN A MAJOR SECOND

Slides that rise by an interval larger than a major second (i.e. leapwise) are not that different from rising stepwise slides. I find that it works well to begin and complete the slide mainly with the highest moving finger, letting the rest of them follow along. For example, in sliding from E up to B, begin the slide with T2 and perform it mostly with that finger, letting T3, B1, and B2 follow along just a tiny bit later. Or perform the entire slide with T2 and simply lift the other fingers completely off their holes at the same time.

SLIDES THAT FALL BY AN INTERVAL LARGER THAN A MAJOR SECOND

These are fairly challenging and are rarely heard in Irish music. To make such slides sound smooth, in most cases you will need to gradually put down all the fingers in question together in a coordinated and smooth fashion. If you wish to pursue this you'll have to experiment with it a good bit.

ADDED-FINGER SLIDES FROM BELOW

So far we have looked at the class of *simple slides*, slides that connect melody notes, "filling in the gap" of the interval between the two notes. Sometimes it sounds lovely to use a slide that does not fill in that gap but that gives inflection to a note in another way.

This typically happens when, in descending from one melody note to another, you slide into the second note from below. For an example, let's look at the first few measures of the single jig or slide *The Star Above the Garter*. It gives a lovely nuance to the G in the third measure to slide up into it from below.

*Figure 9-8. The opening bars of **The Star Above the Garter** with an added-finger slide up to G followed by a simple slide up to C-natural.*

 *Tracks 38 and 39*

To perform this added-finger slide, you put down T3 to move from A to G and at the same time you use B1 to cover all, or better yet, only part of its hole, immediately easing it off its hole to produce the slide. I like to use the same "straightening" technique described above on p. 118 to perform this slide.

This putting down of B1 must be timed just right for it to produce the desired smooth effect, but with practice this soon becomes natural.

This gesture can be beautifully subtle, especially when the slide covers less than one step of the mode. This happens when you slide by covering only part of a tone hole.

Note that the slide up to C-natural later in the same measure is a rising simple slide on a note that ascends leapwise rather than stepwise. I would execute this slide by lifting T2, T3, B1, and B2 cleanly off their holes and at the same time half-holing with T1. This produces a subtle, quick slide from B to C-natural.

ADDED-FINGER SLIDES FROM ABOVE?

In the interest of completeness, it is possible to play an added-finger slide in the context of ascending melodic notes. This would be a falling slide that comes down to the higher melodic note from above. This is something I have rarely, if ever, heard in traditional Irish playing. If you wish to pursue it, have fun.

YET ANOTHER ORNAMENT: THE STRUCK SLIDE

In Figure 9-8, the first slide emphasizes the G in a graceful, soft-spoken way. If you want to emphasize it more assertively, you could cut at the end of the slide. But I think that is a bit strong in this case. If you want to give the note something a bit more special than just the slide, but still want it to treat it gently, you could try a *struck slide*, a variant on the slide that incorporates an aspect of the strike.

Let's look at the first slide in Figure 9-8 again. You move from A to G by placing T3 on its hole. At the same moment, you slide up to G by covering the edge of the B1 hole and immediately tilting the finger off the hole to produce the slide.

To use a struck slide, B1 will approach its hole in a different way. As in the strike, raise B1 enough into the air so that it can come down onto the *edge* of its hole with some velocity, giving a hint of the percussive attack of the strike. This will be a subtle attack because you are striking only part of the tone hole, not the entire hole.

Then, instead of letting the finger rebound as in the strike, keep the finger on the instrument and immediately tilt it up to produce the slide. This takes some practice. It is a subtle effect, but it is noticeably different from the normal slide.

Another good place for a struck slide is the third to last note, a G, in Figure 9-6 on p. 120.

SLIDING INTO A CUT

Above, I mentioned sliding and cutting at the end of the slide. A better way to state this is to say you are sliding into a cut. In the example we just discussed, the G in the third measure of *The Star Above the Garter* (Figure 9-8), we can slide into a cut using an added-finger slide.

Of course you can do the same with simple slides, too, as shown in the opening of *Willie Coleman's Jig* below.

*Figure 9-9. The opening measures of **Willie Coleman's Jig**.*

 Track 40

Here you slide into the G that begins the second measure and cut it when you arrive at the note.

Sliding into a cut has great evocative potential, so use it judiciously. Of course you can slide into multi-note ornaments that begin with cuts, such as the short roll, which we will get to know in Chapter 11. Get ready: sliding into rolls is very satisfying.

STOPPING THE AIR BEFORE OR AFTER A SLIDE

It is often useful to create a brief silence by tonguing before or after a slide.

For example, let's say you slide from B up to the half-hole C-natural (using T1) and then wish go back down to B without sliding down to it. Having sounded the half-hole C-natural, stop the air briefly, move T1 fully back onto its hole and then sound the B. You have in effect silenced the slide back down to B. You can use the same technique when moving from any half-hole fingering to any other note.

Here's another useful application. Let's say you play an E and then want to slide up to G using a very subtle slide. Having sounded the E you can stop the air, take B2 entirely off its hole and at the same time straighten out B1 so that it is covering only part of its hole. Then resume your air and complete the small, microtonal slide up to G by gradually removing B1 from its hole. This idea can be applied whenever you want to use a very small slide.

BREATH SLIDES

You can make the pitch of a note slide down by decreasing the amount of air you are blowing through the whistle. As you do this you also play more quietly, which can be a very nice effect.

You can see that the possibilities for sliding are quite vast.

You could raise the pitch with similar breath techniques, but you don't hear that done much in Irish whistle and flute playing, except to return a pitch to normal after it has already been lowered.

chapter 10: long rolls

The **long roll** is the most commonly used multi-note ornament.

The long roll is something very simple and lovely: *a group of three slurred eighth notes of the same pitch, each one having a different kind of articulation.* The first note is either tongued or slurred into from a preceding melody note, the second note is cut, and the third note is struck. In my notation, what I have just described looks like this.

Figure 10-1. A long roll on G, shown in exploded view.

NORMAL VIEW AND EXPLODED VIEW

Throughout this and the following chapter you will encounter notated musical examples that are given in *normal view, exploded view,* or both.

Exploded view shows what happens inside of each long roll or short roll. (The short roll is the subject of the next chapter.) Each of the roll's constituent notes is depicted, complete with its articulation (cut, strike, or tongue) and inflection (slide).

Normal view represents the roll as a single note with a special symbol above it. This is how I normally notate rolls, for example, in a collection of tune transcriptions. However, the *symbol* over the note tells you only half the story of the roll. The *duration* of the note below the symbol tells you the other half.

This will become clear as you work your way through this and the following chapter. Just remember to pay careful attention to both the symbol *and* the duration of the note below it.

USING AN ACCEPTED SYMBOL

There is a symbol in common usage for rolls in general. Pat Mitchell, in his book *The Dance Music of Willie Clancy*[1] writes that Breandán Breathnach devised this symbol to stand for rolls and cranns in his influential series of tune collections *Ceol Rince na hEireann.*[2]

Unlike Breathnach, I use the symbol very specifically, as shown in Figure 10-2, to indicate the long roll only. I depict other types of rolls and cranns differently. The short roll is the subject of the next chapter. The other types of rolls, and all types of cranns, are advanced techniques that I explore in *The Essential Guide to Irish Flute and Tin Whistle.*

Figure 10-2. The symbol for a long roll, and what it means.

Note that this crescent-shaped symbol is above a dotted quarter note. The long roll is three eighth notes in duration, the same length as a dotted quarter note.

CLEARING AWAY SOME FOG

Almost universally, the long roll has been described and taught as a five-note ornament. This is due to the prevailing custom of thinking of cuts and strikes as grace notes. Add the two grace notes to the three principal notes and you have five notes. The problem is, when you listen to a well-played long roll, you only hear three notes!

Cuts and strikes are not to be thought of as notes. We should think of them as articulations. Once that is understood it follows that the notion of the five-note long roll represents an unnecessary and misleading complication.

ILL-CONCEIVED NOTATION

Figure 10-3 shows some examples of long roll notation taken from current published whistle and flute tutors.

Figure 10-3. Examples of misleading long roll notation taken from other tin whistle and flute tutors.

None of these examples look like what a long roll sounds like. None of them accurately conveys the rhythm of the long roll. They all imply that the specific pitch of the cut and strike are perceivable and significant. None of them show that the sounds of the cut and the strike are qualitatively different from each other. If anyone, not already *knowing* what a long roll sounds like, tried to accurately reproduce what was notated in these examples they would get nothing that sounds like a long roll.

When one is first learning cuts and strikes and cannot yet make them brief enough, a long roll will indeed sound like it has five notes. Perhaps, since we all start out playing them that way, we have retained some vestige of our old perceptions in these notation practices.

But why not notate them the way they sound when played well, especially since that notation is much simpler to read, write, and understand?

THE RHYTHM OF THE LONG ROLL

When learning to play long rolls, it is critically important to learn to play them absolutely dead even, each eighth note articulated right on its beat. You will not always want to play rolls so evenly, but you will need to be able to when playing tunes at very fast tempos. The evenly played roll is your solid base from which you can depart and experiment. Later we will discuss more of the reasons for playing rolls in non-even rhythms.

TRY SOME LONG ROLLS

Let's play the long roll on low G that is shown earlier in Figures 10-1 and 10-2. Remember, you're simply going to play three eighth notes, tonguing only the first one.

Set your metronome at a comfortable tempo somewhere around 60 beats per minute. You are going to play along with the metronome in a cycle (or meter) of four beats, each beat representing an eighth note. Count out the four-beat pattern until you are comfortable with it. Then, on beat one, start playing a low G. Still playing, and without interrupting the air flow, cut the G on beat two, then strike the G on beat three. On beat four stop, and take a breath if you wish. Try it a few more times. This is notated in Exercise 10-1, below. (As mentioned in Chapter 8, traditional players often strike G with B1 and B2 simultaneously.)

Exercise 10-1. *Practicing long rolls on G, shown in exploded view.*

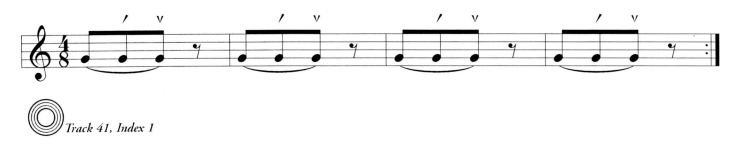

Track 41, Index 1

Notice the subtle differences among the three articulations and how they sound in sequence. Notice how the articulations progress down the instrument and away from you, from your tongue to T2, to B1. The roll has a direction of flow. Can you hear how the long roll resembles spoken language or chant? Realize that you are playing only three notes of the same pitch, but that they are subtly different from each other. Note that the last finger down when you play a G remains still throughout the roll. The last finger will stay down like this for almost all rolls. If you notice tension or gripping in your hands or fingers, find a way to relax.

Experiment with this as you wish and once you are ready, start again and keep the pattern going as shown in Exercise 10-1, above.

Remember that what you are now playing can also be written as shown in Figure 10-4.

Figure 10-4. Practicing long rolls on G, shown in normal view.

Try playing these rolls in the high register too. These fingerings, and the ones for the other long rolls you are about to learn, work for both registers.

CONGRATULATIONS!

You have now grasped what is one of the most pleasing and beautiful gestures in Irish music. Right now it is probably sounding rather stiff and pedestrian, but don't worry. You will come to experience how poetic it can be, and how fluid a long roll can feel, rippling downstream through your fingers.

The G long roll is probably the easiest one to play because the labor is divided between the two hands and you are using fingers that for most people are among their most agile ones.

The F-sharp long roll is the next easiest one. Set up the metronome as before and play these exercises in the same manner you played Exercise 10-1.

Exercise 10-2. *Practicing long rolls on F-sharp, shown in exploded view.* Cut with T3 and strike with B2. Leave B1 in place.

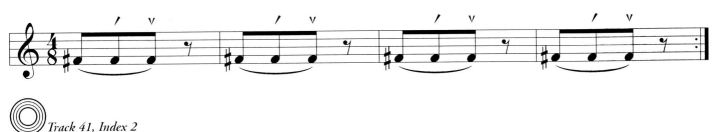

Track 41, Index 2

Next, work with the E long roll. This can be one of the more challenging ones because all of the work is in one hand. Don't forget to let your bottom-hand pinky move with B3 when it's time to strike the E.

Exercise 10-3. *Practicing long rolls on E, shown in exploded view.* Cut with B1 and strike with B3. Leave B2 in place.

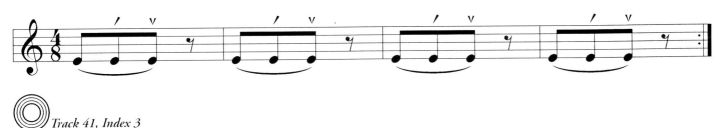

Track 41, Index 3

You cannot do a roll on D because there is no way to strike a D.

Here are two exercises that help you become accustomed to playing long rolls on E, F-sharp, and G.

Exercise 10-4. *Practicing long rolls on E, F-sharp, and G, in jig rhythm.*

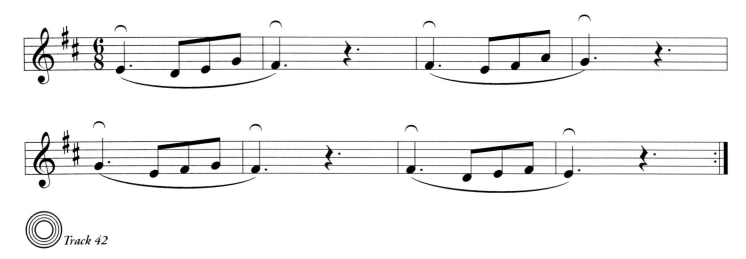

Track 42

Exercise 10-5. *Practicing long rolls on E, F-sharp, and G, in reel rhythm.*

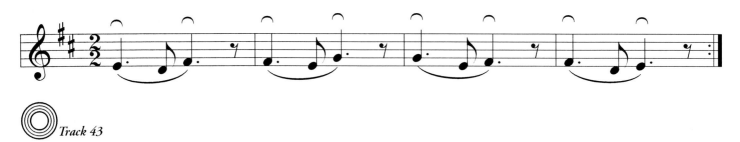

Track 43

THE SPORTING PITCHFORK

In this chapter I present two settings of the jig *The Sporting Pitchfork* to demonstrate how one can use long rolls in a musical context. In the next chapter I do the same with short rolls. In so doing, my primary purpose is to demonstrate the use of long and short rolls, but I vary the tune settings in other ways as well. Bear in mind that I am presenting only my style of variation.

In Chapter 11, on pp. 150-153, in the section called *Summary: All Four Settings of The Sporting Pitchfork,* you can see all four settings of the tune presented together in a score format, so that you can easily make measure by measure comparisons.

By the way, it is hard to say whether this tune is in D Mixolydian or G Ionian. The mode signature is valid for both.

A NEW BREATHING OPPORTUNITY - BREAKING THE LONG ROLL

As with the tune settings in Chapters 7 and 8, I have indicated some potential breathing spots in these settings by placing commas above the staff.

But there are more breathing opportunities than those I have indicated. Each long roll in these tunes settings presents another breathing opportunity.

Whenever a long roll begins on a pulse (i.e. a strong beat) you may omit the second note of that long roll, thereby creating a silence in which to breathe that is one eighth note in duration. When you do this, you are in fact no longer playing a roll, but simply playing an eighth note, then breathing during an eighth note's worth of silence, then playing another eighth note of the same pitch.

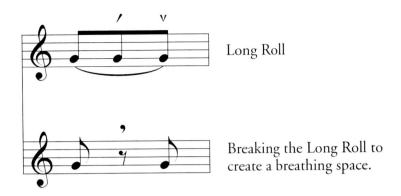

Long Roll

Breaking the Long Roll to create a breathing space.

Figure 10-5. Comparing the long roll, shown in exploded view, with the long roll broken to create a breathing space.

Track 44

We'll cover this and other breathing strategies in depth in Chapter 13.

All of the long rolls you will encounter in this and the next chapter's two settings of *The Sporting Pitchfork* begin on a pulse, so they all present such breathing opportunities.

Here's the first setting of *The Sporting Pitchfork,* which makes use of the three long rolls we have been learning, those on G, F-sharp, and E.

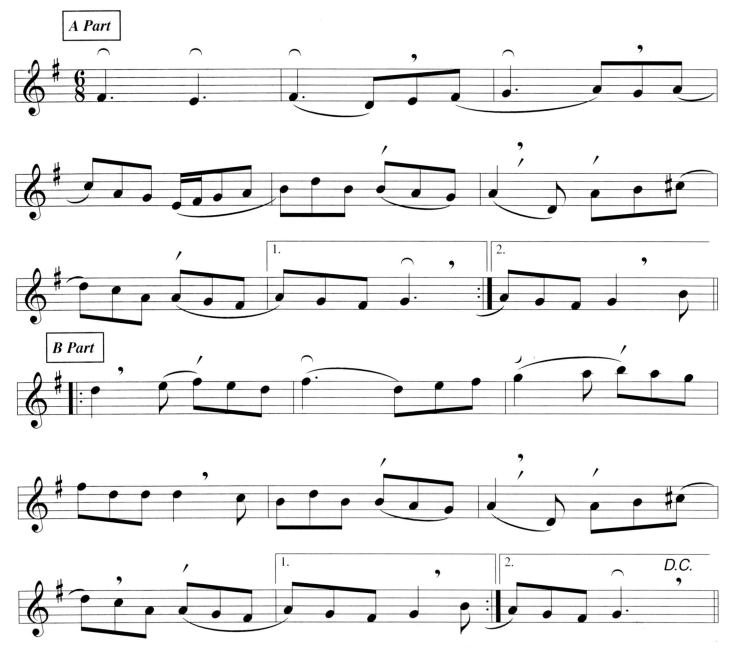

*Figure 10-6. The jig **The Sporting Pitchfork** with long rolls on G, F-sharp, and E.*

 Track 45

TRY LONG ROLLS ON A AND B

Try the A long roll next. This is another of the one-handed rolls, perhaps the most difficult one because of the strike with T3, the least agile of the hole-covering fingers for most people.

Exercise 10-6. *Practicing long rolls on A, shown in exploded view.* Cut with T1 and strike with T3. Leave T2 in place.

Track 46, Index 1

Now try the B long roll. This is also a one-handed roll. It feels different because the cutting and striking fingers are adjacent, with no stationary finger between them.

Exercise 10-7. *Practicing long rolls on B, shown in exploded view.* Cut with T1 and strike with T2. No finger stays down.

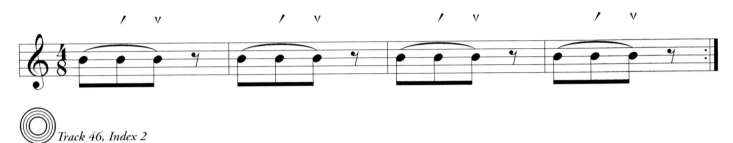

Track 46, Index 2

Here are two exercises for practicing long rolls on E, F-sharp, G, A, and B.

Exercise 10-8. *Practicing long rolls on E, F-sharp, G, A, and B in jig rhythm.*

Track 47

Exercise 10-9. *Practicing long rolls on E, F-sharp, G, A, and B in reel rhythm.*

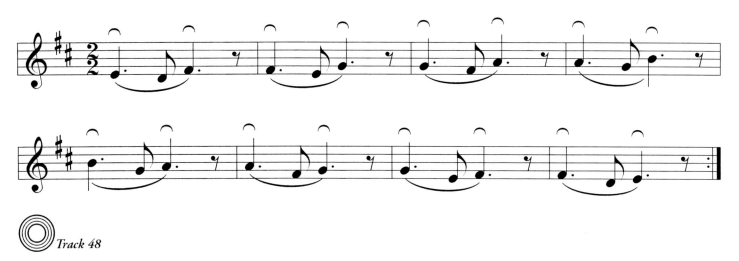

Track 48

ADD SOME A AND B LONG ROLLS TO *THE SPORTING PITCHFORK*

Now that you have learned the five main long rolls, try them out in the following setting of *The Sporting Pitchfork*. Notice the various ways in which this version differs from that shown in Figure 10-6, above. For one thing, you can see that rolls can replace short melodic figures that center around one pitch area. There are other differences too. These kinds of variations are central aspects of improvisation in the language of Irish music.

You should know that I have put more long rolls into this setting of the tune than I normally would play, in order to provide more opportunities to practice them.

Figure 10-7. The jig **The Sporting Pitchfork** *with long rolls on B, A, G, F-sharp, and E.*

 Track 49

LONG "ROLLS" ON C AND C-SHARP

You cannot do "proper" rolls on C or C-sharp because you cannot properly cut these notes. You can, however, simulate rolls on these notes, in the low register, by using strikes with special fingerings. Most players don't use these techniques.

Figure 8-8, on p. 100, showed how to simulate a cut on low C-natural. Figure 10-8, below, shows how to use that fingering, plus another one, to simulate a C-natural long roll.

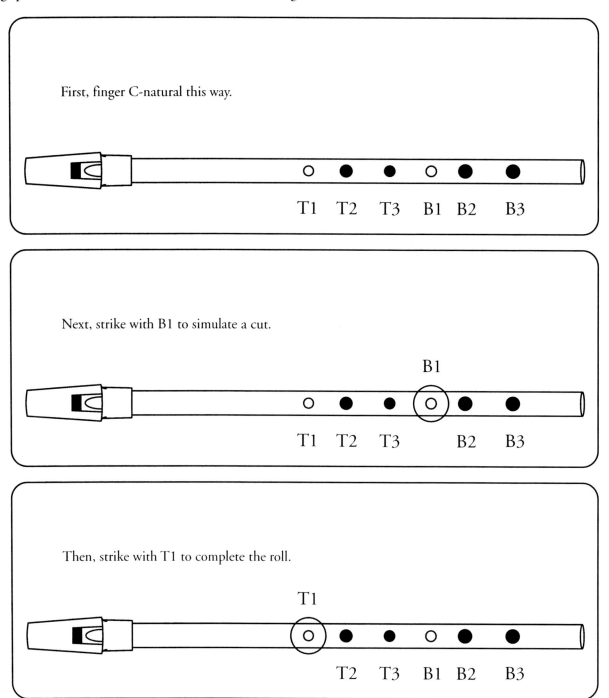

Figure 10-8. A way to simulate a long roll on low C-natural, using strikes.

Another set of fingerings, shown below in Figure 10-9 can also yield a C long roll which, with some whistles, will be more in tune.

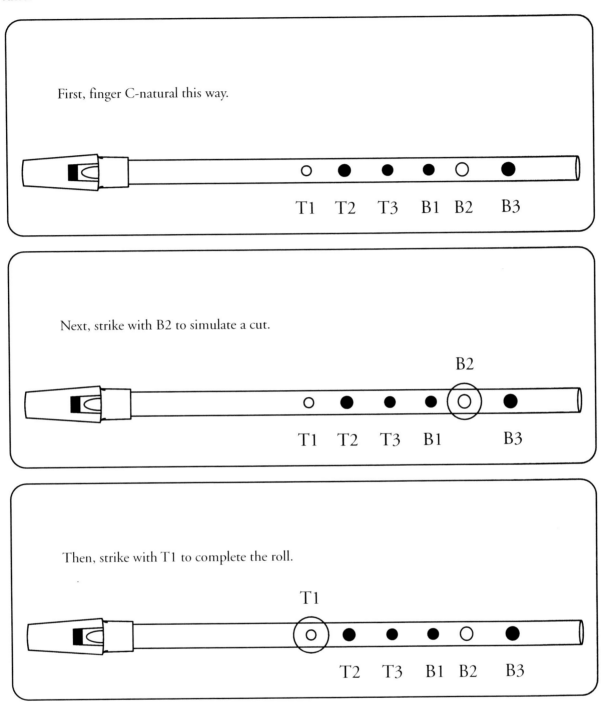

Figure 10-9. An alternate way to simulate a long roll on low C-natural, again using strikes.

In a similar fashion, you can simulate long rolls on low C-sharp, though these are weaker than C-natural rolls on most instruments. First, you can modify the fingerings shown in Figures 10-8 and 10-9 by keeping T2 off its hole to turn these into C-sharp rolls.

Figure 10-10, below, shows another fingering pattern to try.

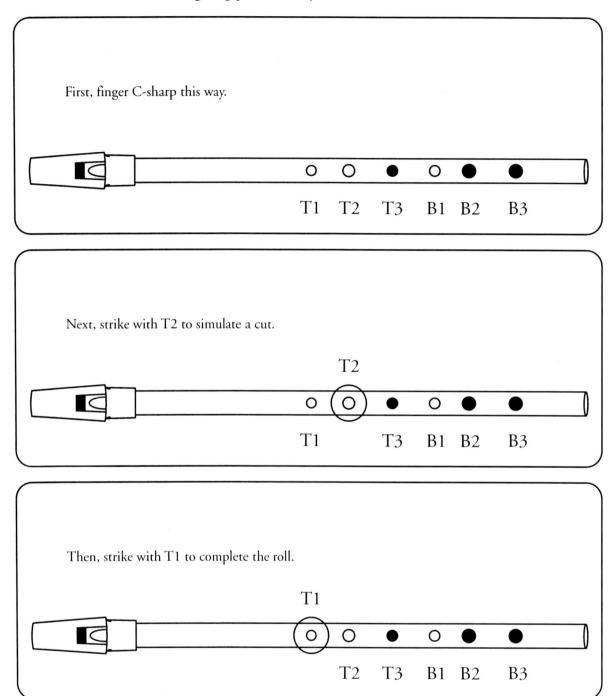

Figure 10-10. Another way to simulate a long roll on low C-sharp.

134

Figure 10-11, below, shows yet another possibility.

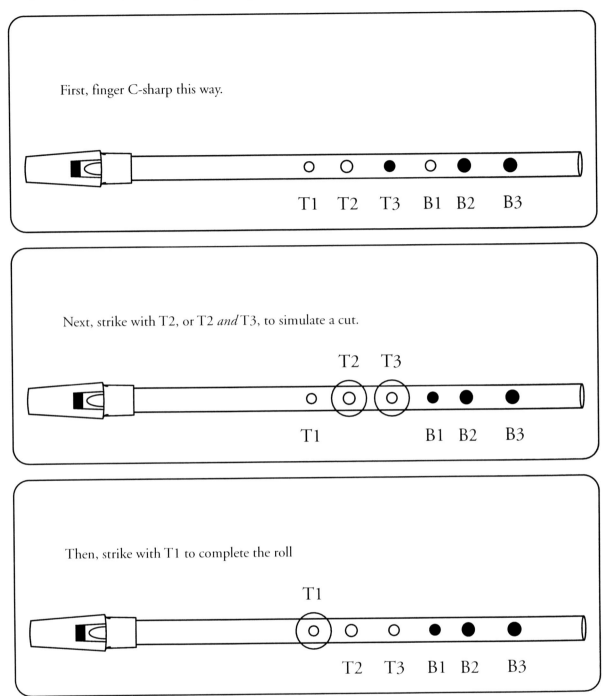

First, finger C-sharp this way.

T1 T2 T3 B1 B2 B3

Next, strike with T2, or T2 *and* T3, to simulate a cut.

T2 T3

T1   B1 B2 B3

Then, strike with T1 to complete the roll

T1

T2 T3 B1 B2 B3

Figure 10-11. Yet another way to simulate a long roll on low C-sharp.

SLOW AND STEADY

Over the months, as you practice your rolls, don't lose track of the steady beat. When you hear that a cut or strike is early or late, take note of that and return your focus to matching the beat. When you are able to stay on the beat consistently, stay with that comfortable tempo for a while and let your muscles really get to know the feeling of placing these articulations where they belong. In other words, practice doing it *right* for a while before going on to a faster tempo. After a while, increase the tempo just a notch or two and see how that feels. If you can't handle it, return to the slower tempo. If you can do fairly well at the new tempo, stick with it until it feels comfortable and stay there for a while. And so on. Don't be in a rush. Our muscles learn more slowly than our minds it seems, but they usually remember things better in the long run. For more on this, see *The Physiology of "Muscle Memory"* in Chapter 15, pp. 178-179.

As you reach the point where you can play good, even, long rolls up to a normal playing speed you will notice something fascinating. The movements (but not the sounds) of the cut and strike, which at slower tempos were separate and discreet events within the roll, are now overlapping. When the tempo rises to a certain point the preparation for the strike can, and should, begin even before you perform the cut. Now you can see and feel the fluidity of the roll, how it is like water in a stream rolling over rocks, one part of the wave flowing up to a crest while just ahead the water is flowing down into a trough. The unbroken stream of your breath provides the smooth downstream flow that encompasses the up and down movements of your fingers. The poetic combination of these elements manifest in the sound of the roll itself, which is a pleasure to the listener's ears. But the player is the luckiest one, for she is able not only to listen to the roll, but to feel and embody it as well.

RHYTHMIC EMPHASIS WITHIN THE LONG ROLL

As I have pointed out earlier, the flow of air that you blow is much like the horsehair of a fiddler's bow as it travels across the string. Just as a fiddler can change the pressure and speed of her bowstrokes to emphasize certain notes and to impart rhythmic stress, weight, or impulse, you can give such life to your music with changes in the qualities of your breath. Just as a fiddler can "lean into" the bow, you can "lean into" the breath.

We have much more capability in this regard on the flute than we have on the whistle, but even very subtle touches, as are possible on the whistle, can help bring your music to life beautifully.

IT'S ALIVE — IT HAS A PULSE

In reels, single jigs, double jigs, slides, hornpipes, polkas, schottisches, flings, barn dances, germans, strathspeys, and marches there are two strong recurrent pulses which could be counted "one, two; one, two," etc. In musical terms, we say these types of tunes are in *duple* meter. Most people tap their foot to these pulses and "one" usually gets a bit more stress than "two." In slip jigs, mazurkas, and waltzes, there are three strong recurrent pulses, which of course are counted "one, two, three; one, two, three" and so on, with "one" getting a bit more stress than "two" or "three." In musical terms, we say these types of tunes are in *triple* meter.

In each tune type these pulses are subdivided into smaller units of time. In reels each pulse is subdivided into four parts, usually notated as eighth notes, and in jigs each pulse is subdivided into three eighth-note parts. In musical terms, we say that reels are in a *simple duple meter* and jigs are in a *compound duple meter*.

In reels, then, there are eight eighth-note beats per measure. The pulse we have been talking about falls on the first and fifth of these eight notes. But the third and seventh notes carry some special weight too, though not as much as the first and fifth. Thus, there are two pulses existing concurrently in reels, the primary pulse on one and five and a secondary pulse on three and seven.

In jigs, the pulse falls on the first and fourth eighth notes and there is no secondary pulse. To keep things relatively uncomplicated we will look only at reels and jigs for now. See Figure 10-12 below.

Figure 10-12. The pulse and its subdivisions in a reel and a jig. The dark shaded areas show the two pulses of the jig and the two primary pulses of the reel, which coincide. The lighter shaded areas show the two secondary pulses of the reel.

As I alluded to above, it is possible to give emphasis to the different notes of the long roll using the breath and differing ways of playing cuts and strikes. Why would we want to do this? *Because rolls can occur in a variety of different contexts in relation to the pulse.* In our practice of rolls so far we have only been playing them such that the first note of the roll falls on a pulse. This is one way that we encounter rolls in tunes, but very often a pulse coincides with the cut (second) note or the struck (third) note of the long roll instead. Soon I will give you a variety of examples.

I feel that rolls sound more musical when you give a bit of emphasis to the note that falls on the pulse. To this same end it helps to make the off-pulse notes a bit more gentle.

I have alluded to how you can accomplish this with breath emphasis. You can "lean into" the on-pulse note with your breath, blowing just a bit harder and louder, taking care not to appreciably raise the pitch of the note.

How Long Rolls Relate to the Pulse

Now that you know how you can control the rhythmic emphasis within the roll, and why you would want to do so, here are some real-life applications.

The first note of a long roll quite frequently falls upon a primary pulse. For examples, see the beginning of the reel *The Banshee* in Figures 10-13 and 10-14 below, and the beginning of *Whelan's Jig* in Figures 10-15 and 10-16 below.

*Figure 10-13. The first two measures of the reel **The Banshee** with long rolls on G.*

*Figure 10-14. The first two measures of the reel **The Banshee** with G long rolls shown in exploded view.*

*Figure 10-15. The first two measures of **Whelan's Jig** with a long roll on E.*

*Figure 10-16. The first two measures of **Whelan's Jig** with the E long roll shown in exploded view.*

137

Long rolls, however, do not always begin on a pulse, primary or secondary. For an example, see the beginning of the reel *The Drunken Landlady* in Figures 10-17 and 10-18 below. (A note to classical players: I do not intend for the notation of the first two notes in each measure of Figure 10-17 to imply emphasis on the start of the second note. Emphasis should instead be placed on the cut notes of these rolls, which fall on secondary pulses, as shown in Figure 10-18.)

*Figure 10-17. The first two measures of the reel **The Drunken Landlady** with long rolls on E which begin on the second eighth-note beat of the measure.*

*Figure 10-18. The first two measures of the reel **The Drunken Landlady** with E long rolls shown in exploded view.*

In Figure 10-18 you can clearly see that the second note of the roll, the cut note, falls upon a secondary pulse (i.e. the third eighth-note beat). The first and third notes of the roll fall on weaker non-pulse subdivisions of the beat (two and four). Therefore, you may choose to give the second note of the roll, the cut note, some emphasis, as explained above, while slightly de-emphasizing the weight of the first and third notes of the roll. You can practice this by using Exercise 10-10, below.

Exercise 10-10. *In a reel, practicing long rolls that start on the second eighth-note beat of the measure.* The cut note of the roll falls on the secondary pulse.

Of course, the cut note of a long roll can fall on a reel's primary pulse as well. In Figures 10-19 and 10-20 you see the beginning of the reel *The Gravel Walk*. At the end of the first measure, and crossing the barline into the second measure, is a long roll on A. Notice that the cut note falls on the primary pulse at the beginning of the second measure.

Figure 10-19. The first two measures of the reel **The Gravel Walk** with a long A roll beginning on the eighth eighth-note beat of the first measure.

Track 54

Figure 10-20. The first two measures of the reel **The Gravel Walk** with a long A roll shown in exploded view.

Notice also the unusual notation in Figure 10-19. The roll symbol appears above an eighth note that is tied across the barline to a quarter note. The total duration of the two tied notes equals three eighth-note beats, the number of beats required for a long roll. There's really nothing unusual about this roll's sound and function in the tune. It's just our convention of using barlines to divide our notated music up into regular, manageable chunks that forces us to notate this roll in an odd-looking way. Actual music, of course, is continuous, not divided up into chunks. There is nothing unusual about the sound of this A roll.

Here is an exercise for practicing this kind of long roll.

Exercise 10-11. *In a reel, practicing long rolls that start on the eighth eighth-note beat of the measure.* The cut note of the roll falls on the primary pulse.

Track 55

Rolls in which the cut note (i.e. the second note) falls on a pulse are less common in jigs, but they do occur. (Remember that jigs have no secondary pulse.) Figures 10-21 and 10-22 show a variation on the beginning of *The Monaghan Jig* that yields just such a situation.

*Figure 10-21. The first two measures of a variation on **The Monaghan Jig** with a long roll on E beginning on the third eighth-note beat of the measure.*

 Track 56

*Figure 10-22. The first two measures of a variation on **The Monaghan Jig** with a long roll on E shown in exploded view.*

Here is an exercise for practicing such long rolls.

Exercise 10-12. *In a jig, practicing long rolls that start on the third eighth-note beat of the measure.* The cut note of the roll falls on the pulse.

 Track 57

In jigs, there are also times when the third note of a long roll, the struck note, falls on a pulse. Figures 10-23 and 10-24 show such a roll in the B part of the well-known jig *The Rose in the Heather.* Take a look at the long roll on E in the fourth measure.

*Figure 10-23. The first four measures of the B part of **The Rose in the Heather,** which includes a long roll on E beginning on the second eighth-note beat of the measure.*

◎ *Track 58*

*Figure 10-24. The first four measures of the B part of **The Rose in the Heather** with long rolls shown in exploded view.*

Here is an exercise for practicing this kind of long roll.

Exercise 10-13. *In a jig, practicing long rolls that start on the second eighth-note beat of the measure.* The struck note of the roll falls on the pulse.

Track 59

In a reel it can happen that the struck note of a long roll falls on either a primary or secondary pulse. In fact, in Figures 10-13 and 10-14 the struck notes of the G long rolls fall on secondary pulse. We hardly notice this though, because the first notes of these rolls are falling on the stronger primary pulses. This is a very common occurrence in reels.

However, it is very unusual for the struck note of a long roll to fall on a primary pulse in a reel.

UNEVEN ROLLS

Once you feel you have gained enough control that you can consistently play the three notes of your long rolls dead even on their beats, you are ready to experiment with the internal rhythm of the roll.

Actually, the only kind of deviation from the even long roll that I hear traditional players make is one in which the cut note is delayed. The struck note seems to stay on the third beat. Thus, the cut and the strike are squeezed closer together than in the even roll. This kind of roll can be heard among players of all instruments, especially when tunes are played at slow or moderate tempos. As the tunes speed up the rolls tend to even out.

The amount that the cut note is delayed is highly individual and changeable. However, it is rarely something as neat and orderly as simply dotting the first note of the roll, that is, placing the second note exactly halfway between beats two and three, as shown below in Figure 10-25.

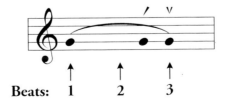

Beats: 1   2   3

Figure 10-25. Uneven rolls are rarely played as shown here, with the second note placed halfway between beats two and three.

Much more often the internal rhythm of the uneven roll is something more like what is shown in Figure 10-26 below.

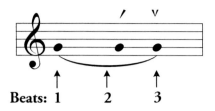

Beats: 1   2   3

Figure 10-26. Uneven rolls are usually played in a fashion similar to what is shown here, that is, the second note is placed closer to beat two than to beat three.

When you are trying to play in tight unison with another musician, there are a great many aspects of their playing that you will want to understand and match. One of them is surely the internal rhythm of their rolls. Hopefully they are listening to you with the same attention and care!

A Special Case of Uneven Rolls

Certain types of tunes, such as hornpipes, mazurkas, and schottisches, are normally played with an *overtly* uneven subdivision of the pulse. That is, the notes tend to alternate "long-short, long-short". The lilt of jigs, reels, and the like is usually more subtle and often goes unnoticed.

A special situation comes up when playing rolls in these uneven kinds of tunes. The rolls are mostly played with the same kind of underlying unevenness. I address this subject in depth in *The Essential Guide to Irish Flute and Tin Whistle*.

Sliding Into the Roll

One of the most pleasing things to do with all the varieties of rolls is to slide into its first note from below. This can be accomplished with either the simple or added-finger slide, or with the struck slide, depending upon the musical context. It is usually best done in a subtle manner without "slurping" the pitch too much.

If you wish to notate sliding into a roll you could do so as shown below in the beginning of the reel *Roaring Mary*.

*Figure 10-27. Sliding into long rolls in the first two measures of the reel **Roaring Mary.***

Track 60

Note that you slide into the first long roll with a simple slide and into the second one with an added-finger slide, which could be a struck slide if desired. Also note how you can slide into the quarter-note high G in the second measure, which has a mid-note cut indicated.

---

[i] Pat Mitchell, *The Dance Music of Willie Clancy*, 2nd ed. (Dublin: Mercier Press, 1977), p. 12.

[ii] Breandán Breathnach, *Ceol Rince na hÉireann, Vol. 1* (Dublin: An Gúm, 1963).

chapter 11: short rolls

The **short roll** can be most easily grasped as a long roll missing its first note. Thus, *the short roll is a group of two slurred eighth notes of the same pitch, each one having a different articulation.* The first eighth note is cut, and the sec-

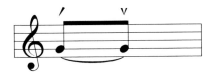

Figure 11-1. A short roll on G, shown in exploded view.

It is essential to understand that the short roll occupies only two eighth-note beats whereas the long roll occupies three (see Figure 11-2 below).

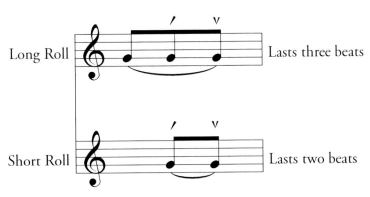

Figure 11-2. Comparison of long and short rolls, shown in exploded view.

Track 61

A NEW SYMBOL

I have modified the symbol in common usage for rolls to create a symbol specifically for the short roll. It is shown below in Figure 11-3.

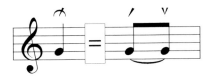

Figure 11-3. The symbol for a short roll on G.

Note well that the short-roll symbol appears above a quarter note. The short roll is only two eighth notes in duration, the same duration as a quarter note.

Notice that the short-roll symbol is the long-roll symbol with a slash through it. This shows that the short roll is a shortened form of the long roll. The slash, being the symbol for the cut, also draws attention to the fact that a cut initiates the short roll.

THE CHALLENGES OF CUTS ARE ALSO THE CHALLENGES OF SHORT ROLLS

Another way to look at the difference between the long and short rolls is that the long roll starts with a "plain" note that gives you one eighth-note beat to prepare for doing a cut on the second eighth-note. The cut in the long roll is the easiest of all cuts, one that separates two notes of the same pitch.

The short roll doesn't allow you any preparation time. It starts with its cut right off the bat. That's one reason why the short roll is more challenging to play than the long roll. Since the short roll begins with a cut, most of the issues raised regarding cuts in Chapter 7 apply equally to the short roll. For example, the challenges of cutting notes when ascending or descending to them almost always apply to short rolls.

You will often find that you will want or need to tongue the start of a short roll. In that case, you will be cutting and tonguing at the same time. This is tricky until you've had a lot of practice. If you need clarification on this, see the section *Cutting and Tonguing at the Same Time* in Chapter 7, p. 94.

Remember that when you cut and tongue at the same time, your cutting finger needs to be in the air, not still on the whistle, at the instant that you tongue. If you cut slightly after you tongue you will hear the cut an instant late and the result will be a kind of jumbled double articulation.

NOW THAT THE FOG HAS CLEARED

By now you are thoroughly familiar with my opinion that cuts and strikes are articulations, not notes or grace notes of any kind. Thus you understand that the short roll is a two-note ornament, and not a four-note ornament as it has been almost universally described in published whistle and flute tutors. Figure 11-4 below shows some examples of unfortunate, ill-conceived short-roll notation taken from such books.

Figure 11-4. Examples of ill-conceived short-roll notation taken from published flute and whistle tutors.

All of these examples are incorrect and misleading. None of them look like what a short roll sounds like. None of them accurately convey the rhythm of the short roll. They all imply that the pitch of the cut and strike are perceivable and significant. If anyone, not already knowing what a short roll sounds like, tried to reproduce what is notated in these examples they would not get anything that sounds like a short roll.

Why not notate them the way they *do* sound, especially when that notation is much simpler to read, write, and understand?

THE RHYTHM OF THE SHORT ROLL

This bears repeating: it is critically important to learn to play your short rolls absolutely dead even, each eighth note articulated right on its beat. You will not always want to play them so evenly, but you will need to be able to, especially when playing tunes at fast tempos.

TRY SOME SHORT ROLLS

Try playing the short roll on low G that is shown above in Figure 11-1. You're simply going to play two eighth notes, cutting and tonguing the first one, then slurring into and striking the second one.

Set your metronome at a comfortable tempo somewhere around 60 beats per minute. You are going to play along with the metronome in a cycle (or meter) of three beats, each beat representing an eighth note. Count out the three-beat pattern until you are comfortable with it. Then, on beat one, cut a low G with T2 at the same moment that you tongue it. (Remember: your cutting finger should be in the air at the moment you tongue. If you cut slightly after you tongue you will hear the cut after the arrival of its parent note.) Still playing, and without interrupting the air flow, strike the G with B1 on beat two. On beat three stop, and take a breath if you wish. Try this short roll a few more times.

Experiment as you wish and once you are ready, start again and keep the pattern going (see Exercise 11-1, below).

Exercise 11-1. *Practicing short rolls on G, shown in exploded view.*

Track 62, Index 1

Remember that what you are now playing can also be written as shown in Figure 11-5 below.

Figure 11-5. Practicing short rolls on G, shown in normal view.

Try playing these short rolls in the high register, too. These fingerings, and the ones for the other short rolls you are about to learn, are correct for both registers.

The G short roll is probably the easiest one to play because the labor is divided between your two hands and you are using fingers that for most people are among their most agile ones. The F-sharp short roll is the next easiest one. Set up the metronome as before and play these exercises in the same manner you played Exercise 11-1. Cut with T3 and strike with B2. Leave B1 in place.

Exercise 11-2. *Practicing short rolls on F-sharp, shown in exploded view.*

Track 62, Index 2

Next work with the E short roll. This can be one of the more challenging ones because all of the work is in one hand. Don't forget to lift your bottom hand pinky when it's time to strike the E. Cut with B1 and strike with B3. Leave B2 in place.

Exercise 11-3. *Practicing short rolls on E, shown in exploded view.*

Track 62, Index 3

Here are two exercises for practicing the short rolls we have worked on so far.

Exercise 11-4. *Practicing short rolls on E, F-sharp, and G, in jig rhythm.*

Track 63

Exercise 11-5. *Practicing short rolls on E, F-sharp, and G, in reel rhythm.*

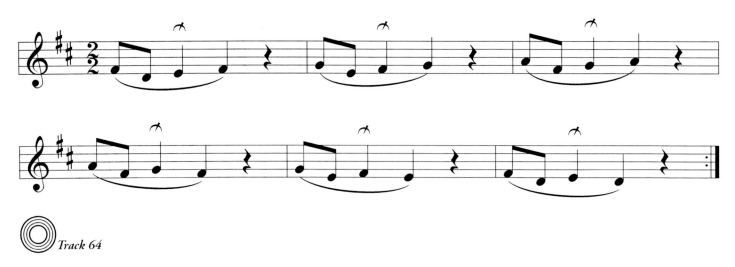

Track 64

USING SHORT ROLLS ON G, F-SHARP, AND E IN *THE SPORTING PITCHFORK*

The following setting of *The Sporting Pitchfork* makes use of the three short rolls we have just been practicing.

As with the tune settings in previous chapters, I have indicated some potential breathing spots by placing commas above the staff. But there are many more breathing opportunities than those so indicated. Each short roll, and long roll, also presents a breathing opportunity.

Whenever a short *or* long roll begins on a pulse you may omit the second note of that roll, thereby creating a silence in which to breathe that is one eighth note in duration. In the previous chapter we saw how that worked with long rolls (see pp. 126-127). When you "break" a short roll, you are in fact no longer playing a short roll, but simply playing an eighth note, and then breathing during the following eighth-note's worth of silence.

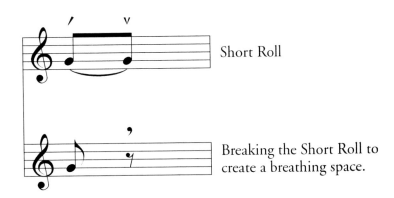

Short Roll

Breaking the Short Roll to
create a breathing space.

Figure 11-6. Comparing the short roll, shown in exploded view, with the short roll broken to create a breathing space.

Track 65

*Figure 11-7. A setting of **The Sporting Pitchfork** using short rolls on G, F-sharp, and E.*

Track 66

MORE SHORT ROLLS

You cannot do a short roll on D because there is no way to strike a D.

Try the A short roll next. This is another of the one-handed rolls, for many people the most difficult one because of the strike with T3, the least agile of the hole-covering fingers for most people. Cut with T1 and strike with T3. Leave T2 in place.

Exercise 11-6. *Practicing short rolls on A, shown in exploded view.*

Track 67, Index 1

Now try the B short roll, which is another one-handed roll. This one feels different because the cutting and striking fingers are adjacent, with no stationary finger between them. Cut with T1 and strike with T2. No finger stays down.

Exercise 11-7. *Practicing short rolls on B, shown in exploded view.*

Track 67, Index 2

Just as with the long roll, don't lose track of the steady beat as you practice your short rolls. When you hear that a cut or strike is early or late, take note of that and return your focus to matching the beat. When you are able to stay on the beat consistently, stay with that comfortable tempo for a while and let your muscles really get to know the feeling of placing these articulations where they belong. In other words, practice doing it right for a while before going on to a faster tempo.

Here are two exercises for practicing all the short rolls.

Exercise 11-8. *Practicing short rolls on E, F-sharp, G, A, and B in jig rhythm.* Note that the B short roll in m. 11 must be tongued. Since it is preceded by a C-sharp, with all finger holds open, this is the only way to sound the cut that begins the B short roll.

Track 68

Exercise 11-9. *Practicing short rolls on E, F-sharp, G, A, and B in reel rhythm.*

Track 69

The following setting of *The Sporting Pitchfork* adds the A and B short rolls to the G, F-sharp and E short rolls.

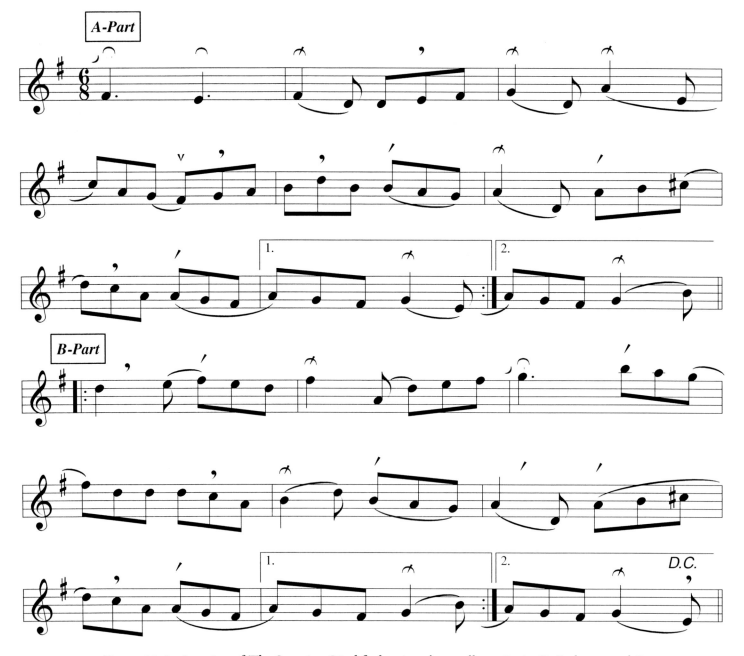

*Figure 11-8. A setting of **The Sporting Pitchfork** using short rolls on B, A, G, F-sharp, and E.*

 Track 70

SUMMARY: ALL FOUR SETTINGS OF *THE SPORTING PITCHFORK*

In Figure 11-9, on pp. 152-153, you may view and compare all four settings of *The Sporting Pitchfork* that are given in this and the preceding chapter. The variations you see here represent only the tip of the iceberg of possibilities, and represent only my own style of playing.

These examples serve to illustrate some possible uses of rolls, cuts, slides, examples of phrasing, and melodic variation. I have put them in score form so that you can easily compare them. Long rolls are introduced in #1 (on E, F-sharp, and G) and #2 (also on A and B), and short rolls in #3 (on E, F-sharp, and G) and #4 (also on A and B).

152

Figure 11-9. The four settings of the jig **The Sporting Pitchfork** given
in Chapters 10 and 11 as figures 10-6, 10-7, 11-7, and 11-8.

MORE SHORT ROLL EXERCISES

Exercise 11-10. *In reel rhythm, practicing short rolls when descending to them stepwise.*

Slur as indicated. Note that you must tongue to sound the B short rolls since they are preceded by C-sharps (all holes open).

Track 71

Exercise 11-11. *In reel rhythm, practicing short rolls when descending to them leapwise (in this case by a third).*

Since each of the following short rolls begins with a leapwise descending cut, you cannot use the normal cut fingering. The optimum cut fingering is shown below the short roll.

Slur as indicated. Note that you must tongue to sound the A short rolls since they are preceded by C-sharps (all holes open).

The B short rolls are preceded by high Ds. You can use either fingering for high D (all holes covered, or venting with T1) and slur from high D into the B short roll. If you use the fingering for high D with all holes covered, you will cut with T1 in the normal manner. If you finger high D with T1 vented, then the cutting finger (T1) is already in the air. Simply put it down an instant after you lift the other five fingers.

153

Track 72

LESS TIME TO PREPARE FOR THE STRIKE

With long rolls, as you reached the point where you could play them well at a normal playing speed, you noticed that the preparation for the strike could begin even before you performed the cut. This lent a grace and fluidity to the feeling of playing the long roll.

With the short roll, things are a bit trickier. You rarely have the time or opportunity to start the preparation for the strike before the cut that begins the short roll. Often, the finger that will be striking is busy doing something else just before the short roll begins.

So, once you get short rolls up to speed you should begin the preparation for the strike at the same time that you perform the cut. Thus you will be lifting two fingers at approximately the same time, the cutting finger and the striking finger preparing to strike.

HOW SHORT ROLLS RELATE TO THE PULSE

Whereas long rolls can be placed in a number of different ways relative to the pulse (see *How Long Rolls Relate to the Pulse* on pp. 137-142 in Chapter 10), short rolls seem to be appropriate in a more limited range of rhythmic contexts. In reels, you never seem to hear them beginning on a beat that is not either a primary or secondary pulse. You could use them in this way, but I feel that when you do so they draw too much attention to non-pulse beats. An example of this awkward-sounding use of a short roll appears below in a variant on the beginning of *Lad O'Beirne's Reel*. (Note also the mid-note cut on G in the first bar.)

*Figure 11-10. A variant on the start of **Lad O'Beirne's Reel** demonstrating an awkward-sounding short roll that begins on a non-pulse beat.*

Track 73

A more musical way of playing this appears in Figure 11-11. Note that a short roll begins on a primary pulse in this example.

154

*Figure 11-11. A more musical variant on the start of **Lad O'Beirne's Reel**.*

Track 74

Another way that many people play the beginning of this reel is shown in Figure 11-12 below.

*Figure 11-12. A common way to play the start of **Lad O'Beirne's Reel**.*

Track 75

In jigs, short rolls can be used starting on pulse or non-pulse beats, though it is uncommon to encounter them starting on non-pulse beats. Here is an example of a short roll starting on a pulse in the single jig *The Lonesome Jig* (also know as *The Rolling Waves, McGuire's March,* and *Maguire's Kick*). Note the mid-note cut in the first bar.

*Figure 11-13. A short roll in the first two bars of **The Lonesome Jig**.*

Track 76

In the next example, we see an appropriate use of short rolls starting on non-pulse beats, namely the second beat in the group of three. This is the beginning of the jig *Tripping Up the Stairs*. Care should be taken to play these short rolls gently so as not to overemphasize the non-pulse beats.

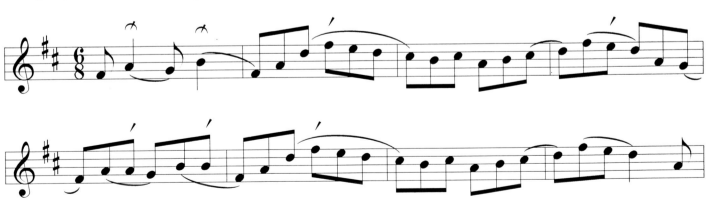

*Figure 11-14. Short rolls in the opening bars of the jig **Tripping Up the Stairs**.*

Track 77

Note that Figure 11-14 could also be notated using mid-note cuts in the fifth bar, as shown in Figure 11-15 below.

Figure 11-15. The music of Figure 11-14 notated with mid-note cuts.

Here is an exercise for practicing this kind of short roll.

Exercise 11-12. *In jig rhythm, practicing short rolls that begin on the second eighth-note beat.*

Track 78

The following interpretation of the jig *The Frost is All Over* shows an example of a short roll starting on the third beat of a group of three eighth notes.

*Figure 11-16. A variant on the opening bars of the jig **The Frost is All Over**.*

Track 79

Once again, care should be taken not to overemphasize the cut of this short roll. The struck note, which falls on the pulse, should get more weight than the cut note.

156

Here are two exercises for practicing this kind of short roll.

Exercise 11-13. *In jig rhythm, practicing short rolls that begin on the third eighth-note beat.* Slur as indicated. Note that you must tongue to sound the second B short roll since it is preceded by C-sharp (all holes open).

Track 80

A Short Roll Preceded by an Eighth Note of the Same Pitch, or is it a Long Roll?

Sometimes a long roll may be interpreted as a short roll preceded by an eighth note of the same pitch, especially when the cut note of the long roll falls on a pulse and is thus emphasized. This is not really wrong, for the last two notes of a long roll are identical to the elements of a short roll. The only factor that really distinguishes these two interpretations is that the notes of any roll, according to my definition, are always slurred together. So, if all three notes in question are slurred together, I would say that there is a long roll being played. If only the last two notes are slurred together, then I would call it a short roll preceded by an eighth note of the same pitch.

Figures 11-17 and 11-18 below show an example of this situation in which only the last two notes are slurred, forming a short roll.

Figure 11-17. An example of a short roll preceded by an eighth note of the same pitch, shown in normal view.

Track 81

Figure 11-18. The same example as Figure 11-17 shown in exploded view.
This shows more clearly that only the last two notes are slurred, forming a short roll.

Figures 11-19 and 11-20 show the same musical example with all three E notes slurred together, thus forming a long roll on E. The distinction between the sounds of these two examples is fairly subtle.

Figure 11-19. The same notes as in Figure 11-17, but played here with a long roll on E.

Figure 11-20. The same example as Figure 11-19 shown in exploded view.
This shows more clearly that the last three notes are slurred, forming a long roll.

Let's look at how both of these variants can be used in the same tune, in this case the first part of the reel *The Drunken Landlady.*

Figure 11-21. The first part of the reel **The Drunken Landlady.**

Comparing the beginnings of the first two measures, the short roll in measure two, with its tongued cut, gives a slight emphasis to the third eighth-note beat. The long roll in measure one has a smoother feeling because we slur into the cut note on the third eighth-note beat. It is a subtle variation, but one that helps develop the rhythmic landscape of the tune.

UNEVEN SHORT ROLLS

Short rolls that occur in hornpipes, mazurkas, schottisches, or other tunes that are played with an overtly uneven underlying rhythm, are played to go along with that uneven rhythm. In these situations, the struck note is delayed but the cut note remains on the beat. I explore this more in *The Essential Guide to Irish Flute and Tin Whistle.*

The kind of uneven playing that is discussed on pp. 141-142 in the previous chapter, i.e. long rolls in which the cut note is somewhat delayed, does not apply in the case of short rolls. Since the short roll begins with the cut note, that note cannot be delayed without serious damage being done. As we have seen from the examples above, when a short roll is used it is almost always placed so as to give emphasis and draw attention to the cut note. Therefore the cut's rhythmic placement must be accurate.

The cut note in the long roll can take on a variety of "characters." It can be strong and emphatic or it can be gentle and subtle. Since it is a note *internal* to the roll, it can be delayed. Not so with the cut in the short roll. It initiates the short roll and so cannot be delayed.

SLIDING INTO THE SHORT ROLL

This subject was discussed in regard to long rolls at the end of the last chapter. There is nothing much different about sliding into a short roll except that when you do so you are also sliding into a cut.

THE ASCENDING ROLL

You can take the idea of sliding into a long roll to its extreme, resulting in a long roll variant that I call an *ascending roll.* Instead of lowering the pitch of the first note momentarily with a slide, in this case you actually play the entire first note one scale step lower than normal. Mary Bergin does this in *Old Joe's Jig,* which appears on her first recording.[i] Figures 11-22 and 11-23 show how the opening of *Old Joe's Jig* could be played without, and then with an ascending roll.

*Figure 11-22. The opening bars of **Old Joe's Jig** beginning with long rolls, shown in normal view.*

Track 84

*Figure 11-23. The opening bars of **Old Joe's Jig** beginning with an ascending roll, which is shown in exploded view.*

Track 85

Is this an altered long roll, or is it really just a short roll preceded by an eighth note?

*Figure 11-24. The opening bars of **Old Joe's Jig** shown beginning with an ascending roll, which is notated using the short roll symbol.*

Good question. I don't have a good answer and I'm not sure that it matters very much. Since most players think of this place in the tune as a long roll on F-sharp, I suppose I would consider this ascending roll to be a variant on that idea. The fact that all three notes are slurred together further supports this.

But since there is an easy way to notate what is happening here using already existing symbols (as in Figure 11-24), I don't feel there's a reason to invent a new symbol for the ascending roll.

[i] Mary Bergin, Feadóga Stáin: *Traditional Irish Music on the Tin Whistle.* Shanachie Records, 1979. 79006.

❖ section 3 ❖

———

tonguing,
phrasing,
and
use of the breath

chapter 12: tonguing

TONGUING AND SLURRING DEFINED

To **tongue**, in the musical terminology of wind instruments, means to use an action of the tongue to articulate or separate notes. You can use the tongue to stop and to start the flow of air.

To **slur** means to connect two or more notes such that only the first note of the group is articulated. A slurred group of notes is played using an uninterrupted, continuous stream of air.

All the air that we blow through our whistles must first pass over our tongues. The tongue is an exquisitely agile, eloquent, and sensitive organ. We have already trained it to an extremely high degree through our mastery of everyday speech.

Every time we use the consonants c, d, g, j, k, l, n, q, s, t, and z, we articulate these sounds with the tongue, and we also use it in more subtle ways to help shape most of the other sounds of speech.

THE PHYSICAL ACTION OF TONGUING

To get a feel for proper whistle tonguing, try the following:

Whisper the syllable "too" and notice where and how your tongue contacts the roof of your mouth. It should touch the hard palate just slightly behind your upper teeth, but not touching the teeth. Now take a deep breath and place your tongue back on that spot. Again, whispering "too," pull your tongue away from the roof of your mouth, but not very far, just a fraction of an inch. This releases your reservoir of air to travel through your lips.

The way that you place and release your tongue determines the consonant of the sound (*t, d, l,* etc.) while the shape of your mouth cavity (which is also determined in large part by your tongue) determines the vowel of the sound (*oo, oh, ah, eh,* etc.). Of course, when playing Irish music you don't give voice to such vowel sounds. We refer to them here simply to help us recognize the shaping that we can give to the mouth cavity. (Actually some players of older generations did occasionally voice vowel sounds while playing. Willy Clancy was one of them. For more on this, see the notes to the transcription of his tin whistle recording of the reel *Woman of the House* in *The Essential Guide to Irish Flute and Tin Whistle.*)

When your tongue is in contact with the roof of your mouth, it prevents air from flowing through. When you pull your tongue away, air is suddenly allowed to flow. You have a great deal of subtle control over how you place, shape, and release your tongue.

RELAXATION AND ECONOMY OF MOTION

Your tongue has a resting position, just as your playing fingers do. When you pull your tongue back from the roof of your mouth, let it relax. Don't place it against your lower teeth or pull it back into your throat. The principles of relaxation and economy of motion apply here, as in every aspect of playing.

When you tongue in whistle playing, your embouchure must be prepared beforehand and it must remain stable. Articulation (performed by the tongue) and air stream shaping and direction (performed by the lips and facial muscles) are separate and distinct. Your jaw need not move at all when you tongue.

GRADATIONS OF TONGUING: SEPARATE VS. CONNECTED, HARD VS. SOFT

There are many subtle aspects of tonguing. Let's look first at how we use tonguing to interrupt and reinitiate the air stream.

When first learning to tongue, the natural inclination is to produce very separate, distinct notes. In doing so, you first whisper the letter "t" to give a clear attack to the start of the flow of air. In this action, you pull your tongue down and away from the hard palate. Second, you replace your tongue to stop the air. After a brief pause you repeat this two-step process.

This way of playing, all with well-separated notes, is sometimes called **staccato** by classical musicians. The Harvard Dictionary of Music defines staccato more specifically as "…a manner of performance, indicated by a dot…placed over the note, calling for a reduction of its written duration…for half or more of its value."[i] A staccato eighth note, for example, would be sustained for at most the length of a normal sixteenth note, that is half or less of its nominal duration.

After some experience with tonguing, one discovers that it is possible to reduce the separateness of tongued notes to almost nothing, to make them very smoothly connected. To do this you use a different sort of tonguing action. Instead of using a two-step process, as described above, in which the air stream is alternately and distinctly started and stopped, you use a one-step process in which the air flow is barely interrupted at all.

Instead of using a hard consonant sound like "t," try using a softer one like "d." When saying "d" in the softest possible way, the tongue action is a gentle "flicking" of the roof of the mouth. This consonant sound comes to resemble the gentle "r" sound of Spanish. Try whispering "doo, doo, doo…" in this smooth and gentle way. You'll notice that the tip of your tongue just barely brushes the hard palate as it goes by.

Playing in this manner produces notes that are softly articulated and very smoothly connected. This manner of playing is what classical musicians call **legato** playing. The Harvard Dictionary of Music defines legato as a manner of performance "…without any perceptible interruption between the notes."[ii] ("Perceptible" is the key word here.) For a wind player, the most legato playing possible is, of course, manifested in the slurring together of notes.

Think of how a fiddler changes the direction of her bowstrokes. An experienced player can do this in an exceedingly smooth fashion, yet theoretically there is by necessity a very brief, barely perceptible interruption in the flow of sound when the bow changes direction. The same potential for smooth articulation exists for tonguing.

In tonguing, there are wide areas of gradation between the extremes of staccato and legato, hard and soft. All of these qualities have a place in Irish music. But to understand their proper places, you must first understand the following.

THE PASTORAL BAGPIPES, THE *PÍOB MÓR,* AND THE AESTHETIC OF LEGATO PLAYING

As has been discussed in Chapter 1, Irish tin whistle and flute stylings owe a great deal to the legacy of the uilleann pipes, which in turn developed out of the older pastoral bagpipe and *píob mór* traditions. These bagpipes could only play in a legato, slurred fashion, with a continuous, unbroken stream of air. Articulations were created solely by the fingers (cuts and strikes) and they did not interrupt the air flow.

Whistle, flute, and uilleann pipe players today don't use these finger articulations out of necessity, as pastoral pipers and *píob mór* players did, but because they are incorporating an established traditional mode of musical expression that had evolved in these older piping traditions.

The uilleann pipes developed into an instrument with a capability very different from those of the pastoral bagpipe and *píob mór:* the ability to stop the flow of air through the chanter by covering all the finger holes while stopping the end of the chanter on the knee. This made staccato playing possible.

In fact, some uilleann pipers play in a predominantly staccato fashion. This is called *tight* or *close* piping and is exemplified by such players as Tommy Reck.[iii]

Uilleann pipers, tin whistle players, and Irish flute players *all* inherited a fundamental and deeply held legato aesthetic from these ancestral bagpipe traditions, and combined it with their own staccato playing capabilities to create a new synthesis: **The music, in all its variety, springs forth from an underlying foundation of legato playing. The appropriate use of staccato playing exists in relation to that foundation, and takes on its meaning in contrast to it.**

Within this broad synthesis exist many different styles of playing, some of which make extensive use of the air-interrupting articulations of tonguing. Nonetheless, they all hearken back to this common root.

As a matter of fact, all of the contemporary melodic instruments of traditional Irish music, including the fiddle, accordion, banjo, etc., derive their styles of playing ultimately from this same piping legacy.

CONTRAST THIS WITH THE CLASSICAL WIND PLAYERS' ORIENTATION

This legato aesthetic is essentially different from that of modern classical music. The classical wind player is taught that all notes are to be tongued unless there is an indication in the notated music, such as a slur, to do otherwise. Most Irish players use tonguing intuitively as a phrasing device *against a general backdrop of slurring*. Classically-trained musicians who wish to learn to play traditional Irish music must come to understand this critical distinction. Tonguing is used extensively in both traditions, but in each it is thought of in very different ways.

A GREATER VARIETY OF ARTICULATION

It seems to me that the traditional Irish musician has a greater variety of articulation available to her than the modern classical wind player has. In classical wind playing, notes are *either* articulated *or* slurred. In Irish traditional music notes can be articulated *and* slurred, because of its fingered articulations, the cut and strike. Classical wind players do not have a common practice of fingered articulations.

THE SUBTLE USE OF TONGUING

Much of the tonguing used in Irish tin whistle playing goes unnoticed because it does not take the music away from its fundamentally legato nature.

ACHIEVING BALANCE

Within the fundamental legato aesthetic of Irish music, there is room for a wide variety of approaches to the question of playing notes in a connected or separated fashion. You should avoid rigid or arbitrary adherence to any concept of how you think you should be playing. If you play all legato or all staccato, the music will be restricted, unable to breathe.

Instead, let your choices be dictated by the music and how you feel about it, how it speaks to you, how you feel moved to express it in the moment. These choices should arise from within you, not be imposed upon the music from the outside, and not predetermined. If you approach the music in this natural way, you will find a balance of staccato and legato, connected and separated playing, that will be your own. The music will be set free and it will breathe.

SINGLE TONGUING AND MULTIPLE TONGUING

The tonguing techniques we have looked at so far fall into the category of **single tonguing**. In single tonguing, one repeatedly uses only one tongue action, represented by a single consonant sound such as "t" or "d". Though we can be quite agile with single tonguing, it is ultimately limited, especially at fast tempos.

Though this is an imperfect analogy, it is instructive to compare the movement of the tongue with the movement of a plectrum by players of the tenor banjo, guitar, or other plucked string instruments. If a tenor banjo player could only use the downstroke of her pick and never the upstroke, she would eventually tire from the repetitive and excessive movement that is required. Using both downstrokes and upstrokes is physically much more efficient and relaxing, and it allows for more agility and fluidity, especially in rapid passages.

We have a similar situation with repetitive single tonguing. Though it may not be as physically tiring as using only downstrokes on the plectrum banjo, there can be a uniformity of sound that comes from using only one tongue action over and over. **Multiple tonguing,** a way of tonguing that makes use of sequences of differing tongue articulations, yields a variety of articulations that can give the music a much more interesting sound. I address multiple tonguing in depth in my book *The Essential Guide to Irish Flute and Tin Whistle.*

---

[i] Willi Apel, *Harvard Dictionary of Music,* 20th printing (Cambridge, Massachusetts: Harvard University Press, 1968), p. 708.

[ii] Willi Apel, p. 396.

[iii] Tommy Reck, *A Stone in the Field* (Danbury, Connecticut: Green Linnet Records, SIF 1008, 1977). Reck also appears on the uilleann pipe anthology *The Drones and the Chanters* (Dublin: Claddagh Records, CC11, 1971). He recorded two 78 sides for the Irish Recording Company (Dublin) in the 1950s. One of these was reissued on *From Galway to Dublin* (Cambridge, Massachusetts: Rounder Records, CD 1087, 1993). He also recorded two 78 sides for Gael-Linn, ca. 1959, but those have not been reissued as of this writing.

chapter 13: musical breathing

The tin whistle and flute are the only instruments of traditional Irish music that are not suited to nonstop playing.

One could see this as a disadvantage. But one can also look at it another way. Since we must create occasional small spaces in the tunes in order to breathe, we tin whistle players are never allowed to forget that music itself needs a chance to breathe once in a while. We *must* breathe, so why not use breathing spaces to enhance our phrasing and clarify how we define musical shapes?

Fine players of other instruments use space in this way too, even though most of them don't have to. Of course singers, the ones who many consider to be the most expressive musicians of all, must leave breathing spaces in their music, just as whistle players must do, and for the same reasons. Insightful instrumentalists know how important it is to make their instruments "sing." A major aspect of achieving this is the creation of space.

One could overcome this apparent limitation by using circular breathing. Later in the chapter I'll elaborate a bit on why I don't recommend this.

THE LANGUAGE ANALOGY RESURFACES

As I wrote in Chapter 6, when speaking we have an intuitive, automatic sense of when it is appropriate to breathe. We do not disrupt meaning by breathing in the middle of a phrase. In fact, we use the necessity of breathing to shape our speech and enhance its clarity and meaning. We use breathing for punctuation. We know that pausing gives emphasis to the next words we speak. So it is in playing the whistle.

All musicians can apply this kind of subtle shaping, or punctuation, to their music. Unfortunately, many don't. For whistle players, pausing for breath is built into the very act of playing. We must learn how to use breathing articulately, in ways that illuminate our interpretation of the music.

ARTICULATE AND INARTICULATE BREATHING

Articulate breathing has the effect of making clear the phrasing and natural contours of a tune. Inarticulate breathing disrupts the music and draws attention to itself.

Often after concerts, listeners come to me and say something like, "It's amazing, you never breathe when you play!" I take this as a high compliment because, though I take frequent, deep breaths, I do so quickly, quietly, and as an integral part of my musical expression. When this is done well, a listener's attention is never drawn to the breathing but only to musical phrasing. Breathing has become my servant, not my master.

NOTE OMISSION AND NOTE SHORTENING

We whistle players must become artistic music editors. *We must learn to omit notes and shorten longer notes* in a musically sensitive way. One can almost never sneak a breath between the notes of an Irish dance tune without detracting from the music. This can only be done successfully on occasion in slow airs and other slow or moderate tunes.

It is revealing to discover that not every note of a tune is indispensable. You can leave certain notes out without compromising the tune. On the other hand, there are many notes that you must not omit, and you must learn to discern the difference.

Note omission and note-shortening choices are fluid; they change all the time, depending upon numerous factors such as varying tempos, whether you are sitting or standing, how well rested or tired you are (which affects how deeply you breathe), whether or not you just ate a large meal, even the altitude of the locale.

Classical musicians often choose and stick with consistent breathing places in each piece of music they play. Many composers who write for wind instruments wisely incorporate rests to accommodate breathing. Leaving out any of a composer's carefully chosen notes is usually frowned upon in classical music.

In Irish music, each player adapts the music in certain ways to her instrument. The whistle player creates her needed breathing spots spontaneously, according to the requirements and moods of the moment. This is, after all, an improvisational music, though extemporization exists within fairly conservative limits in comparison to that of musical genres such as jazz.

Note omission and note shortening contribute in important ways to melodic variation. Soon I will illustrate this with some examples.

WHAT IS A TUNE ANYWAY?

These realizations bring up such questions as: Just what is a tune? Or, what are the "real" notes of a tune?

I don't have a simple answer, but an Irish tune is certainly not an established, unchanging, and unbroken sequence of notes, as you might presume by looking in the numerous printed collections that are available. A tune is something much more fluid and multidimensional, something large and living that music notation cannot contain. When we leave notes out, shorten notes, and change the melody in small ways that are appropriate within the language of Irish music, we are staying true to the tune and keeping it alive.

Each tune has an essence that makes it immediately recognizable, beautiful, and whole, and it carries rich personal associations for the player. With maturity and experience, one comes to intuitively grasp the spirit of a tune and shape it in one's own way.

BREATHE BEFORE YOU HAVE TO

To breathe articulately, you must first attend to the physical requirements of deep breathing and the efficient use of your air supply. These topics are covered in depth in Chapter 3. Plentiful air, and the economic use of it, give you many breathing options.

You may have noticed that when you are about to run out of air your musical energy suffers. If you don't breathe well in the first place, or you use your air inefficiently, then you may not have noticed this, because you may almost always be short of air. When air becomes plentiful for you, you can play with strong, vibrant energy and breath support. It then becomes much easier to breath musically, instead of habitually breathing out of need.

NOTE OMISSION AND NOTE SHORTENING BECOME SECOND NATURE

Like so many other technical aspects of playing this music, note omission and note shortening need to become second nature. As you establish the habit of always tuning in to your body, you will continually be aware of your air supply status. This awareness will be relegated to some subsurface level of your mind, which will keep track of your air while you are occupied with having fun playing music. When you are approaching low air supply, you will feel it in your body, and you will improvise a tasteful way to musically leave out or shorten a note, take a quick, deep breath, and continue on your merry way with a plentiful stock of air. When you do leave out a note in order to breathe, you can still hear that note in your mind's ear if you like. If leaving out a note sometimes derails you or throws you off the tune, try hearing the omitted note in your mind.

These abilities will steadily improve as you become more adept at controlling your breathing and embouchure, and as your knowledge and command of the musical language deepen.

NEVER OMIT A NOTE THAT FALLS ON A PULSE

It is crucial that you never omit a note, or a part of a longer note, that falls on a primary or secondary pulse, unless you wish to create a very conspicuous syncopation (i.e. a strong emphasis on a beat that is normally not emphasized). Omitting an on-pulse note is definitely not consistent with the language of traditional Irish music and represents the epitome of inarticulate breathing. If you omit such a note, knowledgeable players, listeners, and dancers will feel that you are punching a gaping hole into the flow of the tune. If you choose to do so anyway, for dramatic effect, know that you are tinkering with one of the fundamental underpinnings of the music and that many people may see this as an indication of inexperience.

DEVELOP AN ABSOLUTELY DEPENDABLE SENSE OF THE PULSE

It is one thing to understand that you shouldn't omit an on-pulse note. It is quite another to know by second nature which notes those are. You must develop an absolutely reliable sense of the pulse in the tunes you play. *This is the cornerstone of choosing good breathing spots.* A rock-solid sense of the pulse makes breathing choices far easier. Never omitting on-pulse notes narrows the field of candidates for note omission by as much as one-third (in jigs and slip jigs) or one-half (in reels).

If it is difficult for you to sense the pulse of a tune when you play, this means that you need to work on internalizing the music and feeling its rhythms in your body. Learning to dance to the music is a great way to do this. Tapping your foot on the pulse helps many players.

Some cannot play without tapping their foot. When tapping however, be sensitive to those around you. If you tap loudly you may be annoying others. If your loud tapping is not rhythmically accurate, there is no doubt that you are annoying others, whether or not they have the nerve to tell you so.

BREATHING SPOTS IN *THE BANKS OF LOUGH GOWNA*

Below, you will find three settings of the jig *The Banks of Lough Gowna*. The first setting, shown on the top staff, is notated in typical fashion, with no breathing spots indicated. The second and third settings show examples of appropriate breathing places with the kinds of musical adjustments a whistle player might make to incorporate these spaces tastefully into the tune. The location of these breathing spots are indicated with rests and with the comma symbol above each rest.

Also, take note of the variations in ornamentation and phrasing and the small melodic changes that I have incorporated into the second and third settings of the tune.

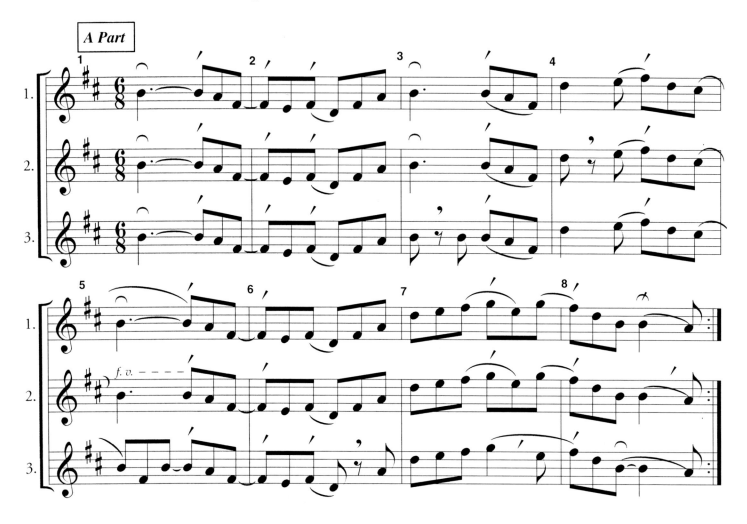

Figure 13-1. Three settings of the jig **The Banks of Lough Gowna.** *The top staff shows the tune without breathing spaces, as one might encounter it in a tune book. Examples of appropriate breathing spaces are shown in the second and third staves. The comma symbol above the staff indicates a breath. The indication "f. v." in measure 5 of the second setting indicates the use of finger vibrato on the dotted quarter note B.*

 *Tracks 86 (staff 2) and 87 (staff 3)*

These breathing places demonstrate three different breathing strategies. Let's take a close look at them.

BREATHING STRATEGY #1: SHORTENING A LONG NOTE

In most dance tunes, though the eighth note is the prevailing subdivision of the pulse, you will find notes that are longer than an eighth note. You can often shorten such notes by one eighth-note's duration, taking a breath during the resulting rest or silence, without disrupting the flow of the tune.

But remember – you never want to leave out a note, or a *part* of a note, that falls on a pulse. Shortening a long note works only if the part of the note you are omitting occurs *off* the pulse. Fortunately, in traditional Irish tunes, this is almost always the case with the longer notes one encounters.

Use of this strategy can be seen in measure 4 of the second setting. Here I shorten a D quarter note to a D eighth note followed by an eighth-note rest.

BREATHING STRATEGY #2: BREAKING A LONG OR SHORT ROLL

This strategy works *only* when the long or short roll begins on a primary or secondary pulse. When a long or short roll starts on a pulse, the second note of that roll necessarily falls on a weak, non-pulse beat and can usually be omit-

169

ted to create a breathing opportunity without disrupting the flow of the tune. Of course, when you do this you no longer have a roll, so you can use whatever articulations you like for the note or notes that remain.

Straightforward examples of this occur in measure 9 of the second setting and measure 3 of the third setting.

The example in measure 12 of the third setting is a bit different. When simply breaking the long roll that is played in measure 12 of the first setting, the result would be a G eighth note, followed by an eighth-note rest, followed by another G eighth note. However, the new phrase (after the newly-created breathing spot) sounds better if you change that last G eighth note to an E. The insight to spontaneously make such changes comes with a deepening knowledge of the language of Irish music, and this can only come from extensive listening and playing.

If you try this breathing strategy with a long or short roll that begins on a non-pulse beat, you will very quickly hear why it doesn't work. For example, take a look at the first two measures of the reel *The Drunken Landlady*.

*Figure 13-2. The first two measures of the reel **The Drunken Landlady**.*

Track 88

These long rolls on E begin on weak, non-pulse beats. If you leave out the middle note of either roll, as shown below, then nothing happens on the secondary pulse and you get a non-idiomatic "hiccupping" effect. A better example of inarticulate breathing in traditional Irish music could hardly be found.

*Figure 13-3. The first two measures of the reel **The Drunken Landlady** showing an example of inarticulate breathing produced by breaking a long roll that begins on a non-pulse beat.*

Track 89

BREATHING STRATEGY #3: OMITTING A "NON-ESSENTIAL" NOTE

Most notes are essential to the spirit and shape of a tune but some are not. Such "non-essential" notes can often be omitted without any ill effect. Their omission can in fact become a refreshing variation in itself. That is why people often don't notice that a breath is occurring in such instances. They are enjoying the well-shaped phrases of music that are caressing their ears, or urging on their dancing feet, and they feel no disruption to the flow of the music. (Or could it be the compelling conversation they're having with someone across the table?)

These nonessential notes almost never occur on primary or secondary pulses. (In fact I can't think of any examples where they do.) What does that leave? Only non-pulse notes. An example can be seen in measure 6 of the third setting of *The Banks of Lough Gowna*, above. The F-sharp in question is a note that links two phrases together, just as the word "and" is used in the second to last sentence of the preceding paragraph (the one that begins, "They are enjoying…" — go back and take a look). When the note is omitted, the two musical phrases remain perfectly intact, but their relationship is changed in an interesting way. Applying this idea to that sentence in the last paragraph, it is as if you had removed the "and" and put in a semicolon. The sense is the same, but the rhythm, phrasing, and some shadings of meaning have changed.

BREATHING AT THE END OF A PART

The A part or B part of a tune will often end in a way that presents an ideal breathing spot, using one of the above strategies. *The Banks of Lough Gowna,* however, is not such a tune. The end of one part continues beautifully into the next and it would be a pity to break the connection. For an example of a tune that does offer such opportunities, see the various settings of the jig *The Sporting Pitchfork* in Figure 11-9 on pp. 152-153.

You will come across many more tunes that offer this breathing option. Even with such tunes, it is often a pleasure to not breathe in those obvious places and instead carry the energy right into the next part of the tune.

DON'T LET BREATHING INTERFERE WITH NATURAL MUSICAL CONTOURS OR FORWARD MOTION

There are plenty of breathing opportunities that fall beautifully into one of these three strategies, but taking advantage of them may nevertheless be disruptive to the tune. This is because such notes are sometimes needed to define the natural contours of the melody or to help maintain its forward motion.

To see what I mean, let's look again at the first two measures of the reel *The Drunken Landlady.*

Figure 13-4. The first two measures of the reel **The Drunken Landlady.**

Below you will see an example of inarticulate breathing in this tune excerpt. I have omitted the last note of the first measure, a non-pulse note that might at first seem to serve simply as a connecting note.

Figure 13-5. The first two measures of the reel **The Drunken Landlady** *with an example of inarticulate breathing.*

In my opinion, this note is an essential note, even though it might at first seem to fit the description of strategy #3. Its omission is too disruptive of the upward sweep and forward motion of the melody.

If you want to breathe somewhere in these measures, you would do better to choose the option shown below in Figure 13-6.

Figure 13-6. An example of an articulate breathing spot in the first two measures of the reel **The Drunken Landlady.**

171

CIRCULAR BREATHING

If you could use circular breathing you could play tunes without ever having to break the constant flow of notes. Wouldn't that be wonderful?

Well, I'm not so sure. Circular breathing is quite difficult on the whistle because the instrument offers so little air resistance or "back pressure." The very few times I have heard it attempted on the whistle the result has sounded anemic, not to mention monotonous.

It is true that the method of air supply for bagpipes is basically a mechanical equivalent of circular breathing. If you mastered circular breathing on the whistle, perhaps you could sound more like a piper. It would be very challenging, though perhaps not impossible, to manage the mechanics of circular breathing, produce a strong and supple tone and still be completely free to use tonguing and note omission in a fully musical way.

I am not an uilleann piper, but I would think that it would be very easy for uilleann pipers to fall into a pattern of playing in an overly verbose, unpunctuated fashion. The use of tight or closed fingerings to produce staccato notes and create space provides one way for pipers to avoid this hazard.

Traditional music very often takes a natural characteristic of an instrument, even when it seems to be a limitation, and turns it into an essential and beautiful element of the art. The implications of non-circular breathing have had a huge impact on the evolution of traditional Irish tin whistle styles over many, many decades. This is a rich legacy in which we have the privilege of partaking. If you wish to explore the possibilities of circular breathing go right ahead, but be careful not to injure the music. And remember, taking a breath is a pleasant thing in life.

SUBTLE BREATH PULSE OR WEIGHT

The flow of air that you blow is much like the hair of the fiddler's bow as it travels across the string. Just as a fiddler can change the pressure and speed of her bowstrokes to emphasize certain notes and to impart rhythmic stress, weight, or impulse, you can give such life to your music with changes in the qualities of your breath. Just as a fiddler can "lean into" the bow, you can "lean into" the breath. I elaborate upon this in Chapter 10, in the sections *Rhythmic Emphasis Within the Long Roll* and *It's Alive — It Has a Pulse,* which appear on pp. 136-137.

❖ section 4 ❖

——

final matters

chapter 14: the language analogy revisited

Now that we have thoroughly explored ornamentation, variation, blowing, phrasing, articulation, and use of the breath, you can see that the depth of Irish tin whistle playing is comparable to the richness of your native language. The possibilities for expression are truly endless.

We have seen how spoken language and tin whistle playing exhibit many parallels in the areas of breath, articulation, phrasing, punctuation, intonation, and inflection; how both embody variation, improvisation, embellishment, and the interpretation of large, complex structures.

REACHING FLUENCY

If you have not grown up immersed in traditional Irish music, then you can also see that learning it is something akin to learning a foreign language. In the early stages you have to give most of your attention to the details and mechanics of the language and the techniques of producing the proper sounds. As your mastery grows, these small scale characteristics become more and more second nature and you are able to continually shift your focus to the larger scale aspects of the language, eventually achieving fluency: the ability to express yourself readily and effortlessly, to think and "speak" in the new language without internal, mental translation. As you progress in this way, your view of the new world that this language makes possible becomes ever wider and wiser.

As you have worked your way through this book, you have been progressing toward fluency in the language of Irish music. Continued playing, listening, and practice will take you ever further down that road. If you are not there yet, you can look forward to a time when you will no longer need to think about the individual elements of ornamentation, about where and how to ornament, about where and how to breathe, about when or how to slide into or out of a note. All of these tools and techniques will simply be at your fingertips, ready to be called upon by your intuition.

With fluency, you can stay in the intuitive, emotional, playful, and interactive part of your mind and spirit. You no longer have to be analytical, though you may choose to be. As your technical prowess and confidence grow, you will continue to relegate technique to muscle memory, freeing the conscious layers of your mind to be more creative, expressive, and interactive. We'll look more at muscle memory in the next chapter.

FROM MONOLOGUE TO CONVERSATION TO COMMUNION

With fluency comes the ability to communicate with others on the highest levels.

Unlike spoken conversation, in Irish instrumental music we "converse" by playing all at the same time. This is not workable in speech. The closest thing to it I can imagine would be a group of people reciting or chanting a poem together, each interpreting it and improvising on it harmoniously while keeping to the meter—or a group of singers improvising together on a song, but then we have left speech and entered back into music.

With this music, becoming fully "conversational" means that you are able to listen so expansively that you are completely aware of what and how you are playing, and, at the same time, you are listening beautifully to the other musicians around you. (Just as you can play beautifully, you can listen with a quality of beauty.) Each musician hears and understands the expressions of the others and all simultaneously tailor their playing such that they bring forth a musical entity that is greater than the sum of its parts. This is the ideal music session, the transcendent experience that Irish musicians live for.

The same kind of expansive interaction can extend outward from a group of musicians to include dancers and listeners.

MUSIC, LIKE LANGUAGE, BECOMES A MIRROR AND A PROJECTOR

As you become fluent and eloquent in Irish music, it becomes a mirror and a projector of your soul. The way you speak reveals and expresses a great deal about who you are and how you see the world. The same is true of playing music, but the "light" that music reflects back to you and projects out to others is of a wholly different spectrum than that of spoken, symbolic language. How does one describe it? Here words truly do fail. But when you listen to the playing of a master musician, you "know" something of their soul, immediately and intimately, and you can feel your own beautiful potential in the unique mirror that their music holds before you.

With growing mastery, the musical waters become clear. The spiritual nature of the music is revealed and becomes apparent to anyone who is receptive to it. In the playing/listening experience, the illusion of separateness begins to dissolve. All master musicians experience the insight that their music does not originate in them but instead flows through them. They become an instrument of something greater. Perhaps the non-symbolic language of music provides a more direct route to this insight than verbal language can.

LOOKING UP INTO A TREE

Being fully musical, like being fully alive, calls for us to learn to be widely perceptive and functional on a variety of planes simultaneously. Here's an illustration, in an experience that we can all have.

One beautiful day, while talking with my young daughter in our backyard, we lay down under a tulip poplar tree. I lay on my back, with the top of my head touching the trunk, and gazed upward. It was a warm, sunny spring day and a very gentle breeze moved through the leaves. I saw the single trunk, the major limbs, the many smaller branches, and the myriad of twigs, which gave rise to tens of thousands of green stems and leaves. The leaves drank in the sunlight and moved in a thousand-fold unison dance to the constantly shifting air. I could see, feel, and take it in *all at once:* the trunk, which continued deep below my back into the soil of the earth and gave unity and structure to the whole tree, the large limbs that divided themselves into smaller branches, all the way out to the tips of the leaves which drank in the sunlight and the atmosphere.

I realized that this way of experiencing the tree, something we can all do if we create a few moments of quiet, is just like the ideal of being fully musical. Imagine that the tree is a tune. From such a vantage point one can listen and play on every level at once and understand how all the levels are interrelated: the details of individual notes, note groupings, motifs and phrases, the larger structures, how those are united into A, B, C, parts, etc., how they form one piece of music, how that piece of music is rooted in a body of music and the soil of a tradition where it is related to every other tree in the forest.

If one were to hover above the tree and gaze down at the dense canopy of leaves, or sit on a branch closely examining a single leaf, one could not see the beautiful whole and feel its rootedness. When playing music, choose to plant yourself at the base of the trunk, looking up.

chapter 15: practice revisited, and some thoughts on "muscle memory"

HUMILITY INSPIRES PRACTICE

Since you have reached this point in the book, it's clear that Irish music has touched you deeply. I hope that your respect for its traditions inspires humility and the desire to join the tradition in the best ways that you can. That means "doing your homework," attentively listening to the older players as well as the new, and honing your own skills so you can play in a conscious and ever-improving way.

If you ever feel that your practice is becoming stale, boring, or unproductive, it is a good time to review the ideas on practice given in Chapter 4.

BUILD YOUR MEMORY BANK OF IDEAL SOUNDS

You can memorize the sounds of the well-played cut, strike, long roll, etc., and store these sounds in a bank of ideal sounds. As you work on training your body to learn the needed skills, continually compare the sounds you are making to the ideal sounds in your memory and imagination. Without self-criticism or judgment, notice well the differences between the reality and the ideal. Those differences are like gold. They show you where to direct your efforts. With patience and self-compassion, keep striving to come closer to your ideals. Little by little you will get there.

REMEMBER: SLOW PRACTICE WILL GET YOU THERE SOONER

We all tend to become impatient with making slow progress. But there is no question that playing too fast too soon significantly impedes us, greatly increasing the amount of time it will take for us to become fine, fully musical players.

It is thrilling to listen to fine, fast playing, and, naturally, we want to be able to play that way ourselves. Many of us, forgetting to listen well to ourselves, go ahead and play faster than we are ready to, do so poorly, and unknowingly reinforce the habits of poor playing. Other musicians will notice you doing this, but most likely they will be reluctant to tell you.

What is the point of playing poorly at a fast pace? It is a short-sighted and self-defeating strategy. Here is a case where the fable of the tortoise and the hare is very apt.

Having reached this point in the book, you know well that Irish music is vastly more than a simple succession of notes. What you see in tune books are simply frozen skeletons of snapshots of settings of tunes, some a bit more fleshed out than others. The nuances that breathe life into the music cannot be written down and cannot be learned in a hurry. When you play too fast too soon, you miss out on them. Why race along flinging frozen skeletons to and fro when you could be sipping and savoring nectar at the banquet table? Playing slowly and well is delicious, and it is a pre-requisite to playing fast and well. I think you will find that the musicians whose fast playing you admire will agree.

For many of us, our metronome is the friend we love to hate. It provides a rigid time reference, and that can be extremely revealing. For example, you want to gain control over your cuts so you can place them wherever you want them. It is easy to fool yourself into thinking that you have gained such control when perhaps you really haven't. Try placing cuts where the metronome tells you to place them, right on a steady beat. When you *externalize* the definition of the beat to a machine, you come to see how your own internal sense of the beat can speed up or fluctuate. It's difficult to maintain a steady beat at an unusually slow speed, especially when you are giving most of your attention to working on a challenging new skill. We want to speed up, even when we are not ready to. Of course we don't want to play like machines, but machines can help us gain insight into how to play better as humans.

THE PHYSIOLOGY OF "MUSCLE MEMORY"

Why should it be that our muscles take longer to learn things than our minds do?

The cut, for instance, is not hard to grasp with the intellect, especially once you have heard it played well. Yet it can take a very long time to gain the needed fine muscle skills.

Research in biology, anatomy, and neurology has begun to address this question. It is intriguing and reassuring to know that during that long learning period you are literally building new nerve pathways that are very persistent and reliable. For help with the following rather scientific discussion, I wish to thank my friend Lawrence Washington, a musician, instrument builder, and molecular biologist.

As we first start learning a new group of movements, such as the fingering motions used to execute a G long roll, we have to think consciously about each component of the group and command the muscles to move. The part of the brain responsible for conscious thought (the cerebral cortex) sends impulses through the muscle-control part of the brain (the cerebellum) and onward to the finger muscles. Since there are so many different, very precise muscle movements in a long roll, its execution is at first slow and tedious, requiring great concentration. The thought process may go something like this: "Do a G long roll: (1) place T1, T2, T3 on their holes, (2) blow, (3) lift T2, (4) replace quickly, (5) raise B1 high, (6) bring B1 down sharply…" and so on, all the while keeping the proper timing, breathing, and a raft of other elements in mind. There is so much to think about that it is no wonder we can feel overwhelmed and frustrated.

But there is comfort to be found in the biology of learning. When we repeat a complex set of muscle motions, specific patterns of nerve pathways are assigned to repeat them. This is a physical process, an actual structural change at the microscopic level of our neurons. Gradually the muscle commands, which originate from the thinking part of the brain, the cerebral cortex, are taken over directly by the muscle-control centers of the cerebellum, which previously had only mediated them. All that remains at the conscious level is the initiating command: "Do a G roll." With that, the cerebellum takes over and commands all the individual movements, which we had to think about one by one when we were first learning. It is as though we have gradually built a very specific machine and now only have to flip a switch for that machine to do its job.

Naturally, once we no longer have to think about each movement of the long roll it becomes possible to perform it quickly and with fluidity. It literally becomes "second nature." In fact, it may be that the movement of a proper cut, for example, is so very quick that most people cannot do it until it becomes established in the cerebellum and we no longer have to "think" about it.

The more times the pattern of movements is repeated, the more strongly the neuronal pattern is established. With the right microscope you would be able to see an increase in the density of the synapses and dendrite branches. The nerve connections become physically stronger, as a path through the woods becomes better defined the more times a family of deer walks along it.

One implication of this fact is that we should take care to practice and repeat only what we want our muscles to learn. If we are early with the timing of a strike as we practice it, and remain inattentive to that fact, our muscles will become expert at playing strikes early.

Of course, in the early stages of learning the cut, for instance, we cannot do them quickly enough. By necessity we practice them "too slow," making them as crisp as we can at that time. But if we remember the sound of the ideal cut, and constantly strive for it in our playing, we continually and gradually revise the pattern of nerve pathways that controls how we execute the cut. Once we finally learn to perform cuts well, the new, improved nerve pathways are well established.

When we keep our ideal sounds well in mind, we establish a feedback loop that continually compares the sensations with the ideal. For instance, when the cerebral cortex tells the cerebellum to execute a long roll, you listen carefully to how it sounds, "think" about it, compare it to the ideal roll, and instruct the cerebellum how to modify the roll toward the ideal. You see how very important it is to listen well to ourselves, and to our models.

Fortunately for the beginner, it does not matter that we execute movement patterns slowly as we learn them. After the neuronal pathways have established their circuits, we can go as fast as our muscles can move. The family of deer walking many times the same way through the woods clear a nice trace. Later they can run as fast as they like down the smooth trail, gracefully as a perfectly timed roll. And the established neural pathway is amazingly persistent. Once made, the additional synapses and increased density of nerve branches stay. We may easily forget how to describe the details of a roll, but the nerves in our brain and fingers have made very strong connections that can be activated anytime we "flip the switch."

fingering chart
for the tin whistle in d
low register

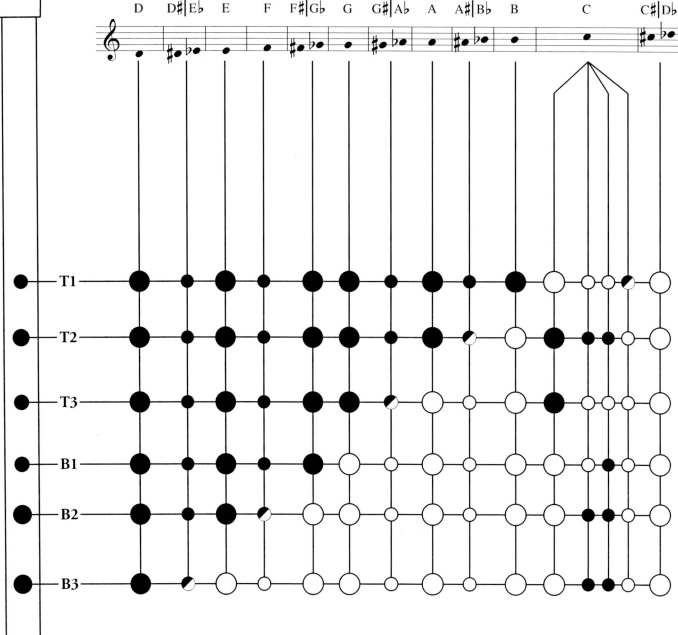

Fingering Chart for Tin Whistle in D. Filled circles indicate closed finger holes, open circles indicate open finger holes, half-filled circles indicate partially covered finger holes. Large circles show the primary, most-used notes of the whistle, small circles the lesser-used notes or fingerings. Note that some notes have more than one fingering. Try these alternate fingerings on your whistle and find out what works best for you. You may also find workable fingerings for your whistle that do not appear in this chart. Note that pitches sound one octave higher than written.

fingering chart
for the tin whistle in d
high register

appendix 6: contents of the companion cd

The companion CD contains most of the figures and exercises from Chapters 1 through 13.

In those exercises that feature a metronome click along with the whistle, the click is heard only in the right channel and the whistle only in the left. As a result, you can adjust the balance of the two, or eliminate either element altogether, by adjusting the left-right balance. "MM" stands for "metronome marking" and indicates the number of beats per minute (bpm).

All selections are played by the author on tin whistle or concertina. Whistle performances are played on a Copeland small D whistle, except for track 5 which is played on an Abell C whistle. Concertina selections are played on a 40-button Wheatstone anglo concertina in D and A.

All selections recorded, mixed, edited, and mastered by the author at Sleepy Creek Recording and Grey Larsen Mastering, Bloomington, Indiana, USA, January and February 2003.

1. **Figure 1-1.** The seven so-called church modes. *Concertina.* **p. 17.**

2. **Figure 1-2.** Comparisons between the Ionian and Mixolydian modes, and the Aeolian and Dorian modes. **p. 18.**

3. **Figure 1-4.** Examples of the two pentatonic modes found in Irish music, the Ionian Pentatonic and the Dorian Pentatonic. **p. 20.**

4. **Figure 1-5.** The first part of *Tuttle's Reel* in D Dorian. *Concertina.* **p. 22.**

5. **Figure 1-6.** The first part of *Tuttle's Reel,* transposed up to E Dorian. *C Whistle.* **p. 22.**

6. **Figure 1-7.** An example of the use of slur notation. **p. 23.**

7. **Figure 5-1.** The D Mixolydian mode. **p. 58.**

8. **Exercises 7-1 through** 7-6. Play a series of notes. *Four preparation clicks for each exercise. MM = 60.* **pp. 75-76.**

9. **Exercises 7-7 through** 7-11. Cuts on repeated notes in various contexts. *Four preparation clicks for each exercise. MM = 120.* **pp. 77-78.**

10. **Exercises 7-12 through** 7-14. Cuts on repeated notes on various subdivisions of the pulse. *Six preparation clicks for each exercise. MM = 120.* **pp. 78-79.**

11. **Exercises 7-15 through** 7-19. Various cuts. **pp. 80-81.**

12. **Exercises 7-20 through** 7-22. Cuts on stepwise ascending notes. *Four preparation clicks for each exercise. MM = 80.* **pp. 81-82.**

13. **Figure 7-15.** A version of *The Lonesome Jig* which makes use of cuts only on repeated notes and stepwise ascending notes. **p. 83.**

14. **Exercises 7-23 through** 7-32. Cuts on notes that ascend by intervals larger than a major second. **pp. 84-86.**

15. **Exercise 7-33.** Practicing a variety of cuts on notes that ascend by intervals larger than a major second. *Three preparation clicks. MM = 80.* **p. 86.**

16. **Exercises 7-34 through** 7-38. Cuts on stepwise descending notes. **pp. 86-88.**

17. **Exercise 7-39.** Practicing a variety of cuts on notes that descend by one step. *Two preparation clicks. MM = 80.* **p. 88.**

18. **Exercises 7-40 through 7-53.** Cuts on notes that descend by an interval larger than a major second. **pp. 88-92.**

19. **Exercises 7-54 through 7-57.** Cutting E, F-sharp, and G while descending leapwise from various notes. *Three preparation clicks for each exercise. MM = 120.* **pp. 92-93.**

20. **Figure 7-16.** A version of the slip jig *The Boys of Ballisodare* that makes use of examples of every class of cuts. **p. 94.**

21. **Figure 7-17.** The first two measures of the slip jig *Hardiman the Fiddler* with a cut placed at the onset of the first note. **p. 95.**

22. **Figure 7-19.** The first measure of the slip jig *Hardiman the Fiddler.* **p. 96.**

23. **Figure 7-20.** The first two measures of the second part of the reel *The Gravel Walk* using a normal cut. **p. 97.**

24. **Figure 7-21.** A variation on the first two measures of the second part of the reel *The Gravel Walk* created by elongating a cut. **p. 97.**

25. **Exercises 8-1 through 8-7.** Practicing repeated strikes on various notes. *Four preparation clicks for each exercise. MM = 120.* **pp. 102-103.**

26. **Exercises 8-8 through 8-14.** Practicing strikes – more examples of usage. *Four preparation clicks for Exercises 8-8 through 8-12, MM = 80. Six preparation clicks for Exercises 8-13 and 8-14, MM = 120.* **pp. 104-106.**

27. **Exercises 8-15 through 8-19.** Practicing strikes on descending notes. *Four preparation clicks for each exercise. MM = 60.* **pp. 108-109.**

28. **Exercise 8-20.** Practicing strikes on stepwise descending notes. *Two preparation clicks. MM = 60.* **p. 109.**

29. **Figure 8-14.** A version of the hornpipe *Bantry Bay* using cuts and strikes only on repeated notes and descending stepwise notes. **p. 110.**

30. **Exercises 8-21 through 8-33.** Strikes on notes that descend by intervals larger than a major second. *Four preparation clicks for each exercise. MM = 60.* **pp. 111-114.**

31. **Exercises 8-34 through 8-36.** Practicing leapwise descending strikes. *Three preparation clicks for each exercise. MM = 60.* **pp. 114-115.**

32. **Figure 8-15.** A version of the hornpipe *Bantry Bay* using cuts and a variety of strikes. **p. 116.**

33. **Figure 9-1.** Sliding up from E to F-sharp. **p. 118.**

34. **Figure 9-4.** A falling slide from F-sharp to E. **p. 119.**

35. **Figure 9-5.** Sliding up from E to F-natural. **p. 119.**

36. **Figure 9-6.** The opening measures of *The Blarney Pilgrim* with simple slides from B up to C-natural and back down to B. **p. 120.**

37. **Figure 9-7.** An excerpt from a variation on the beginning of the jig *The Cliffs of Moher.* **p. 120.**

38. **Figure 9-8a.** The opening measures of *The Star Above the Garter* with an added-finger slide up to G followed by a simple slide up to C-natural. **p. 121.**

39. **Figure 9-8b.** The opening measures of *The Star Above the Garter* with a struck slide up to G followed by a simple slide up to C-natural. **p. 121.**

40. **Figure 9-9.** The opening measures of *Willie Coleman's Jig.* **p. 122.**

41. **Exercises 10-1 through 10-3.** Practicing long rolls on G, F-sharp, and E. *Four preparation clicks for each exercise. MM = 60.* **pp. 124-125.**

42. **Exercise 10-4.** Practicing long rolls on E, F-sharp, and G in jig rhythm. *Six preparation clicks. MM = 120.* **p. 126.**

43. **Exercise 10-5.** Practicing long rolls on E, F-sharp, and G, in reel rhythm. *Four preparation clicks. MM = 120.* **p. 126.**

about the author

Grey Larsen was born in 1955 in New York City. His family moved to Cincinnati, Ohio, the following year. He began piano lessons at the age of four and enjoyed a childhood and youth full of musical exploration, his inner world filled with the keyboard music of Bach and Mozart, the rock, R & B, and Motown sounds on the radio, the songs of contemporary folk music interpreters, and traditional Appalachian and Irish music.

From 1970 to 1972, he studied composition and early music at the Cincinnati College–Conservatory of Music before moving on, in 1973, to continue at the Oberlin Conservatory of Music in Oberlin, Ohio. While pursuing early and modern classical music on the one hand, he came ever more deeply under the spell of traditional music on the other, and for several years he followed both streams with equal energy and dedication. In these and later years, he spent a great deal of time learning traditional Irish music from elder musicians, especially immigrant Irishmen Michael J. Kennedy (1900–1978), Tom Byrne (1920–2001), and Tom McCaffrey (1916–2006), in Cincinnati and Cleveland, Ohio.

Upon completing his Bachelor of Music degree at Oberlin in 1976, the streams forked. He bid a fond farewell to the academic side of music and set a course following his love of traditional music, exploring other waterways that would branch, cross, and rejoin over the decades. He leads a varied and rich musical life as a performer, teacher, author, recording artist, record producer, mastering engineer, and as the Music Editor of *Sing Out!* magazine. Since the early 1970s, he has also devoted himself to the traditional fiddle music of his native Midwest and Appalachia. But that's another story.

He has three children and lives in Bloomington, Indiana, USA.

also by grey larsen:

Selected Recordings
Cross the Water
Dark of the Moon
The Green House
The Orange Tree
Les Marionnettes
The Gathering
Morning Walk
The Great Road
Metamora
Thunderhead
The First of Autumn
Banish Misfortune

Books
The Essential Guide to Irish Flute and Tin Whistle
The Lotus Dickey Songbook

Information at www.greylarsen.com and
www.melbay.com

Index of Tune Titles

Note: Page references in boldface refer to complete versions of tunes.

Note: Complete settings of most of the tunes listed above do not appear in this book. However, transcriptions and recordings of complete settings of those tunes are included in *The Toolbox Tune Collection,* which is available online at <www.greylarsen.com/extras/toolbox>, or by writing to the author at <grey@greylarsen.com> or PO Box 2652, Bloomington, IN 47402-2652.

ζeneral index

Note: Page references followed by "n" refer to footnotes.

A

Abell whistles, 30-31

Accaciaturas, 97n

Accidentals, 19-20

Aeolian mode, 16-17, 19, 31

Anchor points, 35-41
    basic hold, 36-37
    bottom-hand pinky, 40-41
    bottom-hand thumb, 40
    lips, 37-38
    top-hand thumb, 40

Apertures, whistle, 37-38

Appogiaturas, 97n

Articulation, 67. *See also* Tonguing

Ascending rolls, 159-160

Audio recorder use, 52-53

B

Bagpiping. *See* Irish bagpiping

Bane, Joe, 13

Barn dances, 23-24

Basic hold, 36-37

Boehm flutes, 7, 45, 65, 117

Breathing, 166-172
    articulate and inarticulate, 166-167, 170-171
    breathing exercises, 48-49
    circular, 172
    compared to fiddle bowing, 95
    diaphragm exercise, 47-48
    at the end of a part, 171
    examples of breathing spots, 168-169
    forward motion and, 171
    in language analogy, 60, 166
    musical compared to normal, 46-47
    notation for, 82-83
    by note omission and shortening, 47, 166-167, 169-170

posture and, 33-34, 41
    pulses and, 82, 126-127, 167-170
    in rolls, 126-127, 147, 169-170
    subtle breath pulses, 49, 172
    visualization technique for, 46-47
    whistle position during, 42

Breathing exercises, 48-49

Breath slides, 122

C

Casadh, 96

Cassette recorders, use of, 52-53

Chanters, bagpipe, 25, 75, 164

Chips. *See* Cuts

Church modes, 16-17. *See also* Modes

Circular breathing, 166, 172

Clarke tin whistles, 30, 37

Classical music style, 26, 66, 71, 97n, 165-166

Clearing the windway, 42-43

Close piping, 164

C-natural
    fingering of, 21, 57
    long rolls on, 131-133
    piping C, 20-21
    pitch of, 20-21
    sliding and, 119-120
    use of C-sharp instead of, 21

Compound duple meter, 24, 136

Compound subdivision of pulse, 24

Compound triple meter, 24

Coordination exercises, 56-57

Copeland whistles, 29-31, 37

Cross-fingering, 21, 28n, 31, 57-58

Cuiseach, 29

Cuts, 68-97
    as articulations, 67, 68
    compared to grace notes, 71
    delaying, 95-96

elongating, 97
    fingerings of, 71-74, 80-82, 88
    on larger ascending intervals, 84-86
    on larger descending intervals, 88-93
    learning, 68-70
    location in time, 70-71
    lowest available finger rule, 89
    notation of, 75
    optimal fingering rule, 71-72
    in repeated notes, 75-79
    responsiveness rule, 74
    from slides, 122
    on stepwise ascending notes, 79-82
    on stepwise descending notes, 86-88
    strikes used in place of, 87, 107
    tonguing and, 89, 94-95
    in tunes, 83, 93-94

D

Delaying cuts, 95-96

Diaphragm exercise, 47-48

Dorian mode, 16-20, 31

Dorian pentatonic mode, 20

Double graces, 96

Double jigs, 23-24

Drones, bagpipe, 25

Duple meter, 23-24, 136

E

Economy of motion, 57-58, 163

Elongating cuts, 97

Embouchure, 40, 44-46, 48-49, 163

Equal temperament, 44-45

Exercises
    breathing, 48-49
    diaphragm, 47-48
    finger coordination, 56-57

struck, 121-122

    time signature in, 24

Slip jigs, 23-24, 94-96. *See also* Jigs

Slow airs, cuts in, 95

Slurring, definition of, 23, 163. *See also* Slides

Smearing. *See* Slides

Staccato playing, 25-26, 94, 164-165, 172

Strathspeys, 23-24

Strikes, 98-116

    in ascending intervals across register breaks, 107

    compared to cuts, 98

    in larger descending intervals, 111-115

    movements and fingerings of, 98-101

    notation of, 101

    on repeated notes, 102-106

    resting position and, 100-101

    on stepwise descending notes, 108-110

    timing of, 102

    tonguing and, 116

    in tunes, 110, 116

    used in place of cuts, 87, 107

    uses and limitations of, 107-108

Struck slides, 121-122

Subtle breath pulses, 49, 172

Sway, 26-28

Swing, 26-28

T

Tape recorders, use of, 52-53

Taps. *See* Strikes

Tempo, 24, 135-136

"The Thinker" breathing exercise, 48

Third-octave notes, 43

Throating, 67

Thumbs as anchor points, 35-37, 40-41

Tight piping, 164, 172

Tin whistles. *See* Whistles; Pennywhistles

Tips. *See* Strikes

Tonal centers, 14, 17-20

Tonguing, 163-165

    in classical music, 165

    and cuts, 94-95

    definition of, 23, 163

    in descending cuts, 89,

    gradations of, 163-164

    in language analogy, 60

    legato style of Irish music and, 26, 164-165

    physical action of, 163

    in short rolls, 144, 153

    single and multiple, 165

    before or after slides, 122

    and strikes, 116

Transposing whistles, 21-22

Triple meter, 23-24, 136

Tunes

    definition of, 13

    internalization of, 14

    intervals in, 14-15

    names of, 16

    tonal centers of, 14

Tuning whistles, 42

U

Uilleann pipes, 18, 20-21, 25-26, 30, 32, 45, 65, 67, 72, 164, 165n, 172

Uneven rolls, 141-142, 159

Union pipes. *See* Uilleann pipes

Upper grace notes. *See* Cuts

Varsoviennes, 23-24

Waltzes, 23-24

Washington, Lawrence, 178

Whistles. *See also* Whistles, holding and blowing

    accessible modes on, 31

    compared to flutes, 48

    fingering charts for, 180-181

    low D, 21, 30-31, 35

    manufacturers of, 29-31

    melting glue on mouthpieces of, 42

    small D, 21, 29, 74, 180-181

    transposing, 21-22

    windway openings, 37

Whistles, holding and blowing, 33-49

    adjusting overall pitch, 42

    anchor points, 35-41

    basic hold, 36-37

    clearing the windway, 42-43

    covering the finger holes, 21, 35, 41, 56-57

    diaphragm exercise, 47-48

    embouchure, 40, 44-46, 48, 163

    experiments to try, 46

    fingering notation, 34

    holding angles, 38-39

    lips and, 35-38, 40, 43-44, 48

    low register, 41-42, 56, 180

    playing in tune, 44-45

    position during breathing, 42

    posture and, 33-34, 41, 52

    resting position, 35-36, 100-101, 163

    second octave, 43-44, 56, 181

    third octave, 43

Windway openings, 37-38

GCSE
Statistics

Answer Book
Higher Level

Answers: Pages P.1 – P.4

Section One — Data Collection

Planning an Investigation P.1

1) E.g. Do students get higher marks in exams in the afternoon? / Do students get higher marks if they only have one exam per day?
2) The deck of cards has been stacked by Eddie.
3) Poxfix cures chickenpox.
4) Hypothesis 1 – The more TV that students watch, the more overweight they are. Hypothesis 2 – The more TV that students watch, the worse their exam grades are.
5) The hypothesis seems to be true because sales of ice cream have gone up on average by 201 per day after the campaign.
6) a) Students who attend the classes perform better than students who had not attended the classes.
   b) E.g. it might be that the students didn't attend the classes because they were already very good at statistics.

Data Sources P.2-P.3

1) a) Secondary data.
   b) Primary data.
   c) Secondary data.
2) a) Secondary data.
   b) E.g. the data may be biased because Wonderme have a vested interest in promoting their cream. The data is 4 years out of date.

3)

Data	Primary or Secondary
You use data from the 2001 census on the number of rooms in a house.	Secondary
You use results from your experiment measuring sizes of spider webs.	Primary
You use a pie chart from a magazine showing preferred beauty products.	Secondary
You use a grouped frequency table compiled by a supermarket showing the number of times customers visit the supermarket each month.	Secondary

4) a) Secondary data.
   b) The data is not relevant to Cuthbert's project. Only two of the sample are of school age.
5) a) Any sensible answer including: The data is produced by Phloggit Advertising and so may be biased. / The data is not in the format that Kate wants, which means her bar chart might not be accurate.
   b) Secondary data.
6) They could carry out an experiment to compare the results of cleaning with Raz to cleaning with all other brands.
7) a) Primary data as it is unlikely that anyone else has this data.
   b) E.g. they could send a questionnaire to members of the official fan club to find out the age and sex of each person.
8) a) Secondary. It would be more convenient to use data collected by the local council.
   b) They could look at the council's data on levels of recycling before and after the service was set up.
9) a) They also need to know the amount of sweets and crisps being sold in the 10 schools.

   b) To find the sales of sweets and crisps it would be easier to use secondary data because they can use the sales figures from the schools. To find the weights of the students they should use primary data because it is unlikely the schools have the weights of the students on record.
   c) It would take too long and cost too much for the health authority to measure the weight of every student in the 10 schools. So, asking each student their weight in a questionnaire would be more suitable.
10) a) He can be sure that the data directly relates to his investigation.
    b) It's a lot quicker to collect.
11) a) The local council needs to know the time of any road traffic accidents that happen at that junction.
    b) They should use secondary data instead of primary because it would be inconvenient and expensive for the council to monitor the junction themselves.
    c) They could use records about road traffic accidents from the police or car insurance companies.

Types of Data P.4

1) a) Quantitative data is data that can be measured with numbers.
   b) Qualitative data